The Best of SQLServerCentral.com – Vol. 3

Ameet Phadnis
Amit Jethra
Andre Vigneau
Andy Warren
Anthony Bressi
Ashish Kaushal
Brian Kelley
Brian Knight
Bruce Szabo
Chris Cathers
Chris Kempster
Christoffer Hedgate
Dale Elizabeth Corey
David Poole
Denny Figuerres
Dinesh Asanka
Dinesh Priyankara
Don Peterson
Eli Leiba
G Vijayakumar
Goce Smilevski
Haidong Ji
James Luetkehoelter
James Travis
Jeff Moden
Jeffrey Yao
Joe Sack
Jon Reade
Jon Winer
Kevin O'Donovan
Krishna Sonti
Leo Peyasakhovich
Mark Nash
Nicholas Cain
Paul Ibison
Patryk Nowakowski
Ramesh Gummadi
Ramunas Balukonis
Robert Marda
Robert Pearl
Robin Back
Sanket Naik
Santveer Singh
Shiv Kumar
Sotiris Filippidis
Stefan Popovski
Steve Jones
Sureshkumar Ramakrishnan
Vinod Kumar
Wayne Fillis
Wes Brown

The Central Publishing Group
3186 Michaels Ct
Green Cove Springs, FL 32043
U.S.A

Copyright Notice

Disclaimer

The Central Publishing Group, SQLServerCentral.com, and the authors of the articles contained in this book are not liable for any problems resulting from the use of techniques, source code, or compiled executables referenced in this book. Users should review all procedures carefully, test first on a non-production server, and always have good backup before using on a production server.

Trademarks

Microsoft, SQL Server, Windows, and Visual Basic are registered trademarks of Microsoft Corporation, Inc. Oracle is a trademark of Oracle Corporation.

Editors

Steve Jones and Andy Warren

Cover Art

Sylvia Peretz of PeretzDesign.com

The Best of SQLServerCentral.com – Vol. 3

Table of Contents

Introduction

Welcome to The Best of SQLServerCentral.com – Vol. 3!

Once again SQLServerCentral.com had another fantastic year and we decided to reprint some of the best articles, the most popular, and the most read in dead tree format. We wanted to give all our authors a chance to see their names in print as well as give you an off-line resource that you can take with you wherever you may need it-most likely at your bedside to help you drop off at night :), for commutes, holding your coffee cup, whatever. This is our third volume and it's become an annual tradition.

We would also like to thank everyone for their support both on the website as well as by purchasing this book. Your visits to the site, clicking through to advertisers, purchasing products, registering for PASS, all help us continue this community and provide you with a valuable resource that hopefully helps you learn, perform better at your job, and grow your career. We'd like to encourage all of you to submit an article in 2005! This is a community and we aren't looking for the gurus only to contribute. We love hearing about the real world you all live in and deal with on a daily basis. We plan to get at least one article from each author and send you a couple copies of the book. Great for your bookshelf and they make a great Mother's Day present.

Once again, thanks so much for your support and we look forward to 2005.

Andy Warren
Brian Knight
Steve Jones

Administration

This is what we do: administer servers and databases. Everyone has their own set of tricks, tips, scripts tailored to the quirks of their own systems. We can each get sidetracked into dealing with our own systems and miss out on understanding some other sections of SQL Server that we don't work with.

Here's a selection of articles to impart a little more information about the server, Autoclose, AWE, Traces and more. As we compile this 3rd edition, Microsoft SQL Server is a very mature product that is mostly being limited by its architecture as hardware continues to grow in power, loads increase, and many different stresses occur. Nothing earth-shattering here, just some good information that might help you save the day.

A Bit About 64-bit

By Robert Pearl

I recently attended a seminar at MS NYC HQ, discussing in-depth the release of Microsoft's powerful 64-bit SQL Server, and wanted to share my thoughts with your readers. In what is being described as a watershed event, Microsoft is clearly aiming its sights on the enterprise class customer, and to finally quash the notion that SQL Server doesn't scale. Indeed, the release of 64-bit versions of Windows OS, Itanium-2 processor, and SQL Server, is an absolute trifecta that is sure to give ORACLE and DB2 on the UNIX platform a run for its money.

So, what does this mean to the average SQL Server customer and MS SQL DBA? Well, maybe nothing in the short-term, but in the long-term, 64-bit will someday become the norm, and its merits will be discussed here. At least for now, 64-bit will give us the ammunition to fully take on the UNIX SA's in the on-going debate of UNIX vs. Microsoft. But, I digress.

Meanwhile, back at the conference, "scalability" and "availability" were no longer just buzzwords, but actual concepts fully implemented, tested and benchmarked by the TPC-C (Transaction Processing Performance Council). In fact, the highest scores put out by DB2 and Oracle on UNIX, were trounced by SQL Server 2000's 64-bit architecture. (See this MS press release, with links to TPC-C)

Now, on to the highlights of the presentation. One of the more applicable discussions was the comparison between the current 32-bit platform and the new 64-bits. This article will focus on the specific advantages 64-bit has to offer SQL Server 32-bit customers.

The presentation began with a question - "Why 64-bit?" In talking about the challenges of a 32-bit environment, the speaker seems to take aim at the typical application development issues that often plague performance. Although no excuse for poor code, 64-bit may actually compensate for some of these inefficiencies. Among these implications, are:

1. 9 out of 10 times the database is blamed for slow performance;
2. Applications are bound to have inefficient code;
3. Developers will always write un-optimized queries;
4. As soon as one bottleneck is resolved, another one pops up.

Indeed, while 32-bit scalability scales well in most large transaction and data warehousing applications in areas such as supporting up to 32 CPU's and 64 GB of RAM, there are definitely limitations in the way it actually uses these vital resources. And that is precisely what 64-bit promises to solve.

For example, in the 32-bit SQL world, the maximum memory supported is 4GB. Out of this, the OS/Kernel reserves 2GB, and so SQL Server in reality only gets the other two. By setting the 3GB switch in the boot.ini, you can let SQL Server use 3GB, and the Kernel will get 1 GB.

Furthermore, in order to allow SQL Server to use up to 64 GB, one must configure the PAE switch in the boot.ini, as well as enabling AWE (Address Windowing Extension) using sp_configure. However, even this does not maximize the efficiency of your memory. Case in point, the additional RAM becomes available only to your buffer cache, and not your procedure cache, which is limited to only 4GB per instance. There are other 32-bit limitations affecting memory usage (which I won't go into detail), such page life expectancy, and memtoleave (used for out of process memory requests). So, basically, the distribution of RAM in the SQL Server memory pool is not "real" memory, and, as some real-world memory stress tests have shown, can lead to memory contention, lower cache hit-ratio, and of course, slower performance. These limitations are no longer existent in the 64-bit world, and AWE is not used.

Another important measure is CPU utilization and getting the best performance ROI, as well as increased throughput. One of the terms that I became intimately familiar with at the presentation was "context switching". Although you may or may not have frequently heard this term, it is extremely vital to the overall performance of your SQL Server. A typical context switch occurs when the OS or the application is forced to change the executing thread on one processor to another thread executed on another processor. The higher the CPU usage is, or I/O contention, the higher the context switching, and ultimately lower throughput. The number of context switches should be as small as possible.

The worst thing that can occur is when you have your OS resources dedicated to excessive context switching than doing the actual work required by SQL Server. Because it runs as a single process, you end up with increased I/O queues and thread swapping. This leads us to a discussion about parallelism.

Although SQL Server does a good job of dynamically managing most resources, when you get into more high transaction systems and require a higher degree of parallelism, you start getting into more advanced levels of configuration. You then need to become familiar with terms such as: (see this KB article for more info: KB Article - 319942)

1. Affinity Mask
2. Lightweight Pooling
3. Max Async IO
4. Max Worker Threads
5. Memory
6. Priority Boost
7. Set Working Set Size

With 64-bit, you increase CPU parallelism, and it is possible to achieve true parallelism for multi-threaded applications. While context switches are not avoidable on multi-processor machines, it is less of an issue with 64-bit architecture.

To give a practical application of the type of environment most suited for 64-bit SQL Server, it is one where multiple instances are running on a single server. Since there is only so much hardware you can throw at it and still not get optimal performance, this new architecture may be right for you. In fact, I highly recommend it.

Take, for example, where many companies are now consolidating their SQL Server infrastructure and employing them on shared SQL Farm. Currently, I am at a client that is doing precisely this, where they have invested heavily in Hardware, SAN storage, upgraded all the SQL Servers to version 2000, and even moved the server OS to Windows 2003. The SQL Farm is set up as an Active/Active 2-node cluster, which maxes out at eight active instances per cluster (four active per node), with 8 CPU's and 8 GB of RAM. So, if one node fails over, the other node picks up the slack of the other four instances. My client is currently in the process of testing their proof-of-concept server. Now, as anyone knows, this is quite a task, even as it employs a third party product to manage the CPU resources and avoid contention. Nonetheless, they have statically allocated a portion of RAM to each instance, and are struggling with CPU affinity.

Some applications are memory intensive, some are OLTP, others are OLAP, and vary up and down the spectrum in terms of size, transactions, etc. - a potpourri of application databases that need to play nice with each other (not too mention the users). Indeed, they seemed to have taken the 32-bits a bit too seriously, without considering upgrading to 64-bits. This is what I have recommended before they go live. (Whether they listen is another thing, so I hope that they'll read my article!)

Among the general pitfalls of running multi-instances on 32-bit are: instances will compete for resources, application usage is dynamic and user load is unpredictable, a single runaway query can cause all instances to suffer, and the need to manually configure memory and CPU resources per instance.

Since SQL Server works best with dynamic configuration, multiple instances will benefit enormously from 64-bit architecture. Without getting too deep into the OS side of 64-bit (i.e. Windows 2003 64 bit), the Windows System Resource Manager (WSRM) will effectively manage CPU and Memory dynamically, and in turn make SQL Server administration easier. Therefore, there will be no need to "affinitize" resources per instance. (And, think of all those thousands of dollars invested in the 3rd party resource manager.)

I only wish that these clients were there when the presenter presented the perfect scenario to go 64-bits, which is the multi-instance server farm.

The upgrade path to SQL Server 64-bit, from 32-bit databases, is in itself simple as a backup and restore. (Of course, the hardware and 64-bit OS must be in place first.) Data warehousing, high transaction OLTP, and large e-commerce applications are among the beneficiaries of this new 64-bit technology as well.

On the flip side, some of the reasons listed to stay with 32-bit are as follows:

1. Queries are not memory intensive, and are optimized;
2. High levels of CPU parallelisms is not required;
3. Maintenance window is fairly flexible;

4. Large-scale consolidation is not required.

Finally, 64-bits is an extraordinary foray into the world of high-end, multi-threaded, ultra speed processing power that is intended for high availability, performance and scalability. So what about the bottom-line for businesses considering their budget and technology planning? Microsoft believes that the release of 64-bit SQL Server, combined with Windows 2003 64-bit and the I2 processor, will reduce the total cost of ownership (TCO).

In addition, 64-bits will enable consumers to consolidate multiple terabyte databases in a multi-instance environment, with no performance degradation. In turn, licensing fees and management costs will be reduced. While the need for such robust technology currently defines the enterprise class client, it is sure to become as widely used one day by customers, large and small.

Written by: Robert Pearl, President
Pearl Knowledge Solutions, Inc.
http://www.pearlknows.com

Copyright © 2004 - All Rights Reserved.

Note: Not to be reprinted or published without express permission of the author.

An Introduction To Linked Servers

By Krishna Sonti

Introduction

What are Linked Servers?

A Linked Server is a Link to an external (remote) data source. The remote data source can be Oracle, Access, Excel or any other data source that uses an OLE DB provider.

What are Remote Servers?

- Remote servers do not use OLE DB providers
- A remote server configuration allows a client connected to one instance of SQL Server to execute a stored procedure on another instance of SQL Server without establishing another connection
- Both stored procedures and distributed queries are allowed against linked servers; however, only stored procedures are allowed against remote servers.
- Use Linked Servers instead of Remote Servers. Remote servers are for backward compatibility only.

Note: Linked servers can run remote stored procedures for SQL Server and cannot run remote stored procedures for Oracle.

Adding Linked Servers

Syntax

```
sp_addlinkedserver [ @server = ] 'server'
    [ , [ @srvproduct = ] 'product_name' ]
    [ , [ @provider = ] 'provider_name' ]
    [ , [ @datasrc = ] 'data_source' ]
    [ , [ @location = ] 'location' ]
    [ , [ @provstr = ] 'provider_string' ]
    [ , [ @catalog = ] 'catalog' ]
```
Please refer BOL for syntax and *more info*

Example: To add Oracle as a linked server to SQL Server:

This example creates a linked server named **OraLinkServ** that uses the Microsoft OLE DB Provider for Oracle and assumes that the SQL*Net alias for the Oracle database is **OraProduction**.

```
USE master
GO
EXEC sp_addlinkedserver

    @server = 'OraLinkServ',
    @srvproduct = 'Oracle',
    @provider = 'MSDAORA',
    @datasrc = 'OraProduction'
GO
```

Adding Linked Server Login

Sp_addlinkedsvrlogin

Creates or updates a mapping between logins on the local instance of SQL Server and remote logins on the linked server.

Syntax

```
sp_addlinkedsrvlogin [ @rmtsrvname = ] 'rmtsrvname'
    [ , [ @useself = ] 'useself' ]
    [ , [ @locallogin = ] 'locallogin' ]
    [ , [ @rmtuser = ] 'rmtuser' ]
    [ , [ @rmtpassword = ] 'rmtpassword' ]
```

Please refer BOL for syntax and more info

Querying Linked Server

The following are the various methods of querying different linked servers.

LinkedServerName.Dbname.Owner.ObjectName

Select * from LinkSqlServ.Northwind.dbo.Employees

Select * from OraLinkServ..SCOTT.Stores

Select * from LinkMdb...customers

OpenQuery: - Executes the specified pass-through query on the given linked server, which is an OLE DB data source.

Syntax:

```
OpenQuery ( linked_server, 'query' )
```
Examples:

```
SELECT * FROM OPENQUERY(OraLinkServ, 'SELECT Name, Title FROM Scott.Titles')

INSERT OPENQUERY(LinkSqlServ, 'select * from pubs.dbo.jobs') values (15, 'Technical Editor', 100, 300)
```

OpenRowSet: - This method is an adhoc method of connecting and accessing remote data using OLE DB. It creates linked server on the fly.

Syntax

```
OPENROWSET ( 'provider_name'
    , { 'datasource' ; 'user_id' ; 'password'
      | 'provider_string' }
    , { [ catalog. ] [ schema. ] object
```

```
   | 'query' }
 )
```

Removing Linked Server and its Logins

Sp_dropserver - Removes a server from the list of known remote and linked servers on the local SQL Server.

Sp_droplinkedsvrlogin: Removes an existing mapping between a login on the local server running SQL Server and a login on the linked server.

Obtaining Meta data

Please refer BOL for complete syntax.

Sp_tables_ex: Returns table information about the tables from the specified linked server.

sp_columns_ex: Returns the column information, one row per column, for the given linked server table(s). **sp_columns_ex** returns column information only for the given column if *column* is specified.

sp_table_privileges_ex: Returns privilege information about the specified table from the specified linked server.

sp_column_privileges_ex: Returns column privileges for the specified table on the specified linked server.

Sp_linkedservers: Returns the list of linked servers defined in the local server.

Sp_helpserver: Reports information about a particular remote or replication server, or about all servers of both types. Provides the server name, the server's network name, the server's replication status, the server's identification number, collation name, and time-out values for connecting to, or queries against, linked servers.

Sysservers: Contains one row for each server that SQL Server can access as an OLE DB data source. This table is stored in the **master** database.

Sysoledbusers: Contains one row for each user and password mapping for the specified linked server. This table is stored in the **master** database.

xp_enum_oledb_providers: Provides information about OLEDB providers.

Sp_serveroption: Sets server options for remote servers and linked servers.

Sp_serveroption has been enhanced with two new options, **use remote collation** and **collation name**, that support collations in linked servers.

Sp_setnetname: Sets the network names in **sysservers** to their actual network computer names for remote instances of SQL Server. This procedure can be used to enable execution of remote stored procedure calls to computers that have network names containing invalid SQL Server identifiers.

Some Useful Knowledge Base Articles for Linked Servers

Q280106: HOWTO: Set Up and Troubleshoot a Linked Server to Oracle in SQL Server

Q203638: HOWTO: Return Information About SQL Server Linked Servers

Q270119: PRB: 7357/7320 Error While Performing UPDATE, INSERT, or DELETE on Remote Table Using OpenQuery Via Linked Server

Q306212: INF: Troubleshooting Linked Server Error 7391

Q329332: PRB: You Receive Error 7391 When You Run a Distributed Transaction Against a Linked Server

Creating a System Stored Procedure

By Robert Marda

Introduction

In this article I will show you how you can make your own system stored procedure. Simply put, a system stored procedure is any stored procedure with a name that starts with sp_ that is found in the master database. These SPs can be executed from any database and will run from the context of that database. Any time you execute an SP that starts with sp_, SQL Server goes directly to the master database to find it.

Why Make A System Stored Procedure

I resort to making my own system stored procedure if I can't find a way to do what I need to do and I want to be able to do it in any database. Before SQL Server 2000 was released, I created a stored procedure that could script any table with its corresponding non-clustered indexes and primary key. I later designed it to handle default values and clustered indexes. I placed it in the master database so that I could use it in any database and yet only have to maintain one stored procedure. I'm sure there are other reasons. To me you make whatever you need to achieve your company's mission without compromising the integrity of your SQL Servers.

Pit falls

The only problems I am aware of with placing a stored procedure in the master database are: 1. You must be careful to not change anything while in the master database. 2. You must keep a copy of the SP somewhere else because when the master database gets rebuilt your system stored procedures will be gone. This could also happen when applying a service pack and/or during an upgrade to a different version of SQL Server. 3. You must be sure you give access to these SPs to as few people as possible. The ones I have created and fielded have only been used by people with sa permissions on that SQL Server.

A Simple System Stored Procedure

The below stored procedure will give you all the table names that have a specified column name in them:

```
CREATE PROCEDURE sp_FindTableNames
( @ColumnName varchar(128) ) AS

SELECT *
FROM sysobjects
WHERE id IN
(
       SELECT id
       FROM syscolumns
       WHERE name = @ColumnName
)
AND xtype = 'U'
```

Create this stored procedure in your master database on a development SQL Server. Now execute the following code from the Northwind database:

```
EXEC sp_FindTableNames @ColumnName = 'employeeID'
```

Caution

Whenever using system tables you must keep in mind that Microsoft could change the table structure at any time. If they do, then you might have to revise all the system stored procedures you create.

Conclusion

I have not found many reasons to create system stored procedures. However, I believe that creating your own can be useful ,and, with proper testing, will not compromise your SQL Servers.

Distributed Backup Checking

By Kevin O'Donovan

Having just read Santveer Singh's article <u>Which databases are being backed up (another look)</u>, I thought the following might add something. Our situation is slightly more complex. We develop software applications that make use of replicated databases. Our users are distributed across Europe, and in some cases consist of small offices with no real system administration personnel. Consequently, we typically manage their servers for them remotely. Part of this is the backups, and with the number of servers involved this is a bit of a nightmare. I came up with the following solution which, hopefully, might be of use to others as well. In addition to checking back up status, we also use it to monitor disk space for critical disks and replication status, though for conciseness I'll ignore that part for now.

We use maintenance plans to manage our backups. Each system database is backed up once daily, as is each application database. Transaction log backups for application databases are taken every 15 minutes. Backups are done to a separate live disk on the machine, and then backed up to tape as part of the site's daily tape backup. The maintenance plan is set to keep a single full backup and 24 hours of transaction log backups (in the event that anything earlier is needed we can ask the site to pull the relevant tape, but this has not been needed to date). The system I've put in place tells us if the right number of backups exist, if any backups have failed, if any verifies have failed, or if any of the deletes have failed, the failed delete is particularly important as the databases are large, and failures to delete could rapidly fill a disk.

My system is simple enough. It uses msdb.dbo.sysdbmaintplan_history as the source of its information. This table is queried hourly to extract the statistics we require, and the results placed in a table in the database SysAdmin (a database we use on all our servers for holding system management related data and procedures). This table is replicated hourly to one of our local servers. We could have avoided replication since one of the maintenance plan options is to send history information to a remote server. We decided against this for the following reasons:

- We had replication in place anyway
- It was something that could be missed when setting up the maintenance plan
- The current approach generates less network traffic
- We had no idea how reliable the alternative would be

Once the information is in place on our local server, we're free to extract any statistics we require from it. We currently do this in two ways. There is a daily task scheduled on the server that extracts information on problems and mails a report to designated users. Also, I have written an MMC snap-in that displays the current status of all sites and highlights any problems.

The various tables, views and procedures to implement this, are shown below.

BackupList is used to specify which databases should be checked on each server. The server column should match the value returned by @@SERVERNAME for the server in question.

```
CREATE TABLE [dbo].[BackupList] (
    [guid] uniqueidentifier ROWGUIDCOL NOT NULL ,
    [ID] [int] IDENTITY (1, 1) NOT NULL ,
    [Server] [varchar] (50) NOT NULL ,
    [DatabaseName] [varchar] (50) NOT NULL
) ON [PRIMARY]
```

BackupLog is used to store the results of our queries of the maintenance plan histories.

```
CREATE TABLE [dbo].[BackupLog] (
    [guid] uniqueidentifier ROWGUIDCOL NOT NULL ,
    [TestDate] [datetime] NOT NULL ,
        -- Default GetDate() - records time of last test
    [DatabaseName] [varchar] (50) NOT NULL ,
    [Server] [varchar] (50) NOT NULL ,
    [IsSystemDB] [bit] NOT NULL ,
        -- Set if the database is a system database
    [BackupCount] [int] NOT NULL ,
        -- Number of full backups in last 24 hours
```

```
  [BackupFails] [int] NOT NULL ,
      -- number of failed backups in last 24 hours
  [TransCount] [int] NOT NULL ,
      -- number of transaction logs in last 24 hours
  [TransFails] [int] NOT NULL ,
      -- number of failed transaction logs in last 24 hours
  [VerifyFails] [int] NOT NULL ,
  -- number of failed verifies in last 24 hours
  [DeleteFails] [int] NOT NULL
      -- number of failed deletes in last 24 hours<
) ON [PRIMARY]
```

Code

The following procedure performs the actual checks for a specific database

```
CREATE PROC dbo.adm_CheckBackups
  @dbname varchar(50), -- database to check
  @IsSystem bit=0        -- indicates a system database

AS

DECLARE @tlog_fails int, @tlog_count int, @verify_fails int
DECLARE @backup_fails int, @backup_count int, @delete_fails int

-- Return count of failed transaction log backups in the last 24 hours
SELECT @tlog_fails=COUNT(*)
 FROM msdb.dbo.sysdbmaintplan_history
 WHERE database_name LIKE @dbname
 AND activity LIKE 'Backup transaction log'
 AND start_time > DATEADD(hour, -24, getdate())
 AND succeeded=0

-- Return count of transaction log backups in the last 24 hours,
-- whether they succeeded or not
SELECT @tlog_count=COUNT(*)
 FROM msdb.dbo.sysdbmaintplan_history
 WHERE database_name LIKE @dbname
 AND activity LIKE 'Backup transaction log'
 AND start_time > DATEADD(hour, -24, getdate())

-- Return count of failed verifies in the last 24 hours
SELECT @verify_fails=COUNT(*)
 FROM msdb.dbo.sysdbmaintplan_history
 WHERE database_name LIKE @dbname
 AND activity LIKE 'Verify Backup'
 AND start_time > DATEADD(hour, -24, getdate())
 AND succeeded=0

-- Return count of failed full backups in the last 24 hours
SELECT @backup_fails=COUNT(*)
 FROM msdb.dbo.sysdbmaintplan_history
 WHERE database_name LIKE @dbname
 AND activity LIKE 'Backup Database'
 AND start_time > DATEADD(hour, -24, getdate())
 AND succeeded=0

-- Return count of full backups in the last 24 hours, whether they succeeded or failed
SELECT @backup_count=COUNT(*)
 FROM msdb.dbo.sysdbmaintplan_history
 WHERE database_name LIKE @dbname
 AND activity LIKE 'Backup Database'
 AND start_time > DATEADD(hour, -24, getdate())

-- Return count of failed deletes in the last 24 hours
SELECT @delete_fails=COUNT(*)
 FROM msdb.dbo.sysdbmaintplan_history
 WHERE database_name LIKE @dbname
 AND activity LIKE 'Delete old%'
 AND start_time > DATEADD(hour, -24, getdate())
 AND succeeded=0

BEGIN TRANSACTION
-- Clear the previous results for this database on this server
DELETE FROM BackupLog
 WHERE Server=@@SERVERNAME
 AND DatabaseName=@dbname

-- Create a new record with the current information
```

```
INSERT BackupLog(DatabaseName, Server, IsSystemDB, TransCount,
  TransFails, VerifyFails, BackupCount, BackupFails, DeleteFails)
 SELECT @dbname, @@SERVERNAME, @IsSystem, @tlog_count, @tlog_fails, @verify_fails,
        @backup_count, @backup_fails, @delete_fails

-- If there are any problems put things back as they were
IF @@ERROR<>0
    ROLLBACK TRANSACTION
ELSE
    COMMIT TRANSACTION
```

The next procedure calls the check procedure for each applicable database – it is this procedure that is called hourly as an sql server agent job:

```
CREATE PROCEDURE adm_CheckAllBackups
AS

-- First do the user databases specified in the control table
DECLARE cr CURSOR READ_ONLY FOR
 SELECT DatabaseName
 FROM BackupList
 WHERE Server LIKE @@SERVERNAME

DECLARE @dbname varchar(50)

OPEN cr
FETCH NEXT FROM cr INTO @dbname

WHILE (@@fetch_status <> -1) BEGIN
IF (@@fetch_status <> -2)
 BEGIN
   EXEC adm_CheckBackups @dbname, 0
 END

FETCH NEXT FROM cr INTO @dbname

END

CLOSE cr
DEALLOCATE cr
-- finally do the system databases - these are done automatically,
-- and do not need to be specified in the BackupList table
EXEC adm_CheckBackups 'master',1
EXEC adm_CheckBackups 'model',1
EXEC adm_CheckBackups 'msdb',1

-- The distribution database will not exist on all servers, so a
-- check for its existence is performed first
IF EXISTS (SELECT * FROM master..SysDatabases
              WHERE name LIKE 'distribution')
   EXEC adm_CheckBackups 'distribution',1
```

Almost done now – the following view is used to support the summary which is emailed to staff. Notice that the first error checked for is if an update hasn't been received. This would indicate either a replication failure or a failure to run the statistics gathering job on the remote server.

```
CREATE VIEW vBackupReport
AS

select 1 AS Severity, 'Update not received' AS Error
  , Server, DatabaseName, TestDate
 from backuplog where testdate<DATEADD(day, -1, getdate())
union
select 5 AS Severity, 'System Backup not taken' AS Error
  , Server, DatabaseName, TestDate
 from backuplog
 where backupcount=0 and issystemdb=1
union
select 5 AS Severity, 'System Backup failed' AS Error
  , Server, DatabaseName, TestDate
 from backuplog
 where backupfails>0 and issystemdb=1
union
select 9 AS Severity, 'Application Backup failed' AS Error
 , Server, DatabaseName, TestDate
 from backuplog
 where backupfails>0 and issystemdb=0
```

```
union
select 9 AS Severity, 'Application Backup not taken' AS Error
, Server, DatabaseName, TestDate
from backuplog
where backupcount=0 and issystemdb=0
union
select 6 AS Severity, 'Application Backup (transaction) failed' AS Error
, Server, DatabaseName, TestDate
from backuplog
where transfails>0 and issystemdb=0
union
select 6 AS Severity, 'Application Backup (transaction) not taken' AS Error
, Server, DatabaseName, TestDate
from backuplog
where transcount<90 and issystemdb=0
union
select 4 AS Severity, 'Backup Verify fails' AS Error
, Server, DatabaseName, TestDate
from backuplog
where verifyfails>0
union
select 2 AS Severity, 'Backup Delete fails' AS Error
, Server, DatabaseName, TestDate
from backuplog
where deletefails>0
```

The output from this view is formatted a bit and sent by email to a distribution list on our site.

Conclusion

Hopefully, the above might prove useful to someone. It's all fairly simple stuff, but it has made the checking of remote system states far easier for us, and has given us a much greater degree of confidence that every site is working as it should be.

Finding Objects Owned by non-DBO Users

By Santveer Singh

In this article I will show how can we get the list of all the objects (table, Procedure, view or user defined function) owned by non DBO users. I believe this occurred most on Development server where developers don't have DBO rights in Database. To get the list of object we need to create below table and procedure.

Step 1: Create table ObjList using below script:

```
CREATE TABLE [ObjList] (
    [DBName] [sysname] NOT NULL ,
    [Object_Type] [varchar] (20)  NULL ,
    [ObjectOwner] [sysname] NOT NULL ,
    [ObjectName] [sysname] NOT NULL ,
    [cur_date] [datetime] NOT NULL CONSTRAINT [DF_ObjList_cur_date] DEFAULT (getdate())
)
ON [PRIMARY]
GO
```

Step 2: Create Procedure Object_owned_by_non_dbo using below script

```
SET QUOTED_IDENTIFIER ON
GO
SET ANSI_NULLS ON
GO
Create Procedure Object_owned_by_non_dbo
as
declare @dbname varchar(200)
declare @mSql1  varchar(8000)
Set nocount on

DECLARE DBName_Cursor CURSOR FOR
        select name
        from master.dbo.sysdatabases
        where name not in ('master','msdb','tempdb')
        Order by name
```

```
OPEN DBName_Cursor
FETCH NEXT FROM DBName_Cursor INTO @dbname

WHILE @@FETCH_STATUS = 0
 BEGIN
  Set @mSql1 = 'Insert into  ObjList (DBName, Object_Type, ObjectOwner,ObjectName)'+char(13)
  Set @mSql1 = @mSQL1+'Select '''+@dbname+''' as dbName,ObjType =
       Case xtype
                when ''u'' then ''Table''
                when ''V'' then ''View''
                when ''P'' then ''Procedure''
                when ''FN'' then ''UD Function''
                else xtype end
       , SU.name,SO.name  from '+@dbname+'.dbo.sysobjects SO join '+@dbname+'.dbo.sysusers SU
       on SO.uid = SU.uid and  su.name <> ''dbo''
       and SO.xtype in (''u'',''v'',''p'',''FN'')'

  --Print @mSql1
  Execute (@mSql1)

  FETCH NEXT FROM DBName_Cursor INTO @dbname
 END

CLOSE DBName_Cursor
DEALLOCATE DBName_Cursor
GO
```

Step 3: Please execute the below script to retrieve the list.

```
Select * from ObjList

DBName       Object_Type    ObjectOwner    ObjectName        cur_date
----------   -------------  -------------  ----------------  ------------------------
Database1    UD Function    Userv1         IS_FIELD_IN       2004-10-29 16:42:39.127
Database2    Table          Domain1\NT1    Vendor_Top200     2004-10-29 16:42:39.813
Database2    Table          Domain1\NT1    Supplier_Top200   2004-10-29 16:42:39.813
Database2    Table          Domain1\NT1    Emp_Top200        2004-10-29 16:42:39.813
```

Step 3: We can confined the list for specific user or database as below:

```
Select * from ObjList where DBName = 'Database1'

DBName       Object_Type    ObjectOwner    ObjectName        cur_date
----------   -------------  -------------  ----------------  ------------------------
Database1    UD Function    Userv1         IS_FIELD_IN       2004-10-29 16:42:39.127
```

Or

```
Select * from ObjList where ObjectOwner = 'Domian1\NT1'

DBName       Object_Type    ObjectOwner    ObjectName        cur_date
----------   -------------  -------------  ----------------  ------------------------
Database1    UD Function    Userv1         IS_FIELD_IN       2004-10-29 16:42:39.127
Database2    Table          Domain1\NT1    Vendor_Top200     2004-10-29 16:42:39.813
Database2    Table          Domain1\NT1    Supplier_Top200   2004-10-29 16:42:39.813
Database2    Table          Domain1\NT1    Emp_Top200        2004-10-29 16:42:39.813
```

I think you will like this procedure. Please don't forget to send me your comments on this article.

Four of a Kind - Backup Software Shootout

By Wes Brown

All DBAs are faced with the daunting task of backing up databases under their charge, and sometimes a more daunting task of restoring them. In this article we will look at four different backup solutions that can make that job easier. The thing that ties these four products together is compression. All of them offer different feature sets to set them apart and we will touch on those, but the focus here is real time compression and how it can help you. The theory behind compressing the data stream is simple: the results can be dramatic. Almost every return on investment figure uses $200 to $300 dollars per gigabyte saved.

This usually includes things that are easy to calculate like physical disk space, tape, and additional hardware required to store your backup files. It also includes other aspects of cost like the hours it takes to administer the disk and tape systems, and also time to backup and restore. The four solutions we chose for this article were SQL LiteSpeed by Imceda, SQL Safe from Idera, UltraBac from UltraBac Software, and MiniSQLBackup from yohz Software. Let's take a quick rundown of the other features each provides besides compression.

SQL LiteSpeed

Imceda's SQL LiteSpeed has several different options beyond compression. They also provide encryption as an add-on you can buy. New in 3.2 release features object level recovery even from standard Microsoft backups and multiple encryption algorithms to choose from. Backups are also multi-threaded into a single file to increase performance. The standard configuration comes with an MMC snap-in if you require a GUI interface that is easy to use and also includes wizards to convert your SQL Server generated maintenance plans to use SQL LiteSpeed.

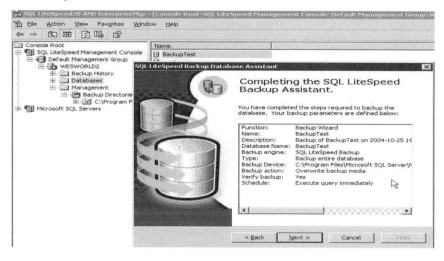

They also have a fully documented extended stored procedure library that is used to replace the backup and restore syntax in your SQL statements. Pricing is per processor and is not currently listed on their web site.

SQL Safe

Idera's SQL Safe is a newcomer to the SQL Server backup world and comes on strong. It was designed to compete with SQL LiteSpeed and offers multi-threaded, encrypted backups just like SQL LiteSpeed. It also has a nice user interface.

One of the features that separate the two products is the lack of extended stored procedures, the addition of a database that keeps an audit trail for backups and restores and a lightweight installer. The lack of extended stored procedures means you will have to use xp_cmdshell if you wish to still use T-SQL scripts to backup your databases. The database it adds initially bothered me. Personally, I like minimal intrusion or things I have to maintain along with my backups. In the process of reviewing the product, I found I like the database and the things it stores for you. It makes it easy to prove to management that you really are saving the money you claimed and also provides a long term audit trail for those of us that have to worry about compliance issues. Pricing is per server and is currently $995 dollars per SQL Server instance.

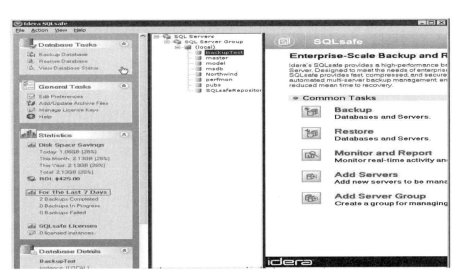

UltraBac

UltraBac Software's offering UltraBac does much, much more than SQL Server backups. I won't list them all here. Agents installed on the target server handle all backups. You will need the base and the SQL Server agent to backup your box. It comes with a GUI that seems a bit cluttered.

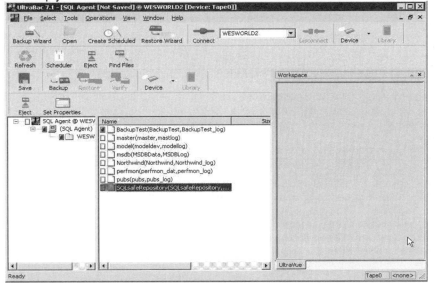

It also comes with a command line interface, but I didn't use it to do the SQL Server backups. I did have some issues backing up a clustered environment, which we will cover later. It was very stable and fast on a standalone SQL Server. One of the qualifications for this round-up was the ability to backup to disk. UltraBac does this by putting a virtual device that it can write to. It doesn't look like your normal file generated by any of the other products, it rolls them in files that are two gigabytes in size until the backup is done. Base pricing from the web site $495 for the base and $695 per SQL Server agent.

MiniSQLBackup

Yohz Software's MiniSQLBackup provides excellent functionality for its price point. It offers GUI, command-line, and extended stored procedure interfaces in the pro version.

Other than compression, it offers mirrored backup. The backup stream gets written to two files-either one will restore the database. MiniSQLBackup Lite is free. MiniSQLBackup Pro is $99 per server.

We will look at both ends of the server spectrum, large and small. This first set of tests is on a smaller hardware solution with a standalone install of SQL Server patched up to version 8.0.818.

Small setup consisted of a single LP1000r NetServer from HP. Dual 1ghz PIII with three 73 gigabyte hard drives striped RAID 0 for speed. I used a copy of the Northwind database populating Categories and Employees with around 900,000 records each to take the database size to 3.7 gigabytes of space used.

I ran all four products and a standard backup to compare them to. All backups were run at the lightest level of compression. If it was settable, everything else was left at default. All backups were performed to the same array.

I gathered performance monitor counters to get a reading on how much stress is being put on the server to perform the backups requested.

Type	Disk Time%	Avg. Queue Length	Disk Read Bytes/sec	Disk Write Bytes/sec	% Proc 0 Time	% Proc 1 Time
Standard Backup	146.75	1.46	21253095.16	21269876.73	1.43	7.11
MiniSQLBackup	35.48	0.35	4776407.02	2555435.72	31.70	45.63
SQL LiteSpeed	104.93	1.04	10012052.02	7169847.49	31.87	11.26
SQL Safe	527.45	5.27	7689851.62	7208673.84	10.13	25.48
UltraBac	1996.66	19.96	15189625.82	10864967.57	40.17	69.52

As you can see SQL LiteSpeed and SQL Safe both used about the same amount of CPU. SQL Safe put more pressure on the disk systems than SQL LiteSpeed. The Disk stats are puzzling I expected them to all use the same amount of disk bytes or be close to each other and a standard backup to be more which it was. That seemed to be the only thing that stayed true.

These are stats reported back ether through the GUI or through query analyzer.

Type	File Size	Time Reported	Time in App	MB/Sec
Standard	3793.27	2.59	3:07	25.57

MiniSQLBackup	2024.07	13.33	16:06	4.97
SQL LiteSpeed	2709.85	5.31	6:27	12.47
SQL Safe	2706.12	6.59	8:00	10.05
Ultrabac	2802.31	4.17	4:07	15.73

These numbers also seemed out of line with my personal experience and with numbers in the second set of the test. I think this may be a side effect of almost zero blank spaces in the random sample data, since it was random letters and numbers and not random whole words.

All products in this first phase of the testing worked as promised and without any issues at all. In part two we will deal with ten times the data on a much larger machine in a clustered setup.

Four of a Kind - Backup Software Shootout Part 2

By Wes Brown

Welcome back. In part one we took a look at four different software packages that have many, many features, but all had one thing in common: the ability to compress backups. If you haven't read part one please review it here. The four solutions we chose for this article were SQL LiteSpeed by Imceda, SQL Safe from Idera, UltraBac from UltraBac Software, and MiniSQLBackup from yohz Software.

The hardware and software configuration for the next set of test shows the other end of the spectrum. The server is an HP LH6000 with six 700mhz PIII processors with eight gigabytes of ram attached to an older EMC 3700 with 128 disks available. The OS is Windows 2000 Enterprise configured as a cluster with SQL Server 2000 Enterprise built 8.0.818 installed on it. The sample data is a typical set of data you would find in any company's CRM solution. The actual data size is 42.6 gigabytes in an 89.8 gigabyte database spread across eight files in a single-file group. The tests were set up this way to make sure that the software you use to backup your smaller machines is still appropriate on your most critical servers.

Unfortunately, UltraBac failed to backup the cluster. I did speak to their technical support and followed all the instructions and recommendations they made. Even as far as loading a secondary machine separate from the cluster setting up a network alias to the cluster name in the client network utility, nothing worked. Similarly, MiniSQLBackup also wouldn't backup the cluster. I got in contact with Yohz Software. They were very responsive and within a week had a new build that did backup the cluster successfully.

I ran all four products and a standard backup to compare them to. All backups were run at the lightest level of compression, if it was settable, everything else was left at default. All backups were written to a different set of drives separate from the data and log drives that were allocated to SQL Server.

I gathered performance monitor counters to get a reading on how much stress is being put on the server to perform the backups requested.

Type	CPU	% Avg Disk Time Backup Drive	Avg Queue Length Back up Drive	Avg Read Bytes/Sec Backup Drive	Avg Write Bytes/Sec Backup Drive	% Avg Disk Time DB Drive	Avg Disk Queue Length DB Disk	Avg Read Bytes/sec DB Drive	Avg Disk Write Bytes/sec DB drive
SQL Standard	1.59	70.63	0.71	0.00	14887214.30	283.22	2.83	1487610 5.52	1521.16
MiniSQLBackup	14.56	15.35	0.15	151.97	3825357.96	148.96	1.49	2300542 1.18	1414.37
SQL LiteSpeed	12.57	33.89	0.34	0.57	5869727.27	391.09	3.91	3090952 3.40	1641.73
SQL Safe	12.49	28.07	0.28	432.87	4929578.58	112.84	1.13	2569351 6.68	1393.89

UltraBac	0.00	0.00	0.00	0.00	0.00	0.00	0.00	0.00	0.00

These numbers are well within what I expected. It just goes to show you testing on real world data always generates the best results. The numbers are broken up into two sets; the first four samples shows average CPU utilization and the stress put on the set of disks the backup files were placed on. The second set is the drives that the database files were on. The load, as we expected, is greater on the CPU; but, in some cases, much less on the disk subsystems. The only exception to this is SQL LiteSpeed, but it makes up for the added stress by being the quickest in the field.

These are stats reported back either through the GUI or through query analyzer.

Type	File Size	Time reported by command output	Time in App	MB/Sec
Standard	34,516,316	39.59	39.37	14.88
MiniSQLBackup	5,736,467	25.45	25.45	23.14
SQL LiteSpeed	6,586,690	18.06	18.57	32.62
SQL Safe	6,586,829	22.66	22.46	26.00
UltraBac	0	0	0	0

As you can see, all solutions that did operate in the clustered environment did pretty well. Even the least expensive product produced a compressed file much smaller than the original backup with a significant savings in backup time.

Backing up a SQL Server in record times with great savings on disk space is one thing, what about restoring these databases in a timely manor? I've never been in a restore situation where time wasn't a factor.

In part one of this article we used a smaller machine configuration. All of the backups taken were also restored. No additional parameters were passed to the restore statements all databases were restored over the top of the original database.

Type	Time Reported in QA	Time Reported In App	MB/Sec
Standard Restore	8:29	7.90	8.388
MiniSQLBackup	0	7.24	9.152
SQL LiteSpeed	8:00	6.58	10.072
SQL Safe	9:06	7.34	9.035
UltraBac	0	5.57	8.037

These times may look a little strange. Two of the apps I used the GUI to restore the database just like I did to back them up. All of the restores generally took less time than the standard SQL Server restore commands. SQL Safe edged in when it came to the report in milliseconds, but the time in Query Analyzer shows a small increase over the standard restore. I may chalk this one up to the fact the command is run by calling the xp_cmdshell. Overall, in the smaller server configuration, UltraBac had the times to beat in the backup process and restore. It did turn in the lightest amount of compression overall. SQL LiteSpeed was the next best and had a decent amount of compression.

In the cluster configuration these were the numbers returned for the restore:

Type	Time Reported in QA	Time Reported In App	MB/Sec
Standard Restore	48.27	47.73	12.34
MiniSQLBackup	0	36.56	16.11
SQL LiteSpeed	36.15	35.63	18.65
SQL Safe	32.32	31.59	18.64
UltraBac	0.00	0.00	0

In our clustered real world data set all programs beat the standard restore times by a significant margin with SQL Safe turning the best time overall.

Lessons Learned

To be honest with you, I had a mild bias when starting these tests. I have been a long-time user of SQL LiteSpeed and really expected it to just walk away with most of the test scores. I was initially skeptical that SQL Safe could do so well in these tests, being so new on the market and being a direct competitor against SQL LiteSpeed, who has had years to perfect the product. Another great surprise to me was how well a $99 tool stood up against this field. I wasn't surprised when it failed to run in a clustered setup, but what did shock me is how quickly Yohz software turned around a new build of MiniSQLBackup that did work, and work well. The only disappointment was UltraBac. It did perform well in the standalone, which was a plus, but configuration failed to run in a cluster setup no matter what I tried. Also, the GUI left much to be desired. It feels like they are trying to be all things to all people, and not doing SQL Server backups justice. Personally, I would say it is a coin toss between SQL LiteSpeed and SQL Safe as the top two contenders. SQL LiteSpeed was faster on backup and SQL Safe was faster on restores. Both have a great feature set . Without complete pricing information I would be hard pressed to pick the best between these two great products. Both Products have new releases in the works; 4.0 of SQL LiteSpeed is due in the middle or late November, SQL Safe has 1.2 due out now. If you must have compression in your backup scheme and you are on a tight budget, MiniSQLBackup is a great alternative. At ten times less the cost of even SQL Safe it is a fantastic value.

If you have any questions about this article, or methods used in the evaluation feel free to send email to admin@wesworld.net.

How To Find SQL Server Objects

By Ashish Kaushal

How many times do we as SQL developers or DBAs find ourselves shuffling through objects in Enterprise Manager or expanding the left pane of Query Analyzer, trying to find a table or view for which we have no clue except a nearly correct name, and the only way we would know that it is the right object is looking at its meta data or text. Well, it might not be an everyday kind of thing, but it does happen from time to time (or perhaps not in an idealistic situation where all databases are well documented and all names follow a well defined naming convention with no exceptions; and most of all, the employees never quit).

A better why to find a SQL Server object, such as a table, a procedure, or a trigger, would be to query the sysobjects system table in the local database (of course, one has to be certain about which database that object is supposed be in). For example:

```
Select * From sysobjects
Where name like 'ClientInvoice%'
```

(Script I)

Executing the above query displays all the objects in current database whose name starts with "ClientInvoice". If the type of the object to be searched is known, then the query can be changed to provide only that type of object whose name start with "ClientInvoice". This might return a much smaller and more readable resultset. For example:

```
Select * From sysobjects
Where xtype = 'U' And name like 'ClientInvoice%'
-- 'U' for user table
```

(Script II)

The main shortcoming of above methods is that the sysobjects table is database specific. If one does not know which database contains the object, then the above query has to be run in all the databases to find the object.

Is there an easier way to write a query which searches all the databases in a single step to locate a specific object and/or of a specific object type? The answer is yes, by using the handy sp_MSforeachdb procedure.

For example:

```
Exec sp_MSforeachdb
'Select * From ?..sysobjects where xtype= ''U''
And name like ''ClientInvoice% '''
```

(Script III)

Sp_MSforeachdb is an undocumented (also means unsupported) procedure available in both SQL Server 7 and SQL Server 2000. It takes one string argument, which in our case is same as Script II, but there is one important difference, if we look carefully at Script III, it has "From ?..sysobjects" instead of simply "From sysobjects" as in Script II.

Why ? This is important, because sp_MSforeachdb uses dynamic SQL internally, and "?" is the placeholder for the name of the database, and it keep substituting "?" with the name of each database as it loops through all the database names, thereby accessing the sysobjects table in each database in a cycle in sequence. Suppose if there are n databases, if we do not supply "?", then sp_MSforeachdb of-course loop through the n databases but keep accessing sysobjects table of the current database (that is the database we are running this query in) n-times.

Now that we know "?" is, the placeholder for the name of database, why not try to write a script which could provide a result set with name of database, name of object, and type of object.

-- Part 1

```
Declare @sqlstr
nvarchar(200)

-- Part 2
/* drop the temporary
table if already exists */
If Object_Id('tempdb..#tblDBObjects') is Not Null
Drop table# tblDBObjects
/* create temporary table */
Create TABLE #tblDBObjects (
dbName sysname,
objName varchar(200),
objtype char(2)
)

-- Part 3
/*assign string value to
variable */
Select @sqlstr = 'sp_msforeachdb ''Insert tblDBObjects select ''''?'''' as
DBName, name, xtype From ?..sysobjects'''
/* execute SQL string */
Exec sp_executesql @sqlstr

-- Part 4
/* select from temp
table */
Select * From #tblDBObjects Where name like 'ClientInvoice%'
RETURN
```

(Script IV)

Explanation of the Above Script

Part 1 of the script simply declares variable with the nvarchar datatype. This is because the string, which is to be executed with the sp_executeSQL procedure, must be of nvarchar type.

Part 2 checks to see if the temporary table with the name tblDBObjects already exits. If temporary table tblDBObjects exits, it drops it. Then it creates a temporary table with the name #tblDBObjects. '#' tells that the table should be temporary, so is created in the tempdb database. A temporary table is automatically dropped once the script completes execution successfully.

Part 3 create a SQL string which inserts the values in #tblDBObjects as it loops through databases and select values from the sysobjects table. The reason for using this string and sp_ExecuteSQL is that it could enable us to provide object type as an input in case we want to write a stored procedure and pass the object name, as well as object type, as input parameters. Providing object types would extract smaller result set and might also speed up operation where there are too many enormous databases. This has been explained in Script V.

Part 4: Once the temp table has been populated, records can be pulled out as needed.

Here's a Stored Procedure May Want to Use to Find Objects

```
Create PROC FindObject_usp
(
@objname varchar(200) = Null
, @objtype varchar(20) = Null
)
As
Declare @sqlstr nvarchar(200)

-- Insert wildcard, if exact search is not required.
-- Set @objname = '%' + @objname + '%'
-- Its better to supply custom wild card in the input parameter @objname

/* drop the temporary table if already exists */
If Object_Id('tempdb..#tblDBObjects') is Not Null
Drop table #tblDBObjects
/* create temporary table */
Create TABLE #tblDBObjects (
dbName sysname,
objName varchar(200),
objtype char(2)
)
Begin
If @objtype = 'CHECK'

Select @sqlstr = 'sp_msforeachdb ''Insert #tblDBObjects select ''''?'''' as
DBName, name, xtype From ?..sysobjects where xtype = ''''C'''''''''
If @objtype = 'Default'

Select @sqlstr = 'sp_msforeachdb ''Insert #tblDBObjects select ''''?'''' as
DBName, name, xtype From ?..sysobjects where xtype = ''''D'''''''''
If @objtype = 'FOREIGN KEY'

Select @sqlstr = 'sp_msforeachdb ''Insert #tblDBObjects select ''''?'''' as
DBName, name, xtype From ?..sysobjects where xtype = ''''F'''''''''
If @objtype = 'Log'

Select @sqlstr = 'sp_msforeachdb ''Insert #tblDBObjects select ''''?'''' as
DBName, name, xtype From ?..sysobjects where xtype = ''''L'''''''''
If @objtype = 'Scalar function'

Select @sqlstr = 'sp_msforeachdb ''Insert #tblDBObjects select ''''?'''' as
DBName, name, xtype From ?..sysobjects where xtype = ''''FN'''''''''
If @objtype = 'Inlined table-function'

Select @sqlstr = 'sp_msforeachdb ''Insert #tblDBObjects select ''''?'''' as
DBName, name, xtype From ?..sysobjects where xtype = ''''IF'''''''''
If @objtype = 'Stored procedure'

Select @sqlstr = 'sp_msforeachdb ''Insert #tblDBObjects select ''''?'''' as
DBName, name, xtype From ?..sysobjects where xtype = ''''P'''''''''
If @objtype = 'PRIMARY KEY'

Select @sqlstr = 'sp_msforeachdb ''Insert #tblDBObjects select ''''?'''' as
DBName, name, xtype From ?..sysobjects where xtype = ''''PK'''''''''
If @objtype = 'Replication filter stored procedure'

Select @sqlstr = 'sp_msforeachdb ''Insert #tblDBObjects select ''''?'''' as
DBName, name, xtype From ?..sysobjects where xtype = ''''RF'''''''''
If @objtype = 'System table'

Select @sqlstr = 'sp_msforeachdb ''Insert #tblDBObjects select ''''?'''' as
DBName, name, xtype From ?..sysobjects where xtype = ''''S'''''''''
If @objtype = 'Table function'

Select @sqlstr = 'sp_msforeachdb ''Insert #tblDBObjects select ''''?'''' as
DBName, name, xtype From ?..sysobjects where xtype = ''''TF'''''''''
If @objtype = 'Trigger'

Select @sqlstr = 'sp_msforeachdb ''Insert #tblDBObjects select ''''?'''' as
```

```
DBName, name, xtype From ?..sysobjects where xtype = ''''TR''''''''
If @objtype = 'User table'

Select @sqlstr = 'sp_msforeachdb ''Insert #tblDBObjects select ''''?'''' as
DBName, name, xtype From ?..sysobjects where xtype = ''''U''''''''
If @objtype = 'UNIQUE constraint'

Select @sqlstr = 'sp_msforeachdb ''Insert #tblDBObjects select ''''?'''' as
DBName, name, xtype From ?..sysobjects where xtype = ''''UQ''''''''
If @objtype = 'View'

Select @sqlstr = 'sp_msforeachdb ''Insert #tblDBObjects select ''''?'''' as
DBName, name, xtype From ?..sysobjects where xtype = ''''V''''''''
If @objtype = 'Extended stored procedure'

Select @sqlstr = 'sp_msforeachdb ''Insert #tblDBObjects select ''''?'''' as
DBName, name, xtype From ?..sysobjects where xtype = ''''X''''''''
If (@objtype = '') Or (@objtype is Null)
Select @sqlstr = 'sp_msforeachdb ''Insert #tblDBObjects select ''''?'''' as
DBName, name, xtype From ?..sysobjects'''
End
/* execute SQL string */
If (@sqlstr <> '') Or (@sqlstr is Not Null)
Exec sp_executesql @sqlstr
/* If @objname is not supplied it should still return result */
If (@objname = '') Or (@objname is Null)
Select * From #tblDBObjects
Else
Select * From #tblDBObjects Where objName like @objname
RETURN
```

(Script V)

The above script creates a stored procedure which takes two optional parameters: @objname (name of the object to be searched) and @objtype (type of the object to be searched). Different types of object type and their abbreviations can be found in SQL online help for sysobjects string). Stored procedure FindObject_usp creates different SQL string based on different object types, e.g., @objtype parameter; if @objtype is not provided it selects all the objects from sysobjects table and inserts into #tblDBObjects temp table. It is evident that in case of enormous databases if object type is known, providing @objtype parameter makes query much faster. Once #tblDBObjects table has been populated it can be queried with @objname parameter with or without a wild card as needed.

We can execute the FindObject_usp procedure, for example, to find a object of type Check constraints whose name starts with 'CK_B' as;

```
Exec FindObject_usp
'CK_B%', 'check'
```

Or

```
Exec FindObject_usp1
'xp_%', Null
```

Conclusion

I assume that this procedure would be used by database administrators on an as-needed basis. This is not something which would run on database servers most of the time, but if performance is an issue, you could substitute the use of a temp table with a table datatype. Once the procedure is in place somewhere in a dbadmin or similar database where DBA scripts are kept you can start using it, which would hopefully make a DBAs life much easier.

Published with the express written permission of the author. Copyright 2004.

Monitoring Drive and Database Free Space

By Mark Nash

It's 13:30 AM and you get a call from the Applications On-Call person. Application XYZ is down, looks like a SQL Server problem. You find that a drive or database is out of space, causing the SQL Server to crash. Now the difficult part: find some free space and hope the SQL Server will successfully recover!! We will not even consider the Application downtime, corrupt databases, etc…

We began addressing this issue several years ago, as the number of SQL Servers at our institution increased (currently 60+). We have since developed a system of stored procedures/SQL jobs that monitor drive/database space, send email/page notifications as necessary, produce weekly reports and record the information for historical review. We feel they are worth sharing. Possibly you can use all or part of this system.

For this system to properly function, all SQL Servers must have the ability to send email. We use 'xp_sendmail'. We decided several years ago that all our SQL Servers would use email to notify us of problems. We use 2 types of email accounts. The first is for events that can wait for the next workday; e.g., problems on development SQL Servers, where an email will suffice. The second is for events that require immediate attention; e.g., a failed DBCC check on a production SQL Server, where an email-generate page is used. In the following examples, we will be using the first email type.

Drive Space Monitoring.

Monitoring of space begins at the Disk Drive level. We run the 'Disk Drive Space Info' job hourly, using SQL Server Agent. The basic job steps are:

- Step 1 – Create DrvSpace Table.
- Step 2 – Get Drive Space Data.
- Step 3 – Alter Table DrvSpace
- Step 4 – Enter Drive Total Space.
- Step 5 – MonitorEmailLowDriveFreeSpace

Here is a detailed look at these steps:

Step 1 – Create DrvSpace Table. This step simply creates an empty table 'DrvSpace' in tempdb for each run.

```
use tempdb
go
If exists (select name from tempdb..sysobjects where name = 'DrvSpace' and type = 'U')
 begin
    drop     table DrvSpace
 end

Create table DrvSpace (
    DriveLetter    char(02)   null,
    MB_Free        float      null)
```

Step 2 – Get Drive Space Data. This step executes xp_fixeddrives, and inserts the output into table DrvSpace.

```
use tempdb
go
INSERT DrvSpace EXECUTE master..xp_fixeddrives
```

Step 3 – Alter Table DrvSpace. This step alters table DrvSpace by adding a column for Total Drive Space.

```
use tempdb
go
Alter Table DrvSpace ADD MB_Total float NULL
```

Step 4 – Enter Drive Total Space. This step requires editing. Here you enter the Total Drive Space in GB for a given drive. In this example the 'C' drive has 3.99 GB of Total Drive Space. This portion of code needs to be repeated for each drive on the server that will be monitored.

```
use tempdb
go
update DrvSpace
 set MB_Total = (3.99 * 1024)
```

```
where DriveLetter = 'C'
```

Step 5 – MonitorEmailLowDriveFreeSpace. This step executes the Stored Procedure sp_Monitor_Email_Low_Drive_Free_Space'. As executed here, it will look for local drives with under 10% (0.1) free space. Email notifications are sent, identifying these drives. This procedure is actually more flexible than displayed here: the C: Drive is handled separately with a 15% free space limit and any other Drive can be specified as an 'exception' with its own specific free space limit. Documentation embedded in this Stored Procedure details its operation.

```
EXEC msdb.dbo.sp_Monitor_Email_Low_Drive_FreeSpace 0.1
```

Code:sp_Monitor_Email_Low_Drive_FreeSpace.sql

Database Space Monitoring

Now that we have Drive Space Information, we gather Database Space Information and current SQL Server Disaster Recovery Information. We run the 'Database Info' job daily, using SQL Server Agent. The basic job steps are:

- Step 1 – Initialize Tables in msdb.
- Step 2 – Capture Space Info on all DBs.
- Step 3 – MonitorEmailLowDBFreeSpace
- Step 4 – Current SQL Server Disaster Recovery Info

Here is an detailed look at these steps:

Step 1 - Initialize Tables in msdb. This step simply creates a table 'DASD' in msdb. This table name is a throwback to earlier days, when Disk Drives were referred to as Direct Access Storage Devices. We elected to use the msdb database, rather than create a new database for just one table. The size of DASD is managed in Step 3.

```
use msdb
go
if not exists (select name from msdb..sysobjects
               where name = 'DASD'
               and type  = 'U')
begin
  create table msdb..DASD
  ( createDTM varchar(20),  SQL_Server varchar(30),
    db_name varchar(30),     group_name varchar(30),
    group_alias varchar(30), total_DB_space varchar(10),
    group_type varchar(20), free_DB_space varchar(10),
    total_drive_space varchar(10), free_drive_space varchar(10),
    drvLetter varchar(5), db_maxsize int, db_growth int
  )
end
```

Step 2 - Capture Space Info on all DBs. This step execute Stored Procedure 'sp_Monitor_Capture_DB_Space_Info', which captures space information on all databases. It also combines relevant Disk Drive information (drives containing that database's files), and writes this information to table DASD. An issue with this Stored Procedure is that it queries system tables to obtain its information. This may become a problem with MS SQL 2005, and will have to be addressed as more information on MS SQL 2005 system tables becomes available. Documentation embedded in this Stored Procedure details its operation.

```
EXEC msdb..sp_Monitor_Capture_DB_Space_Info
```

Code:sp_Monitor_Capture_DB_Space_Info.sql

Step 3 - MonitorEmailLowDBFreeSpace. This step executes Stored Procedure 'sp_Monitor_Email_Low_DB_FreeSpace'. As with Disk Drives, an overall Free Space % can be set for all databases, with 2 exception databases/sizes specified. Free Space on databases with no growth is computed from un-allocated database space, while Free Space on databases with max size limits included potential yet unused database size in its computations. Databases with no growth limits are not included in Free Space computations or Emails. Emails from the Disk Drive Free Space portion of the system are considered sufficient. This Stored Procedure also purges all rows in DASD > 1 year old, except for those generated on Fridays, thus leaving 1 space recording/week/database. Finally, this Stored Procedure sends Emails notifications on any database , other then *'tempdb'*, that was created 1 or 4 days ago, keeping track of over ambitious Application Staff. Documentation embedded in this Stored Procedure details its operation.

```
EXEC msdb.dbo.sp_Monitor_Email_Low_DB_FreeSpace 0.1
```

Code:sp_Monitor_Email_Low_DB_FreeSpace.sql

Step 4 – Current SQL Server Disaster Recovery Info. Finally, this step executes Stored Procedure 'sp_MSSQL_Recovery_Info', which captures disaster recovery information on all databases. It has nothing to do with Space Usage, it was just convenient to run it here. The output of this Stored Procedure is saved to a local Drive. This information is finally copied to a central information server using ftp, along with similar information from all MS SQL Servers. Documentation embedded in this Stored Procedure details its operation.

```
EXEC msdb..sp_MSSQL_Recovery_Info
```

Code:sp_MSSQL_Recovery_Info.sql

Weekly Database Space Reports

We generate weekly Database Space Reports from a Support Server, using osql commands in bat files. These jobs are scheduled using the standard W2K Scheduler. The prior week's reports are overlaid with the current week's reports. These reports are viewed as needed and are a wonderful source of information for Disk Drive Space Predictions. The Stored Procedure sp_DASD_Report is run locally on each SQL Server.

An example of this weekly report follows.

```
Date      SQL SERVER  DB Name       TotalDB MB  FreeDB MB  Autogrow  Max DB Size  Free Disk MB
--------  ----------  ------------  ----------  ---------  --------  -----------  ------------
20040326  SQLSERVER   AdminReports       46.69      18.93  YES               500         15065
20040402  SQLSERVER   AdminReports       46.69      18.70  YES               500         14331
20040409  SQLSERVER   AdminReports       46.69      15.70  YES               500         13927
20040416  SQLSERVER   AdminReports       51.38      20.86  YES               500         12490
20040423  SQLSERVER   AdminReports       51.38      20.02  YES               500         11652
20040430  SQLSERVER   AdminReports       51.38      18.99  YES               500         10920
20040507  SQLSERVER   AdminReports       51.38      17.48  YES               500          9861
20201225              AdminReports
20040326  SQLSERVER   Management       3243.88    1423.38  YES  Unrestricted         15065
20040402  SQLSERVER   Management       3243.88    1423.38  YES  Unrestricted         14331
20040409  SQLSERVER   Management       3243.88    1345.60  YES  Unrestricted         13927
20040416  SQLSERVER   Management       3243.88    1345.59  YES  Unrestricted         12490
20040423  SQLSERVER   Management       3243.88    1345.59  YES  Unrestricted         11652
20040430  SQLSERVER   Management       3243.88    1345.59  YES  Unrestricted         10920
20040507  SQLSERVER   Management       3243.88    1345.59  YES  Unrestricted          9861
20201225              Management
20040326  SQLSERVER   Employee       131072.00   10749.23  NO    131072.00         53093
20040402  SQLSERVER   Employee       131072.00    9828.36  NO    131072.00         53093
20040409  SQLSERVER   Employee       131072.00    9363.62  NO    131072.00         53093
20040416  SQLSERVER   Employee       131072.00    8423.04  NO    131072.00         53093
20040423  SQLSERVER   Employee       131072.00    7513.55  NO    131072.00         53093
20040507  SQLSERVER   Employee       131072.00    6848.62  NO    131072.00         53093
20201225              Employee
```

Code:sp_DASD_Report.sql

Conclusion

We have far too many SQL Servers to visit each day and review Database/Drive Free Space. This system allows us to focus on other aspects of Database Administration, knowing we will be informed if Free Space is becoming an issue on any of our SQL Servers.

Code: sp_Monitor_Email_Low_Drive_FreeSpace.sql
sp_Monitor_Capture_DB_Space_Info.sql
sp_MSSQL_Recovery_Info.sql
sp_Monitor_Email_Low_DB_FreeSpace.sql

sp_DASD_Report.sql

Moving System Databases - A Checklist

By Christoffer Hedgate

Moving a database in SQL Server is normally as simple as detaching it from the server, moving it to its new location and then attaching it again. However, that only counts for user databases. Moving system databases requires quite a bit more work. Since I had to do this a couple of times during the last weeks, I wrote down a simple checklist that I could follow to make sure it was done right, so I did not screw up the servers and could speed up the process as much as possible. And since I guess I will be doing it again sometime in the future and inevitably will lose the notes I scribbled down, I thought I could just as well post them here for safe-keeping. If anyone wants to use this checklist go ahead, but remember to do the steps in the exact order of the list, and make sure you have all the necessary backups before starting. To be completely clear, doing this wrong can completely screw up your databases, and I cannot take any responsibility if anything does go wrong. Also note that the checklist was written for the specific situation I encountered. Your system databases might have more data files and/or other file paths and names than those in the list, so you might need to make some changes. Have fun!

1. Make sure you have backups of all user databases plus master, model and msdb.
2. Moving msdb and model
   1. In Enterprise Manager, right-click the server and choose Properties.
   2. Click Startup Parameters.
   3. Add a new parameter "-T3608" (without the quotes)
   4. Stop SQL Server.
   5. Start SQL Server, and make sure that SQL Agent is NOT started.
   6. Run the following command in Query Analyzer:

```
use master
go
exec sp_detach_db 'msdb'
go
exec sp_detach_db 'model'
go
```

   7. Move the data and log files for both msdb (normally msdbdata.mdf and msdblog.ldf) and model (normally model.mdf and modellog.mdf) to their new locations.
   8. Run the following in Query Analyzer:

```
use master
go
exec sp_attach_db 'model'
   , 'PATH_TO_MODEL_DATAFILE\model.mdf'
      , 'PATH_TO_MODEL_LOGFILE\modellog.ldf'
go
```

   9. Remove the -T3608 flag in Enterprise Manager/Server/Properties/Startup Parameters.
   10. Stop SQL Server.
   11. Start SQL Server.
   12. Run the following in Query Analyzer and check that the file paths are correct:

```
use model
go
exec sp_helpfile
go
```

13. Run the following in Query Analyzer:

```
use master
go
exec sp_attach_db 'msdb'
    , 'PATH_TO_MSDB_DATAFILE\msdbdata.mdf'
        , 'PATH_TO_MSDB_LOGFILE\msdblog.ldf'
go
```

14. Run the following in Query Analyzer and check that the file paths are correct:

```
use msdb
go
exec sp_helpfile
go
```

15. Finished!
3. Moving tempdb
    1. Run the following in Query Analyzer:

```
use master
go
alter database tempdb modify file (name = tempdev
    , filename = 'PATH_TO_NEW_LOCATION_OF_TEMPDB_DATAFILE\tempdb.mdf')
go
alter database tempdb modify file (name = templog
    , filename = 'PATH_TO_NEW_LOCATION_OF_TEMPDB_DATAFILE\templog.ldf')
go
```

    2. Stop SQL Server
    3. Start SQL Server
    4. Run the following in Query Analyzer and check that the file paths correspond to those stated in step 1:

```
use tempdb
go
exec sp_helpfile
go
```

    5. Stop SQL Server.
    6. Move the original data and log files for tempdb to some new location, or rename them, just so that you are sure that SQL Server can not be using them.
    7. Start SQL Server.
    8. Run the following in Query Analyzer and check that no error occurs:

```
use tempdb
go
create table test (a int)
insert into test (a) values (1)
select * from test
drop table test
go
```

    9. Remove the original data and log files for tempdb.
    10. Finished!

NOTE: Steps 5 through 8 are, of course, not really necessary. They are just included as a quick extra check to really make sure that nothing went wrong. Skip them if you wish.

4. Moving master

Note: In this scenario we are not only moving the master database, we are also moving all of the files that SQL Server uses in its 'data location' (as specified when installing SQL Server). The situation I encountered was that SQL Server's data location was specified to be something like D:\ (though with the program files as normal on C:\Program Files\Microsoft SQL Server\), but now the entire D:\ drive needed to be removed, so we needed to move everything SQL Server had stored there, plus all references to it, to avoid problems in the future. If you are only moving the master database you only need to follow the applicable steps of, course.

   1. In Enterprise Manager, right-click the server and choose Properties.
   2. Click Startup Parameters.
   3. Remove all of the three parameters that are already there (if there are more, remove the three that correspond to the three below in step 4).
   4. Add the three following parameters:
      -dPATH_TO_NEW_LOCATION_OF_MASTER_MDFFILE\master.mdf
      -ePATH_TO_NEW_LOCATION_OF_SQLAGENT_ERRORLOG\ERRORLOG
      -lPATH_TO_NEW_LOCATION_OF_MASTER_LOGFILE\mastlog.ldf

      In my case the values of these parameters where as follows:
      -dE:\MSSQL\Data\master.mdf
      -eE:\MSSQL\LOG\ERRORLOG
      -lE:\MSSQL\Data\mastlog.ldf
   5. Stop SQL Server.
   6. Move the files as specified below:

```
OLD_PATH_TO_MASTER_MDFFILE\master.mdf --> NEW_PATH_TO_MASTER_MDFFILE\master.mdf
OLD_PATH_TO_MASTER_LOGFILE\Data\mastlog.ldf --> NEW_PATH_TO_MASTER_LOGFILE\mastlog.ldf
OLD_PATH_TO_SQL_DATA_LOCATION\BACKUP --> NEW_PATH_TO_SQL_DATA_LOCATION
             (the entire folder with everything in it)
OLD_PATH_TO_SQL_DATA_LOCATION\JOBS --> NEW_PATH_TO_SQL_DATA_LOCATION
             (the entire folder with everything in it)
OLD_PATH_TO_SQL_DATA_LOCATION\LOG --> NEW_PATH_TO_SQL_DATA_LOCATION
             (the entire folder with everything in it)
OLD_PATH_TO_SQL_DATA_LOCATION\REPLDATA --> NEW_PATH_TO_SQL_DATA_LOCATION
             (the entire folder with everything in it)
```

   7. Make the following changes to the registry (using regedit):

```
         HKEY_LOCAL_MACHINE\SOFTWARE\Microsoft\MSSQLServer\MSSQLServer
   BackupDirectory = NEW_PATH_TO_SQL_DATA_LOCATION\BACKUP

   HKEY_LOCAL_MACHINE\SOFTWARE\Microsoft\MSSQLServer\Replication
      WorkingDirectory = NEW_PATH_TO_SQL_DATA_LOCATION\REPLDATA

   HKEY_LOCAL_MACHINE\SOFTWARE\Microsoft\MSSQLServer\Setup
      SQLDataRoot = NEW_PATH_TO_SQL_DATA_LOCATION\

   HKEY_LOCAL_MACHINE\SOFTWARE\Microsoft\MSSQLServer\SQLServerAgent
      ErrorLogFile = NEW_PATH_TO_SQL_DATA_LOCATION\LOG\SQLAGENT.OUT
      WorkingDirectory = NEW_PATH_TO_SQL_DATA_LOCATION\JOBS
```

      Note: This checklist does not cover servers using full-text search. If your server does use FT, then you will need to expand steps 6 and 7. Just move the FT directory in step 6 and search the registry for any references to it and change them as necessary.
   8. Start SQL Server.
   9. Finished!
5. If you are using SQL Agent on your server do not forget to make sure that it is running.

Conclusion

So there we are, all system databases moved. Again, please note that this was mainly meant as a checklist for myself, but feel free to use it as a base for your own checklist when you need to move system databases. I urge you to read through it several times so you are sure what it says and what you are doing. Most of the steps here come from the Microsoft article Moving SQL Server databases to a new location with Detach/Attach, which will probably help you more than this list. I simply compiled them into an easy-to-follow, step-by-step list that I could use to cut the down-time as much as possible.

Scheduled MS Cluster Failovers using Automation Server Objects

By Anthony Bressi

If you are working in an Active-Passive clustered SQL Server environment, there are often times when you need to initiate a failover so that you can perform routine maintenance tasks on the Passive server - to apply service packs, install software, etc. In this article Iwill outline a quick and easy way to perform scheduled failovers using the MS Cluster Service Automation Classes.

Microsoft's Cluster Automation Server Objects enable developers and DBAs to manage their MS Cluster server through Component Object Model (COM) objects using COM aware languages such as Visual Basic and C++ and aware scripting languages like VB Script. In this article we will use Visual Basic 6.0 to develop a short application that can be scheduled to failover a server cluster. This article assumes that you are familiar with creating and running projects in Visual Basic and therefore skips basics such as variable declaration in an effort to keep the sample code blocks short.

To develop code using the Cluster Automation Server objects you will need to download The Platform SDK if you do not already have it installed locally. At the time of this writing it can be downloaded from Microsoft at http://www.microsoft.com/msdownload/platformsdk/sdkupdate/psdk-full.htm.

To start, make a new "Standard.exe" project in Visual basic and add a reference in your Project references to "Microsoft Cluster Service Automation Classes.", msclus.dll.

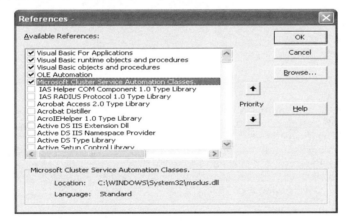

Next, copy the code below and paste it into your project - the Form_Load method is fine. Modify the code to fit your environment:

```
'Create your cluster object
Set oCluster = New Cluster

'Open your connection, below change to name of your cluster
oCluster.Open ("MyCluster")

'Hook into Resource Groups collection
Set oClusGroups = oCluster.ResourceGroups
```

```
'Retrieve a specific group, change below to name of the group you want to work with
Set oClusGroup = oClusGroups.Item("My Cluster Group")
```

Now you are hooked into your Cluster and a specific resource group. Next, determine your Active node:

```
'Determine the Active node
sActiveNode = oClusGroup.OwnerNode.Name
```

By knowing which node is Active in a simple Active/Passive, 2 server configuration you can easily determine which node is passive. We will skip that If Then statement and assume we assigned our passive node's name to a new string variable called sPassiveNode.

At this point, we have our cluster server objects all set up and know which server is active and which is passive. We are almost ready to failover. But before we failover it is a good idea to make sure that the secondary node is healthy:

```
Set oSecondaryNode = oCluster.Nodes.Item(sPassiveNode)
Dim bOkay As Boolean
bOkay = True

'check each network interface
For i = 1 To oSecondaryNode.NetInterfaces.Count
        If Not oSecondaryNode.NetInterfaces.Item(i).State = ClusterNetInterfaceUp Then
                bOkay = False
        End If
Next
```

If everything is fine on the passive node we will initiate failover. The "Move" method used below moves a group and its resources from the current active node to another node. If no other node is specified, it chooses a "preferred" node based on its own predefined criteria. Since we are only using 2 nodes in our example, we leave out the optional cluster Node parameter but still pass in our Timeout parameter of 180 seconds.

```
'Move group over to the passive node
If bOkay Then
        varReturn = oClusGroup.Move(180)
End IF

'the move statement returns a variant that lets us know if the method timed out, if it didn't
time out we assume success
If CBool(varReturn) Then
        Debug.Print ("Failover timed out")
End If
```

Summary

The intention of this article was to provide an introductory look into the Cluster Service Automation Classes. The code presented in this article is very basic and should be built upon with your own functionality such as logging and error catching as well as other general programming practices. Those general practices are outside the scope of this article. In our example we only failed over 1 group; if you want to failover several groups the failover code above will fit neatly into a function that can be called as needed. For more information on Windows clustering visit http://msdn.microsoft.com/library/default.asp?url=/library/en-us/dnanchor/ht ml/anch_winclustering.asp.

Anthony Bressi is owner of Agilist Technologies Inc. which specializes in software for SQL Server Database Administrators and SQL Server developers. Mr. Bressi has over 8 years of hands-on experience in the Microsoft SQL Server development environment.

Top Ten Features of Enterprise Manager

By Dale Elizabeth Corey

More than once, I have heard, "I never knew that feature existed in Enterprise Manager", so I thought I would conjure up a Top Ten List for Enterprise Manager. However, I will not say that there may be other features that are not equally as important and these are not necessarily in any order. The nice thing about Enterprise Manager (see Figure 1) is that it can make some of the daily mundane chores a lot easier.

Enjoy the read and be sure to leave me "pithy" comments. ☺ I welcome suggestions for other good tips and tidbits.

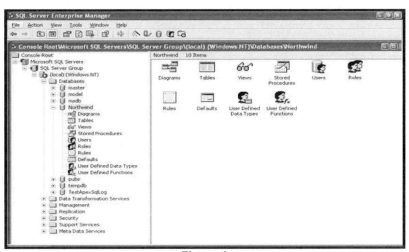

Figure 1

Enterprise Manager's Top Ten Features:

1. **Configuration Properties** – This is pretty much self explanatory. If you haven't already checked out my article on this, **Exploring SQL Server 2000 Configuration Properties**, you should. It's a great outline/definition of each of the property settings in Enterprise Manager.
2. **Query Designer under Databases/Tables** – If you are stuck building a complex query with joins or you are new to building queries, you need to check out my article on using Query Designer (Visual Basic Tools) in Enterprise Manager. It explains how Query Designer's Query By Example (QBE) can be utilized to your advantage. Check it out at **Building Joins the Easy Way**.
3. **Databases/Views** – You can look into the details of your views through Enterprise Manager. Views are virtual tables defined by queries. Basically, it's a filter. You can easily manage your views by expanding a server group, then the server. Look under **Database** and then **Views**. By right clicking on a view, you can easily create, design, and open views. You can also easily manage triggers and permissions as well as generate scripts and display dependencies (Figure 2). You can also see the view's properties by right clicking on the view in question and clicking on **Properties** (Figure 3).

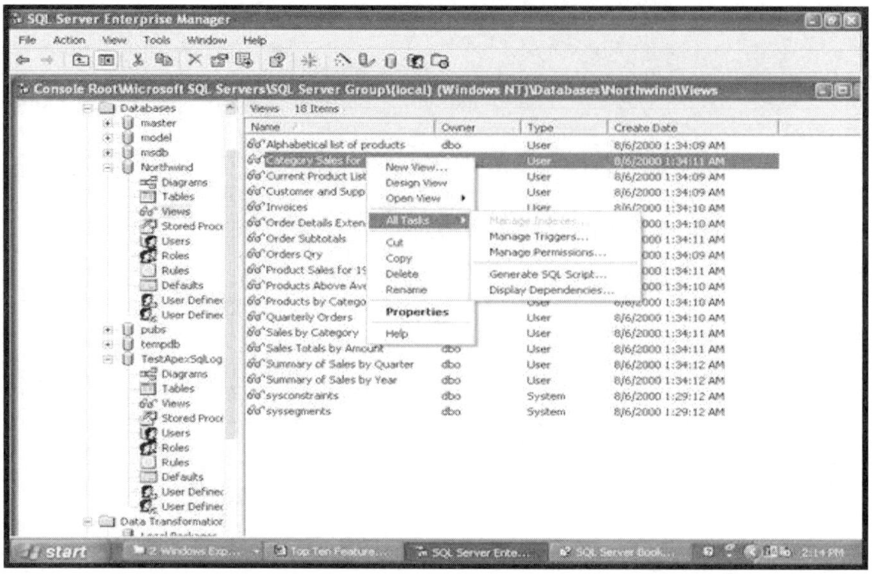

Figure 2

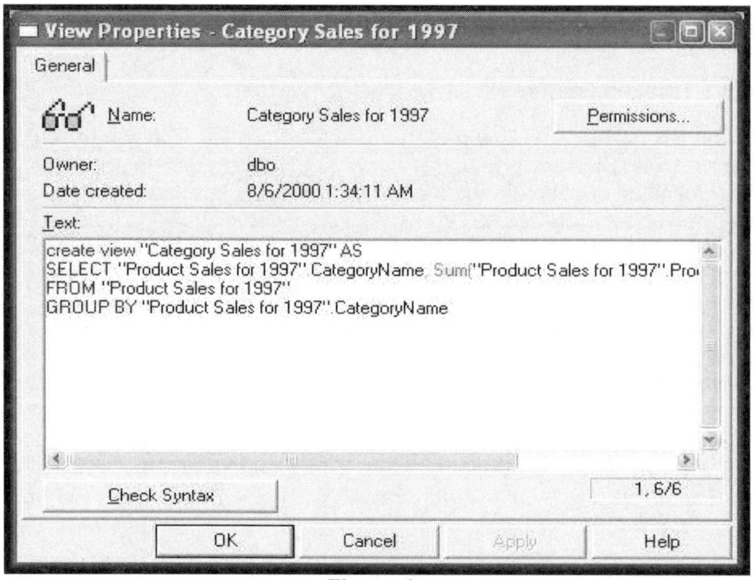

Figure 3

4. **Databases/Stored Procedures** – Stored procedures are programs written in the Transact-SQL programming language. They are programs stored on the SQL Server and are executed on the server. This makes processing faster, more secure, with less traffic, and modular 'cause the procedure only has to be created once. Applications execute stored procedures so they can process results (i.e. inserting a customer into the database through the client interface). You can easily manage your stored procedures by expanding a server group, then the server. Look under **Database** and then **Stored Procedures**. By right clicking on a stored procedure, you can create new stored procedures. You can also easily manage permissions as well as create new publications, generate scripts, and display dependencies (see Figure 4). You can also see the stored procedure's properties by right clicking on the stored procedure in question and then clicking on **Properties** (Figure 5).

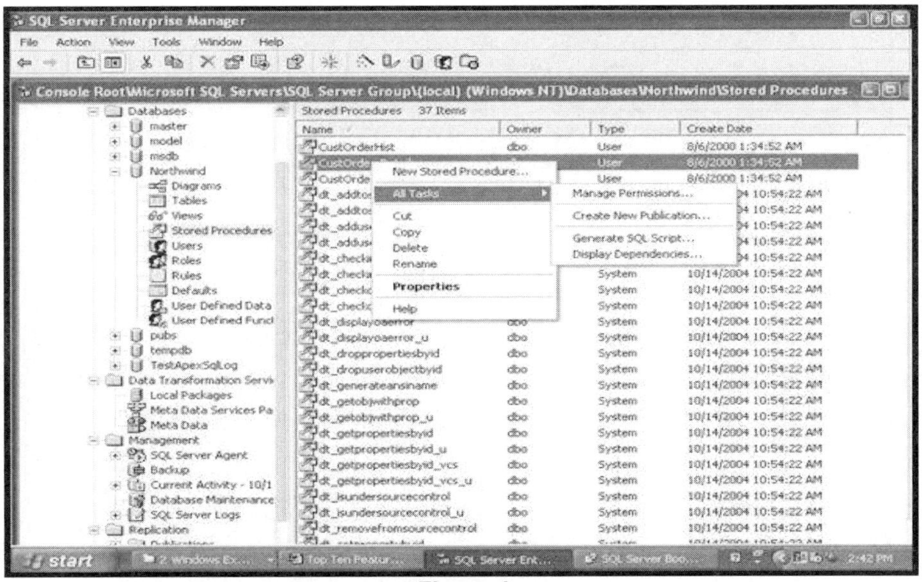

Figure 4

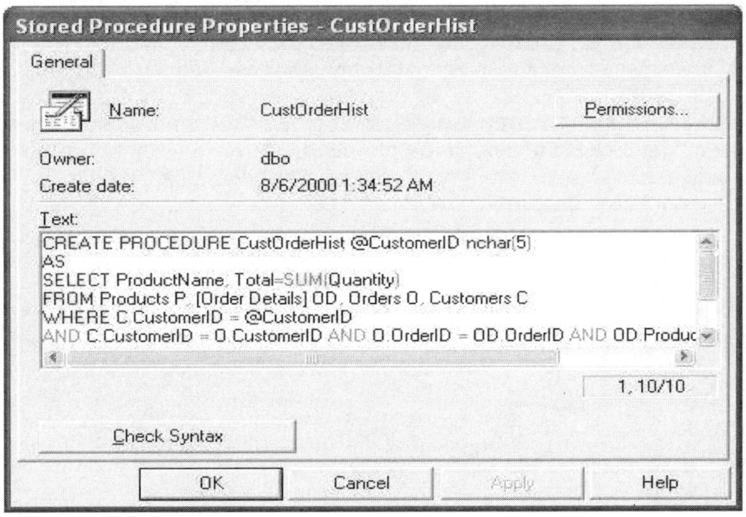

Figure 5

5. **Management/SQL Server Agent/Jobs** – If you ever need to run scheduled tasks (i.e. backups, DTS packages, replication) during certain times/ intervals, this option is a must for setting them up easily. Also, if you need to set up alerts via email/paging, for example, this is where to do it (see Figure 6). Make sure that if you need to set up tasks to run regularly, you need to set up the SQL Agent to **Autostart when the Operating System Starts** (see Item 1 above on where to find this under configuration properties) and also to **Autostart SQL Server Agent if it stops unexpectedly**. You can find this after expanding a server group, then the server. Look under **Management** and then right-click **SQL Server Agent**. You can find it under **Properties.**

Figure 6

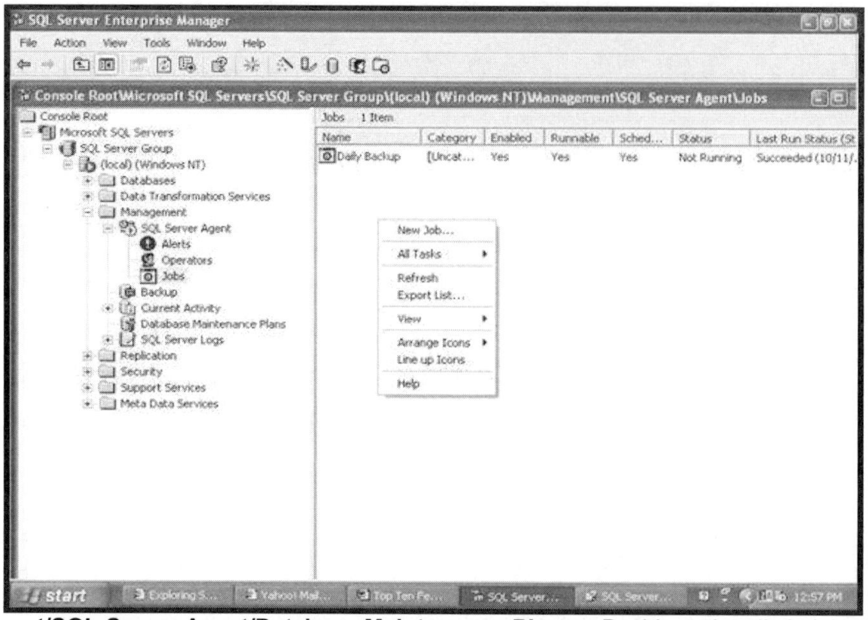

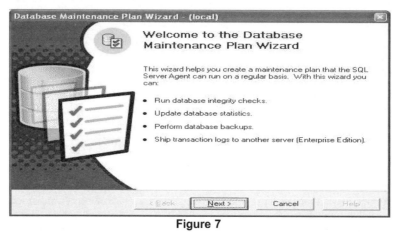

6. **Management/SQL Server Agent/Database Maintenance Plans** – Besides primarily helping you with backing up your databases and transaction logs, the wizard (see Figure 7) will help you to reorganize the data on the data and index pages, compress data files, update index statistics, perform internal consistency checks of data and data pages, and set up log shipping (for synchronizing databases with standby servers). You can find the wizard after expanding a server group, then the server. Look under **Management** and then right-click **Database Maintenance Plans.** If you want to just set up an immediate backup job or to schedule one a backup job, you can expand a server group, then the server. Look under **Management** and then right-click **Backup.**

Figure 7

7. **Management/SQL Server Agent/SQL Server Logs** – A new error log is created every time you open a new instance in SQL. The error log allows you to check on processes like backups, restores, and scripts to make sure they have been completed (see Figure 8). You can view the error logs after expanding a server group, then the server. Look under **Management**, click on **SQL Server Logs**, and then click on the log you want to see.

Figure 8

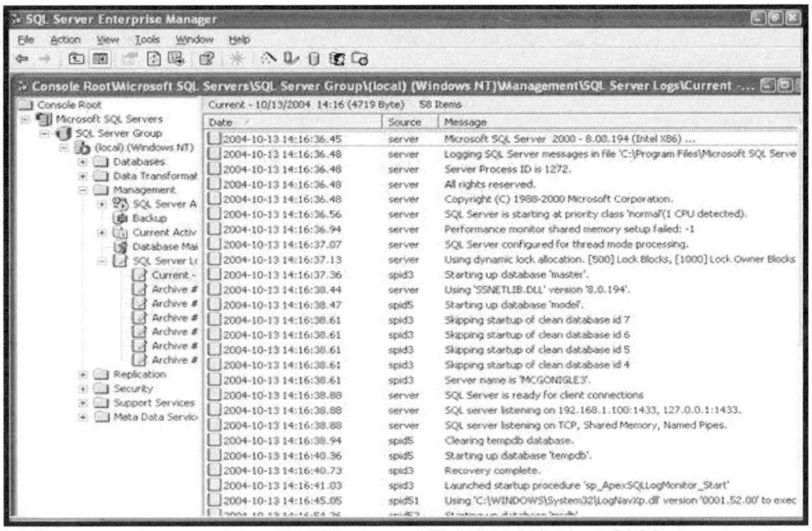

8. **Security/Logins** – You can grant a Windows NT 4.0 or Window 2000 user or group login access to SQL Server. You should only grant database access to individual Windows NT 4.0 and Windows 2000 users if the user needs to perform exclusive activities other than the Windows NT 4.0 or Windows 2000 groups that have already been granted access to the database, and of which they are a member. You can add or delete users/groups login after expanding a server group, then the server. Look under **Security**, click on **Logins**, and then right click and choose **New Login**. Otherwise, right click the user/group you want to delete and choose **Delete** (see Figures 9 and 10).

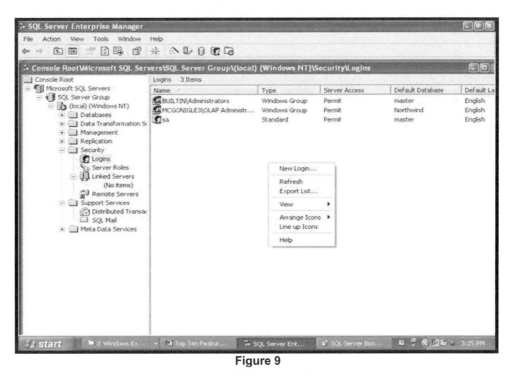

Figure 9

Figure 10

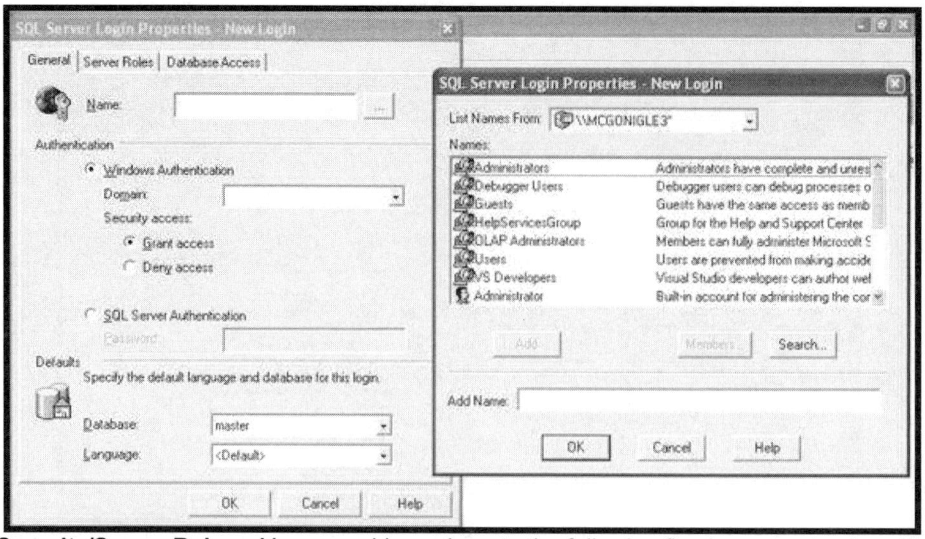

9. **Security/Server Roles** – You can add members to the following fixed server roles (see Figure 11). Look under **Security**, **Server Roles**, right click on the appropriate Server Role and then choose **Properties.** Under the **General** tab, choose **Add** (see Figure 12).

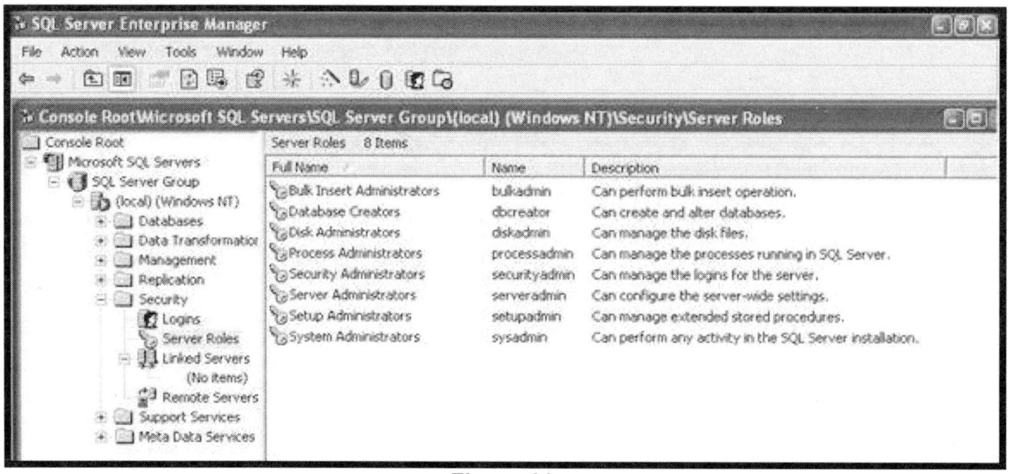

Figure 11

Figure 12

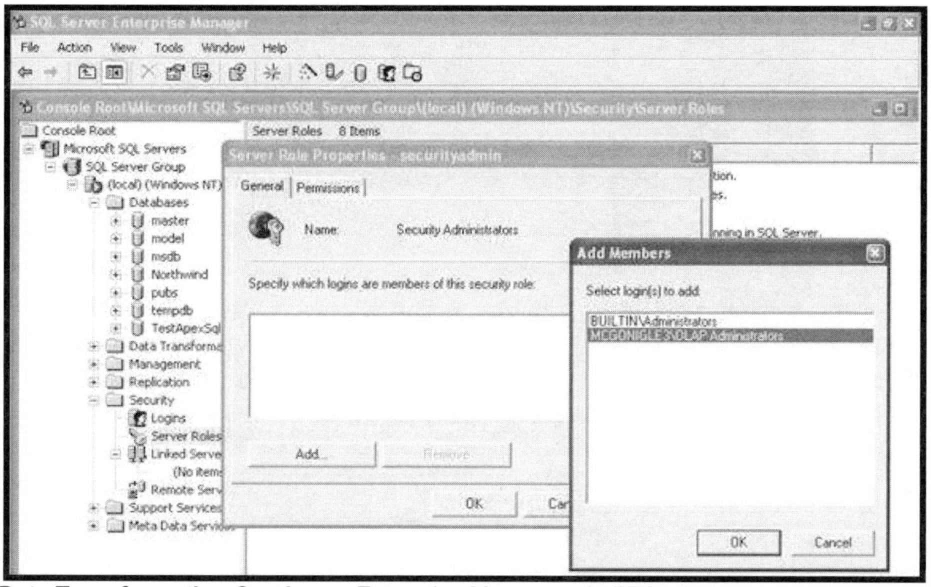

10. **Data Transformation Services** – Enterprise Manager, via DTS, allows you to easily shuffle data back and forth that derives from different sources and formats. These sources include SQL Server, Access, Excel, Oracle, dBase, Paradox, ODBC, HTML, and other OLE DB providers. The simplest way to implement a DTS package is to right click on **Databases** and choose **All Tasks,** then choose **Import Data** or **Export Data** (see Figure 13). (Note: there are other places in the console tree that you can find this option.) That will bring up the DTS Wizard (see Figure 14). You will be guided through screens to choose your source and destination for the data (Figures 15 and 16). For more intermediate and advanced DTS packages, you can use **DTS Designer** by right clicking **Database Transformation Services** and choosing **New Package**. Of course, you can also programmatically write and compile DTS packages (i.e., Visual Basic, C++).

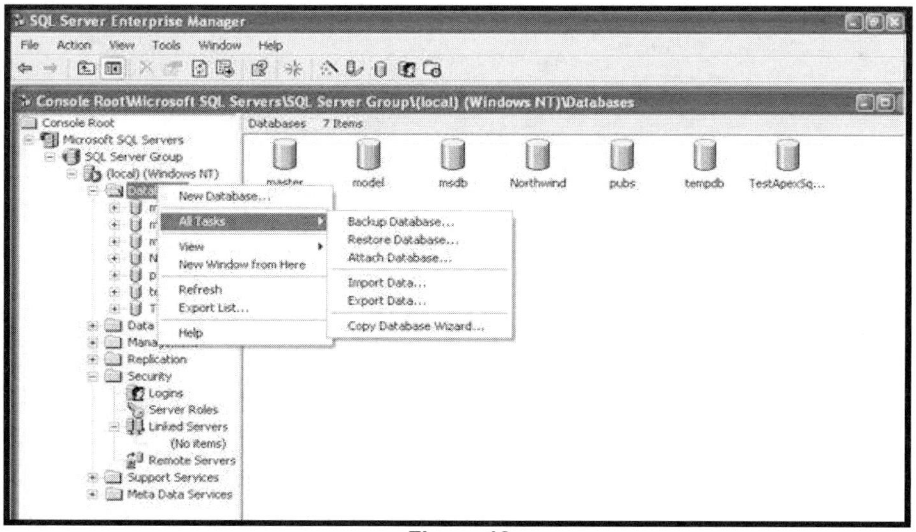

Figure 13

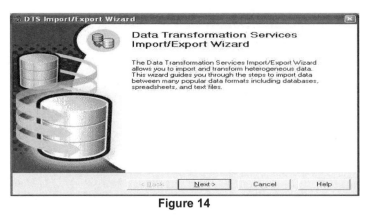

Figure 14

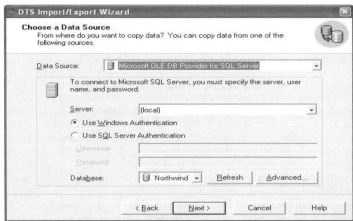

Figure 15

Figure 16

Some Enterprise Manager Tips:

- Right clicking on **Databases** will give you options for **Backup/Restore/Attach Databases, Import/Export Data,** and the **Copy Database Wizard**.
- Right clicking on a database under **Databases** (see Figure 17), will give you further options for Importing/Exporting, Maintenance, Scripting, Backup/Restore, Shrink/Detach/Take Offline, Copy Subscription Database, and View Replication Conflicts.

Figure 17

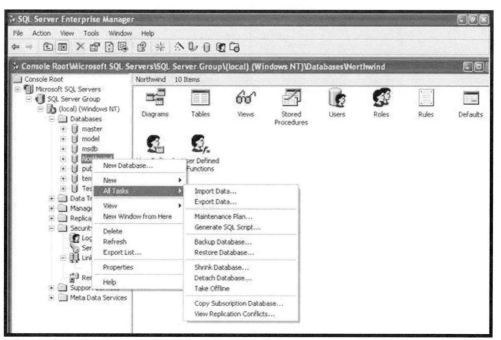

- Do not forget to choose **Refresh** from the right click menus or from the Toolbar, **each** time you make a change (i.e. create a table) in Enterprise Manager. Otherwise, the results will not display.

Tracing Deadlocks

By Shiv Kumar

This article is to identify and track the source for the cause of deadlock. Typically, in a system integration solution, you wouldn't encounter deadlock in your testing. This deadlock might creep in production or in live phase as your solution talks to different systems which is connected live with users. In a production environment turning the profiler and searching for the deadlock on is really painful and, moreover, the performance is also affected to a small extent.

Here are the steps to identify the source for the deadlock:

- Enable the Trace flag 3604 followed by 1204. The trace flag 3604 is not documented in SQL 2K books online. This option sends the trace to the client.

- The trace flag 1204 returns the type of locks participating in the deadlock and the current command affected. The deadlock information is automatically sent to the error log

- DBCC TRACEON (3604)

- DBCC TRACEON (1204)

Now any deadlocks happening in SQL server will be logged into the error log file, ERRORLOG. You can access the file either through enterprise manager or through explorer. In enterprise manager you can see it under Management / SQL Server Logs or under <Drive:>\\Program Files\Microsoft SQL Server\MSSQL\LOG.

The deadlock information appears in the file as

```
Deadlock encountered.... Printing deadlock information
2004-02-28 09:31:20.86 spid4
2004-02-28 09:31:20.86 spid4      Wait-for graph
2004-02-28 09:31:20.86 spid4
```

```
2004-02-28 09:31:20.86 spid4      Node:1
2004-02-28 09:31:20.86 spid4      RID: 7:1:35443:0              CleanCnt:1 Mode: U Flags: 0x2
2004-02-28 09:31:20.86 spid4       Grant List 0::
2004-02-28 09:31:20.86 spid4         Owner:0x5c53dfa0 Mode: U       Flg:0x0 Ref:0 Life:00000001
SPID:61 ECID:0
2004-02-28 09:31:20.86 spid4         SPID: 61 ECID: 0 Statement Type: UPDATE Line #: 167
2004-02-28 09:31:20.86 spid4         Input Buf: Language Event: Sproc_TPS_Reports

2004-02-28 09:31:20.86 spid4       Requested By:
2004-02-28 09:31:20.86 spid4         ResType:LockOwner Stype:'OR' Mode: U SPID:58 ECID:0 Ec:
(0x6EF235F8) Value:0x658cb560 Cost:(0/297FC)
2004-02-28 09-: 31:20.86 spid4
2004-02-28 09:31:20.86 spid4      Node:2
2004-02-28 09:31:20.86 spid4      RID: 7:1:76320:0              CleanCnt:1 Mode: X Flags: 0x2
2004-02-28 09:31:20.86 spid4       Grant List 1::
2004-02-28 09:31:20.86 spid4         Owner:0xdabf560 Mode: X        Flg:0x0 Ref:0 Life:02000000 SPID:58
ECID:0
2004-02-28 09:31:20.86 spid4         SPID: 58 ECID: 0 Statement Type: DELETE Line #: 158
2004-02-28 09:31:20.86 spid4         Input Buf: Language Event: EXEC Sproc_TPS_CaptureMissingEvent
2004-02-28 09:31:20.86 spid4       Requested By:
2004-02-28 09:31:20.86 spid4         ResType:LockOwner Stype:'OR' Mode: U SPID:61 ECID:0 Ec:
(0x5A507578) Value:0x8c32720 Cost:(0/0)
2004-02-28 09:31:20.86 spid4       Victim Resource Owner:
2004-02-28 09:31:20.86 spid4         ResType:LockOwner Stype:'OR' Mode: U SPID:61 ECID:0 Ec:(0x5A507578)
Value:0x8c32720 Cost:(0/0)
```

Let's analyze the log file. In the above case 2 nodes were involved in deadlock. Node :1 belongs to SPID : 61 and Node :2 belongs to SPID :58. To know the source query that was under execution during deadlock, it can be found from the input buffer. This line can be found from the line starting with "input Buf:" For Node:1 its "Sproc_TPS_reports" and for Node :2 its "Sproc_TPS_CaptureMissingEvent".

Now that we know the query source we need to know what was the statement and the line no# that caused the deadlock. This can be retrieved from "Statement Type" present just above the "Input Buf" statement. In this case it's "Update Line #167" for SPID:61 and "Delete Line #158" for SPID : 58.

Now that you know the line no# , you can attack the query to optimize it for avoiding deadlock. The problem lies in if there are multiple calls to stored procedure within this stored procedure Sproc_TPS_Reports or Sproc_TPS_CaptureMissingEvent? Then this line no # and statement type can't say much to pinpoint the object involved in the deadlock. The next step is to look at the line next to "Node :1" or "Node :2". In this example it's RID: X: X: X: X. The RID indicates that the data is fetched from heap directly and it's a row lock. The SQL server can lock on the following items

Items	Description
RID	is a row identifier. It is used to individually lock a single row within a table. The format is RID: *db_id:file_id:page_no:row_no*
Key	is a row lock within an index. Used to protect key ranges in serializable transactions The format is KEY: *db_id:object_id:index_id*;
Page	is a lock, when entire 8-KB data page or index page will be locked. The format is PAG: *db_id:file_id:page_no*
Extent	is only used for allocation. When it's used, entire extent will be locked The format is EXT: *db_id:file_id:extent_no*
Table	lock is used when a large percentage of the table's rows are queried or updated. This lock includes all table's data and indexes The format is TAB: *db_id:object_id*;
Database	is used when you restore the database. The format is DB: *db_id*

From the above table it's clear that except for Extent and Database Items, you can trace the deadlock object with ease. Anyway, extent and database will not be encountered in your custom code stored procedure. Other than the extent and database, key and table have the object_id in it. So by just executing the query "select object_name(<object_id>)"., you can determine the object name easily. For other lock items RID and page you can determine the object name from the Page_no. This can be determined through an undocumented DBCC command DBCC PAGE. The syntax for this is:

DBCC PAGE ({db_id|dbname}, pagenum [,print option] [,cache] [,logical])

where:

db_id|dbname - Enter either the dbid or the name of the database
pagenum - Enter the page number of the SQL Server page that is to be examined
print option - (Optional) Print option can be either 0, 1, or 2

0 - (Default) This option causes DBCC PAGE to print out only the page header information.

1 - This option causes DBCC PAGE to print out the page header information, each row of information from the page, and the page's offset table. Each of the rows printed out will be separated from each other.

2 - This option is the same as option 1, except it prints the page rows as a single block of information rather than separating the individual rows. The offset and header will also be displayed.

cache - (Optional) This parameter allows either a 1 or an 0 to be entered.

0 - This option causes DBCC PAGE to retrieve the page number from disk rather than checking to see if it is in cache.

1 - (Default) This option takes the page from cache if it is in cache rather than getting it from disk only.

logical - (Optional) This parameter is for use if the page number that is to be retrieved is a virtual page rather then a logical page. It can be either 0 or 1.

0 - If the page is to be a virtual page number.

1 - (Default) If the page is the logical page number.

So just pass the parameter that you get from RID / Page Lock items. In the above case it would be DBCC Page(7,1,35443,3)

The output for this will appear in client as below. For ease in understanding, only the portion that is of interest is copied here.

```
PAGE: (1:35443)
---------------
BUFFER:
-------
BUF @0x0196D440
---------------
bpage = 0x7BA22000        bhash = 0x00000000       bpageno = (1:35443)
bdbid = 7                 breferences = 0          bstat = 0x9
bspin = 0                 bnext = 0x00000000
PAGE HEADER:
------------
Page @0x7BA22000
----------------
m_pageId = (1:35443)      m_headerVersion = 1      m_type = 1
m_typeFlagBits = 0x0      m_level = 0              m_flagBits = 0x0
m_objId = 2029457433      m_indexId = 0            m_prevPage = (1:37670)
m_nextPage = (1:106590)   pminlen = 5              m_slotCnt = 8
m_freeCnt = 7408          m_freeData = 7996        m_reservedCnt = 0
m_lsn = (77495:484:39)    m_xactReserved = 0       m_xdesId = (0:9175698)
m_ghostRecCnt = 0         m_tornBits = 0
```

of all these info , the data of m_objID is of interest(which is highlighted in bold). The value is 2029457433. Now that you know the object ID you can determine the object name by executing the query

```
SELECT object_name(2029457433)
```

Now that you have traced the source, you can work out to find the solution for avoiding the deadlock.

T-SQL

The basis of any relational database system is the SQL manipulation language. In this section we've compiled the best articles that work with the T-SQL language in SQL Server. Complicated queries, unusual methods of getting data, a look at some of the more interesting ways that people have written their queries.

ADO.NET – A Data Access Layer

By Patryk Nowakowski

Purpose

With the release of ADO .NET, Microsoft has fundamentally changed the way of database applications development. The new version of ADO introduced with .NET Framework is extremely flexible and gives developers a wide variety of tools for handling common database programming tasks. This comes with special regard to so-called disconnected data structures; i.e., objects residing in memory that hold copy of data in the database. These structures allow developers to easily manipulate data in client applications (often referred to as "presentation layer"). This approach may be called a thick client as a vast part of data manipulation is performed on client side. Thanks to ADO .NET, users can slice and dice data and make changes to it with as little effort put in application preparation as possible. Off-line objects need to be filled with data from database and commit changes made by user. It appears as though this task is not so easy, especially if we consider the vast number of techniques for retrieving and especially updating data in the database.

Experienced database developers might get fed-up with repeatedly performed tedious tasks such as opening a database connection, fetching results from DataReader object to a DataTable, and so on. On the other hand, not every developer has to be familiar with database programming, and he might get confused with all those off-line structures and various techniques to bring them alive. The purpose of this article is to introduce a custom framework that handles common database access scenarios and isolates widows / Internet presentation layer development from data access layer by exposing several comprehensive routines. Its main goal is to incorporate most elegant solutions and comply with highest standards of SQL Server development using the benefits of ADO .NET.

If you are not familiar with the basics of ADO .NET, I guess it would be worth taking a while to read this article from Microsoft's MSDN before you continue.

The most basic task – retrieving information from the database

This was actually the moment I first came up with an idea of dbHelper. I was developing an application which processes enormous number of data. Results were presented to the user who could check whether they were correct and possibly apply some changes, yet the "crazy things" done in the server side were the key point of the application. In order to verify the results, user had to access several databases on different servers. In this project I was responsible for developing the solution on SQL Server. My teammate was developing the front-end. After some time it became clear that the easiest way for an effective cooperation was for me to provide him with a library that handles all database access tasks. And so it began...

Retrieving information from database in enterprise scale applications is often handled by stored procedures. Major benefits of this approach are:

- better performance;
- better security;
- each operation can be logged on the SQL Server side;
- reduction of network traffic;
- very elegant solution thanks to programming abstraction;
- well, actually I guess there are hundreds more... This article could give you some perspective on what I named above.

Quite often it is desirable to maintain a log of who accessed a specific set of information, and when. (In our case we had to make sure that the user did actually control the results). This task could have been handled by the client application, but it would have required additional coding for each and every data access operation, not to mention that such action would have had to take place two times for each operation (to handle beginnings and endings).

So my approach was to:

- create a stored procedure handling SELECT statements
- create second stored procedure that writes to application log and would be invoked by the first SP

- and finally create a function that uses the stored procedure to retrieve data into ADO .NET objects.

Before we start: our "data retrieval procedure" is going to use **sp_executesql** in order to execute dynamic SQL statements. As **sp_executesql** can process any valid SQL statement, we have to ensure that the SQL command passed to the procedure is actually a SELECT statement. If not, then we should be able to throw a custom error.

In order to process custom error messages, we will have to add a new error type to **dbo.sysmessages** in master database. We accomplish this task by running the following code in QA (assuming that your user belongs to either **sysadmin** or **serveradmin** role. If not then you'll have to ask your SQL server admin to run this code for you):

```
DECLARE @next_cust_msg_id INT

USE master

SET @next_cust_msg_id=COALESCE((SELECT MAX(error)+1
 FROM dbo.sysmessages WHERE error>50000),50001)

EXEC sp_addmessage @msgnum = @next_cust_msg_id, @severity = 16,
        @msgtext = N'Procedure dbo._spsys_select expects a valid SELECT statement to be passed as
@command parameter.
        Parameter ['%s'] does not contain SELECT keyword.',
        @lang = 'us_english'

SELECT @next_cust_msg_id
```

Note: You can browse the contents of dbo.sysmessages table in master database, but you cannot modify it unless your instance of SQL Server is configured to "Allow modifications to be made directly to the system catalogs".

The code above simply creates a new row in dbo.sysmessages table. The trick is that the primary key in this table has to be greater or equal 50001 for custom errors, so we have to check for first free error number and use it in our calls to RAISERROR function.

dbo._spsys_select - stored procedure for data retrieval

a) parameters

- @command NVARCHAR(1000) – SQL SELECT statement;
- @user AS VARCHAR(100) – user currently logged on to client application;
- @rows_returned AS INT OUTPUT – rows returned as a result of our query.

b) execution

- create an entry in log table by performing a call to dbo._log_task SP;
- check whether @command really contains a valid SELECT statement;
- construct an input to sp_executesql
- execute @command
- check for errors, if there is an error then create a proper entry in application log
- return 0 if everything worked OK.
- Pretty straight forward, isn't it?

So far you can:

1. execute this procedure in QA:

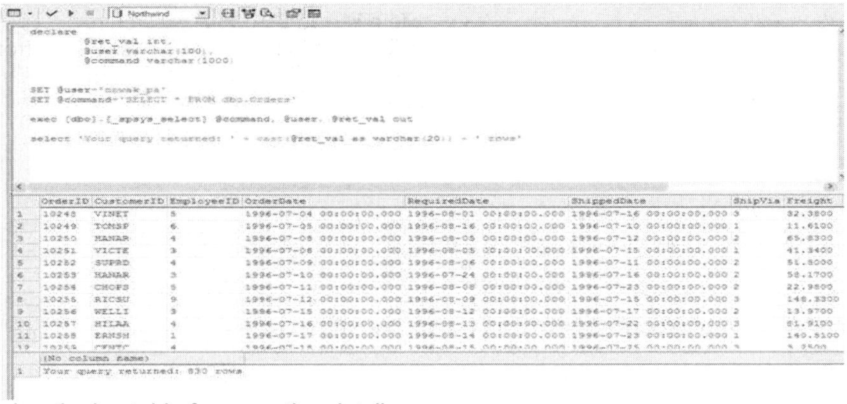

2. view the log table for execution details:

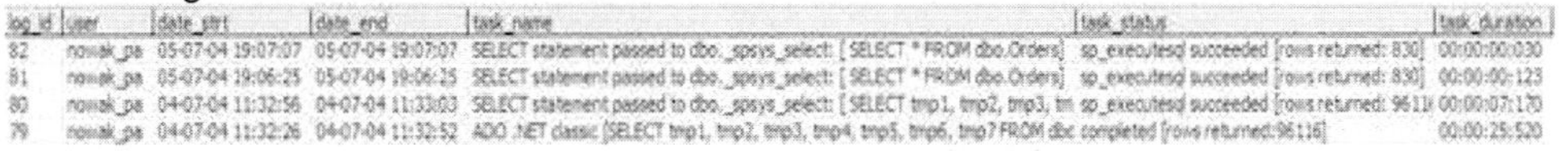

Now we can move on to actually using this thing in live application.

The very beginnings of our custom data access layer

First let's briefly discuss the architecture of our C# .NET solution. It involves two projects:

- windowsClient: our client (or data presentation layer) that is going to use our custom DAL component to retrieve data from the database.
- dbHelper: our class library that is going to be linked into the windowsClient project.

Even though dbHelper class is implemented in C# you may use it in your VB .NET applications also.

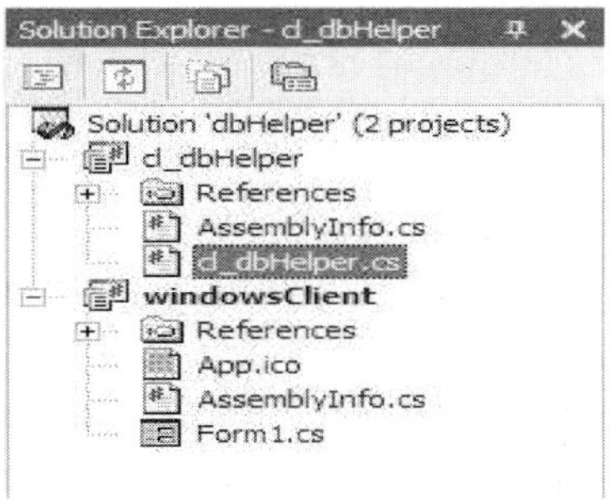

The working application should look like this:

windowsClient's sole purpose is to test the dbHelper class, so I didn't care too much about the design.

How it works:

First check whether the connection string is valid for your SQL Server configuration. If not, then you'll receive an error when application starts, because dbHelper class is instantiated when application form is being loaded. If so, then use the **change** button next to connection string TextBox to adjust the configuration. Next thing to do is to input a valid SELECT statement into the first textbox. You can execute your query both using dbHelper and using a simple function. They both do exactly the same thing including logging into the log table. What differs is the execution performance and code involved into retrieving result. The core function for data retrieval using SP is:

```
public bool execSpsysSelect(string command, string dtTablename)
```

which takes as parameters your SQL query and the name that should be assigned to newly created DataTable object that is going to hold the result. Function returns false if your query returned an empty set and thus no DataTable object has been created.

In order to display the result, the DataGrid control's DataSource property is set to the newly created DataTable object which resides in the default DataSet called dsDbHelper. All you need to display the result is to add the following code to Button's OnClick event handler:

```
if (this.dbh.execSpsysSelect( this.txtSQL.Text, "res"))
    this.dataGrid1.DataSource=this.dbh.dsDbHelper.Tables["res"];
```

Seems nice, especially if you compare it to classic ADO.NET:

```
int logid=this.dbh.execLogTask("ADO .NET classic ["+this.txtSQL.Text+"]",null,true,-1);

System.Data.SqlClient.SqlConnection c = new System.Data.SqlClient.SqlConnection();

c.ConnectionString=this.txtConnStr.Text;

System.Data.SqlClient.SqlCommand cmd = new System.Data.SqlClient.SqlCommand();

cmd.Connection=c;
```

```
cmd.CommandTimeout=3600;
cmd.CommandText=this.txtSQL.Text;

c.Open();

System.Data.SqlClient.SqlDataAdapter da = new System.Data.SqlClient.SqlDataAdapter(cmd);

System.Data.DataSet ds = new DataSet("adonet");

da.Fill(ds,"nonadores");

this.dataGrid1.DataSource=ds.Tables["nonadores"];

this.dbh.execLogTask( null,"completed [rows returned:"+
ds.Tables["nonadores"].Rows.Count.ToString()+"]",false,logid);
```

Note: *dbh.execLogTask* is a function included into dbHelper that handles calls to the dbo._log_task SP in order to create log entries in logs table.

Performance

With very simple queries simple ADO .NET performs slightly (I mean really!) better to dbHelper. The difference in execution time is hardly ever over one second. This is possibly due to the fact that dbHelper uses time expensive method FillSchema in order to create the DataTable object that is further filled by a DataReader object. It also has to populate SqlParameter collection for SqlCommand that executes the SP. Finally, in this case, we're kind of using cannon to kill a fly, aren't we?

For more complex queries things turn better for dbHelper that performs up to about 10%-20% better. You might want to check it out on my example. It creates 2 tables with 7 columns of random numbers. It is for you to choose the number of records in each table. The SQL script to recreate and populate those objects is included in the companion package.

To test performance I like to use the IN clause…

Before you ask

Anyone who goes through the code of the *execSpsysSelect* function will notice that I create the DataTable object before I check whether query returned any rows. One could also ask why don't I use the *@rows_returned* value.

Well, I don't use it simply because it is not set until I finish retrieving the result from SELECT statement. The @@ROWCOUNT variable is set after the SELECT statement is completed. In this case SELECT statement is considered to be finished after you close the DataReader object.

Things to do

Ideally, a custom DAL library should perform additional tasks that ADO .NET does not handle:

- retrieve additional metadata such as column description and its **default value**. (Actually I've read on several newsgroups that it is not possible to retrieve column's default value from SQL Server and apply it to DataColumn object. Believe me - it is!)
- properly set ReadOnly flag for columns such as columns with DATETIME() default value that indicates when a given record was created;
- analyze SELECT commands passed to it and implement techniques such as usage of DataRelation object to increase performance and facilitate handling updates, which leads to…
- **handle updates to database** – this is a challenge using different techniques for optimistic / pessimistic concurrency;
- introduce multithreading to prevent client application from hanging when a large query is begin processed.
- use XML to store / parse data and be able to communicate through XML Web Service

I'm going to take you through all this in future articles.

An Efficient Set-based Solution for Islands and Gaps

By Goce Smilevski

Introduction

Alexander Kozak described an efficient row-based solution for the problem of identifying islands and gaps in sequential numbers in his article, Islands and Gaps in Sequential Numbers. The set-based solutions described there were not very efficient, especially when the input data was too fragmented. This article provides the logical next step, since it describes an efficient set-based solution: one that performs equally well for small and large fragmentation of the input data.

For easier reading and testing, here is the table structure and a small (but illustrative) set of test data, copied from the Kozak's article.

```
CREATE TABLE gaps(gapID int NOT NULL PRIMARY KEY)
INSERT INTO gaps values(1)
INSERT INTO gaps values(2)
INSERT INTO gaps values(3)
INSERT INTO gaps values(4)
INSERT INTO gaps values(6)
INSERT INTO gaps values(7)
INSERT INTO gaps values(8)
INSERT INTO gaps values(10)
INSERT INTO gaps values(14)
INSERT INTO gaps values(15)
INSERT INTO gaps values(16)
INSERT INTO gaps values(17)
INSERT INTO gaps values(38)
```

Listing 1: The original test table structure and data

For any further details on the solutions proposed in the previous article, please refer to the link above. The solution proposed here requires at least SQL Server 2000 (so much of ANSI portability :-)), though I think an ORACLE equivalent can be easily implemented.

The Pitfall of Set-Based Solutions and How To Eliminate It

The proposed set-based solutions used two intermediate rowsets, one for the lower and one for the upper bound of islands or gaps and there is nothing wrong there. To obtain the final result set, these two rowsets are JOINed. Alexander Kozak himself detected that set-based solutions had one major pitfall: for large fragmentation of input data, set-based solutions performed poorly. Due to the large number of records in each rowset, the JOIN took too much time.

So, how can you optimize those JOINs ? The execution plan of all three set-based solutions shows several things:

- A MERGE JOIN is used to obtain each intermediate rowset, and
- NESTED LOOPS are used to JOIN two rowsets into the final result.

The MERGE JOIN is said to be a more efficient way for JOINing rowsets that are already ordered. So the two intermediate rowsets are obtained in the most efficient way, but the matching between each island/gap's lower bound to its corresponding upper bound is performed less efficiently. The solution of this part of the puzzle leads to the solution of the problem.

The trick used here originates from the logical order of islands/gaps bounds. Lets take a look at the desired result. For islands, it should be:

```
island_start    island_end
1               4
6               8
10              10
14              17
38              38
```

For gaps, it should be:

```
gap_start      gap_end
5              5
9              9
11             13
18             37
```

When two columns in any of the result sets are considered separately (as an intermediate rowset), the following is noticed: *when they are ORDERed, the first row in the lower bound rowset corresponds to the first row in the upper bound rowset, the second row in the lower bound rowset corresponds to the second row in the upper bound rowset, and so forth*. My opinion is that matching island/gap's bounds with correlated subqueries using <= operator was the major reason for inefficiency of the set-based solutions described by Kozak.

Now, let's consider how to number a rowset. MS SQL Server doesn't give too many choices - the IDENTITY function/property is usually used for that purpose. It can be used as a column property or as a derived column in SELECT ... INTO statement. But, since the solution should be set-based, it should return a result set that can be easily SELECTed or used otherwise in SQL statements. That is why a stored procedure with a temporary tables was not a choice. The other alternative is to use the IDENTITY as a column attribute. So our table should have one IDENTITY column that will number the rows of intermediate rowsets. Due to the desired set-based nature, I decided to use a *multi-statement table valued function*. Each of the four intermediate rowsets (lower and upper bounds for islands and gaps) should be returned by UDF of this kind. The result table of the UDF should contain one IDENTITY column (for numbering) and one bound column (for the lower or upper bound).

Finding Islands

The final result is a JOIN of two rowsets, returned by two UDFs. Here is the code of the function that retrieves the islands lower bounds:

```
CREATE FUNCTION dbo.udfFindIslandStarts()
  RETURNS @res_tbl TABLE
    (row_num int identity(1, 1) NOT NULL PRIMARY KEY,
     island_start int NOT NULL)
AS
BEGIN
  INSERT INTO @res_tbl (island_start)
    SELECT gapID FROM gaps AS g1
    WHERE NOT EXISTS (SELECT gapID FROM gaps AS g2
                      WHERE (g2.gapID = g1.gapID - 1))
    ORDER BY gapID
    OPTION (MERGE JOIN)
  RETURN
END
GO
```

Listing 2: The UDF for finding island lower bounds

The ORDER BY ensures the proper ordering of bounds in all four UDFs, so the numbering can be used. The MERGE JOIN hint is added to ensure that the execution will use that method to make the JOIN. The result set of

```
SELECT * FROM dbo.udfFindIslandStarts()
```

looks like this:

```
row_num      island_start
----------   ------------
1            1
2            6
3            10
4            14
5            38
```

which means that the first island starts at number 1, the second starts at number 6, etc.

Similarly, the code that finds the island upper bounds is:

```
CREATE FUNCTION dbo.udfFindIslandEnds()
  RETURNS @res_tbl TABLE (
    row_num int identity(1, 1) NOT NULL PRIMARY KEY,
    island_end int not null)
AS
BEGIN
  INSERT INTO @res_tbl (island_end)
    SELECT gapID FROM gaps AS g1
    WHERE NOT EXISTS (SELECT gapID FROM gaps AS g2
                      WHERE (g2.gapID = g1.gapID + 1))
    ORDER BY gapID
    OPTION (MERGE JOIN)
  RETURN
END
GO
```

Listing 3: The UDF for finding island upper bounds
The result set of

```
SELECT * FROM dbo.udfFindIslandEnds()
```

looks like this:

```
row_num     island_end
----------- -----------
1           4
2           8
3           10
4           17
5           38
```

which means that the first island ends at 4, the second one ends at 8, etc. And finally, the SQL statement that retrieves the final result:

```
SELECT
  t1.gap_start, t2.gap_end
FROM
  dbo.udfFindGapStarts() AS t1
  INNER JOIN dbo.udfFindGapEnds() AS t2
    ON (t2.row_num = t1.row_num)
OPTION
  (MERGE JOIN)
```

Listing 4: The final SQL statement that finds the islands

Another MERGE JOIN hint is necessary, to ensure optimal execution.

Finding Gaps

Similarly, another two UDFs do the job for gaps. Here is the first one:

```
CREATE FUNCTION dbo.udfFindGapStarts()
  RETURNS @res_tbl TABLE (
    row_num int identity(1, 1) NOT NULL PRIMARY KEY,
    gap_start int NOT NULL)
AS
BEGIN
  INSERT INTO @res_tbl (gap_start)
    SELECT gapID + 1
    FROM gaps AS g1
    WHERE NOT EXISTS (SELECT gapID FROM gaps AS g2
                      WHERE (g2.gapID = g1.gapID + 1))
    ORDER BY gapID + 1
    OPTION (MERGE JOIN)
  RETURN
END
GO
```

Listing 5: The UDF for finding gap lower bounds

The result set of

```
SELECT * FROM dbo.udfFindGapStarts()
```

looks like this:

```
row_num    gap_start
---------- -----------
1          5
2          9
3          11
4          18
5          39
```

which means that the first gap starts at 5, the second one starts at 9, ... OOOPS ! At the end, there is one obsolete record, that means that a gap starts at 39. Obviously, 39 is not in the result set, and it is here due to the specific rule for finding gaps - dealing with data that does not really exist. This last record will be ignored in the final result.

At last, the code that finds gap upper bounds:

```
CREATE FUNCTION dbo.udfFindGapEnds()
  RETURNS @res_tbl TABLE (
    row_num int identity(0, 1) NOT NULL PRIMARY KEY,
    gap_end int NOT NULL)
AS
BEGIN
  INSERT INTO @res_tbl (gap_end)
    SELECT gapID - 1
    FROM gaps AS g1
    WHERE NOT EXISTS (SELECT gapID FROM gaps AS g2
                      WHERE (g2.gapID = g1.gapID - 1))
    ORDER BY gapID - 1
    OPTION (MERGE JOIN)
  RETURN
END
GO
```

Listing 6: The UDF for finding gap upper bounds
The result set of

```
SELECT * FROM dbo.udfFindGapEnds()
```

looks like this:

```
0          0
1          5
2          9
3          13
4          37
```

Another phantom row here, the first one, that is a result of the effort of the UDF to find a gap before the first record.

This last UDF is little unusual. If the IDENTITY starts at 1, the row_num column in the result set will be shifted by 1, yielding into a result set like this one:

```
row_num    gap_end
---------- -----------
1          0
2          5
3          9
4          13
5          37
```

This will require a little correction in the JOIN condition, so that corresponding row_nums are matched. But, that "little" correction may become expensive, if it is done for large number of rows. That is why, the IDENTITY here starts at 0.

And finally, the SQL statement for gaps, that JOINS two UDF results.

```
SELECT
  t1.island_start, t2.island_end
FROM
  dbo.udfFindIslandStarts() AS t1
  INNER JOIN dbo.udfFindIslandEnds() AS t2
  ON (t2.row_num = t1.row_num)
OPTION
  (MERGE JOIN)
```

Listing 7: The final SQL statement that finds the gaps

Due to the JOIN condition, two phantom records do not appear in the result set.

Testing and Results

I used the UDF from the script I contributed to SQLServerCentral earlier to load test data into the gaps table. After the loading, I deleted each third record (as Kozak did in his tests) to simulate large data fragmentation. The upper bound value in test tables and charts is the upper bound of input data.

Since I was interested in the performance of core statements, I wrote stored procedures that created temporary tables and simply filled them wit the result of two final SQL statements. So, the times measured were the times necessary to load the data into these temp tables. I didn't SELECT all those data to the client. I modified Kozak's row-based solution accordingly, by commenting the last SELECT statement.

First test starts finding islands and gaps at upper bound of 100,000, ending at upper bound of 1,000,000, with a step of 100,000.

Upper bound	Old (islands)	Optimized (islands)	Optimized (gaps)
100.000	12	7	7
200.000	24	15	15
300.000	36	22	25
400.000	48	30	34
500.000	59	39	42
600.000	72	46	51
700.000	84	54	61
800.000	96	62	70
900.000	109	72	79
1.000.000	120	79	91

The Excel chart based on this test data shows this:

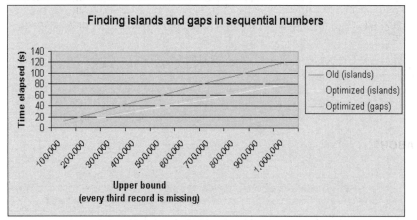

56

Second test starts finding islands and gaps at upper bound of 1,000,000, ending at upper bound of 10,000,000, with a step of 1,000,000. The time measured and the chart based on them are shown below:

Upper bound	Old (islands)	Optimized (islands)	Optimized (gaps)
1.000.000	131	81	89
2.000.000	248	166	188
3.000.000	377	306	354
4.000.000	591	454	490
5.000.000	722	644	648
6.000.000	870	711	799
7.000.000	1037	837	944
8.000.000	1149	932	1034
9.000.000	1285	1005	1150
10.000.000	1440	1143	1280

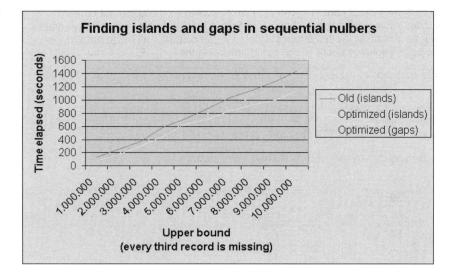

Conclusions

Obviously, when pre-ordered result sets should be JOINed, the MERGE JOIN is the most efficient way. Ordering can be achieved by using IDENTITY columns in table valued UDFs to obtain a numbered result set. Regarding the islands and gaps problem, it seems that the SQL Server feature that usually causes fragmentation of sequential number (IDENTITY columns) helped to efficiently detect that fragmentation ... something like "fight fire with fire" :-).

Be Prepared

By Stefan Popovski

@@ERROR versus XACT_ABORT

Be Prepared! Have you ever been a boy scout? That's the right motto for scouts and for SQL Server developers in case of implementing error handling strategy. I never know where things can go if code in stored procedures isn't full of a lot of "IF @ERROR<>0" statements.

Some better winds comes with Yukon. Like in .NET programming languages, Yukon has a structured exception handling.

```
BEGIN TRY
    BEGIN Transaction
        SELECT 'error simulation' / 0
    COMMIT Transaction
END TRY

BEGIN CATCH TRAN_ABORT
    DECLARE @err int
    SELECT @err = @@error
    PRINT '@@error: ' + ltrim(str(@err))
    ROLLBACK
END CATCH
```

But till Yukon comes, we have to be prepared to set up errors ambush just using @@ERROR and RETURN parameter.

We have one more tool to beat errors: XACT_ABORT. If I execute SET XACT_ABORT ON, I will force atomicity in transaction, and rolling back every open transaction in case of "any error". But XACT_ABORT ON is incapable in case of errors which source comes from Diferred Name Resolution.

When a stored procedure is executed for the first time, the query processor reads the text of the stored procedure from the syscomments system table of the procedure and checks that the names of the objects used by the procedure are present. This process is called deferred name resolution because objects referenced by the stored procedure need not exist when the stored procedure is created, but only when it is executed.

When a stored procedure is created it is allowed to use non existing table name. So a "typing error" in object name will pass without any warning. In addition, if you imagine that many languages have similar letters but in different ASCII code, then these errors become very dangerous.

For example, in the Macedonian language (using Windows Cyrillic, CodePage 1251)

```
'T' <> 'T'.

SELECT ASCII ('T')       English - Latin              T

84

SELECT ASCII ('T')       Macedonian - Cyrilic         T

210
```

Object names are checked in resolution stage. If an object does not exist (or the name is not correctly written), the error will fire.

Example 1: SET XACT_ABORT OFF / ON - Error simulation"Non existing table"

```
CREATE TABLE [TabExist] ([p1] int,[p2] [char] (16)) ON [PRIMARY]
GO
CREATE PROCEDURE ProcAbortSample AS
INSERT INTO TabExist Values(1,'ProcAbortSample')
INSERT INTO TabNonExist Values(1,'ProcAbortSample')
INSERT INTO TabExist Values(2,'ProcAbortSample')
GO
CREATE PROCEDURE ProcCallerSample AS
DECLARE @Ret INT
BEGIN TRANSACTION
INSERT INTO TabExist Values('1','ProcCallerSample')
SET @Ret = 1001
EXEC @Ret = ProcAbortSample
PRINT 'Return parameter of ProcAbortSample is: ' + str(@Ret)
PRINT 'IF Return parameter after exec ProcAbortSample is 1001 Return is not affected'
COMMIT TRANSACTION
GO
```

```
DECLARE @RetFinal INT
DELETE FROM TabExist
SET XACT_ABORT OFF
EXEC @RetFinal = ProcCallerSample
PRINT 'Return parameter of ProcCallerSample is ' + str(@RetFinal)
GO

PRINT 'IF next <SELECT * FROM TabExist> yield any row then
INS statements are not rolled back'
SELECT * FROM TabExist
```

Result...

```
Server: Msg 208, Level 16, State 1,
Procedure ProcAbortSample, Line 3
Invalid object name 'TabNonExist'.
Return parameter of ProcAbortSample is:       1001
IF Return parameter after exec ProcAbortSample is 1001 Return is not affected
Return parameter of ProcCallerSample is         0
IF next <SELECT * FROM TabExist> yield any row then INS statements are not rolled back
p1
p2
-----------        ----------------
1
ProcCallerSample
1
ProcAbortSample
```

This is OK because I executed <SET XACT_ABORT OFF>. But if I'm going to execute the same batch with SET XACT_ABORT ON, the result will be the same.

```
DECLARE @RetFinal INT
DELETE FROM TabExist
SET XACT_ABORT ON
EXEC @RetFinal = ProcCallerSample
PRINT 'Return parameter of ProcCallerSample is ' + str(@RetFinal)
GO
PRINT 'IF next <SELECT * FROM TabExist> yield any row then INS statements are not rolled back'
SELECT * FROM TabExist
```

Result...

```
Server: Msg 208, Level 16, State 1, Procedure ProcAbortSample, Line 3
 Invalid object name 'TabNonExist'.
Return parameter of ProcAbortSample is:       1001
IF Return parameter afrer exec ProcAbortSample is 1001 Return is not affected
Return parameter of ProcCallerSample is         0
IF next <SELECT * FROM TabExist> yield any row then INS statements are not rolled back
p1          p2
-----------     ----------------
1               ProcCallerSample
1               ProcAbortSample
```

Conclusion:

SET XACT_ABORT ON is unable to force atomicity in case of errors caused by referencing non-existing objects. So we need another weapon in order to shot these errors. There is no other way except using @@ERROR and RETURN parameter in combination and rollback transaction explicitly.

Example 2 - Using @@ERROR to handle "Non existing table" error

```
IF EXISTS(SELECT Name FROM Sysobjects where name ='ProcCallerSample')
DROP PROCEDURE ProcCallerSample
GO
```

```
CREATE PROCEDURE ProcCallerSample AS
DECLARE @Ret INT
BEGIN TRANSACTION
INSERT INTO TabExist Values('1','ProcCallerSample')
SET @Ret = 1001
EXEC @Ret = ProcAbortSample
IF @@Error <> 0
        BEGIN
    PRINT 'Error is caught, it follow Rollback'
    ROLLBACK TRANSACTION
    RETURN 1002
        END
COMMIT TRANSACTION
GO

DECLARE @RetFinal INT
DELETE FROM TabExist
EXEC @RetFinal = ProcCallerSample
PRINT 'Return parameter of ProcCallerSample is ' + str(@RetFinal)
GO
PRINT 'IF next <SELECT * FROM TabExist> yield zero rows then INS statements are rolled back'
SELECT * FROM TabExist
--------------------------------------------------------------------------------
```

Result

```
Server: Msg 208, Level 16, State 1,
Procedure ProcAbortSample, Line 3 Invalid object name 'TabNonExist'.
Error is caught, it follow Rollback
Return parameter of ProcCallerSample is        1002
IF next <SELECT * FROM TabExist> yield zero rows then INS statements are rolled back
p1
p2
----------- ----------------
(0 row(s) affected)
--------------------------------------------------------------------------------
```

This is just one case of complex error handling logic that has to be implemented in order to catch all possible errors. There is a different case of behavior depending on the type of error. Errors can cause statement termination, scope abortion, batch abortion or connection termination. There is no universal cure for all situations.

Finally, all that we have is @@Error and Return parameter. When we use them in combination, we can catch most errors from procedure of first level downward.

In the next article, Be Prepared – Part 2, I will discuss error handling blocks depending on nested level of stored procedures.

Calculating Work Days

By Jeff Moden

Overview

One of the more serious questions in project scheduling, employee planning, and accounting of time is "How many workdays are there?" In other words, given a start date and an end date, how many weekdays (usually a "workday") are there in the date range including the start date and the end date?

The normal response I get to that question varies but has been limited to "It can't be done in SQL", "Ya gotta use a CURSOR", or "You have to build a table". This article will take you through all of the logic behind building a nasty fast "Work Day Calculator" function, the crux of which is a single SELECT statement. A fully commented production-worthy UDF is available at the end of this article.

For those in a hurry...

For those of you who are in a hurry, think that real programmers don't document their code, don't care about user-friendliness, or are one of those who reads the last page in a book before reading the rest, let me save you some time... here's the core of the code sans any type of comments, user support, or supporting code. As promised, it's a single SELECT statement...

Example 1: Raw Code Summary

```
SELECT
    (DATEDIFF(dd, @StartDate, @EndDate) + 1)
  -(DATEDIFF(wk, @StartDate, @EndDate) * 2)
  -(CASE WHEN DATENAME(dw, @StartDate) = 'Sunday' THEN 1 ELSE 0 END)
  -(CASE WHEN DATENAME(dw, @EndDate) = 'Saturday' THEN 1 ELSE 0 END)
```

...and now, for the rest of us...

Building the parts of the "Work Days" algorithm

Beware of slow speeds and inaccuracies

Most of the methods I've seen for doing this included either CURSORs (yeeech!), WHILE loops, or the creation of sequence or date tables. All of these methods either employ (what I call) "RBAR" programming (pronounced as "*ree-bar*" and stands for "**R**ow **B**y **A**gonizing **R**ow"), or the creation and yearly maintenance of what usually turn out to be some rather lengthy but still finite date or sequence tables. There had to be a better way... something that didn't involve time consuming loops or lookups in tables... something direct... something that was nasty fast.

Some of the methods I found are direct but frequently are in error as well. For example, taking the total number of days in the date range, dividing by 7, and then multiplying by 5 provides a really fast *estimate* for large date ranges, but for small ranges can be quite inaccurate percentage-wise. There had to be a better way... something that is 100% accurate *all* the time... something that doesn't care about Leap Years, whether either of the dates occurred on a weekend or weekday, and something that is easy to understand.

The UDF at the end of this article is 100% accurate all the time, and is, as I said before, nasty fast. Let's start breaking the problem down...

The following sections explain how we're going to create "the basis" of a User Defined Function (UDF) to find the number of work days (week days) in a given range of dates. The basic principle is simple... count up all of the whole days in the date range and then subtract all weekend days.

How many whole days in a date range?

There are several ways to figure out how many whole days there in a date range. Many of them are quite cumbersome and some of them are incorrect because they include the "Time" element. I've found that the easiest and most accurate method for calculating whole days is to use SQL Server's "DATEDIFF" function. The DATEDIFF function uses the following syntactical format:

Example 2: DATEDIFF Syntax

```
DATEDIFF(datepart, startdate, enddate)
```

Let's try using it with something real easy to figure out on our own... how many whole days are there in the date range from the 1st of January to the 10th of January for any year? That's right, 10, if you count the 1st and 10th as part of the date range. Let's try it in code ("dd" is the *datepart* name for "days" and must NOT be included in quotes)...

Example 3: DATEDIFF Usage (typical)

```
SELECT DATEDIFF(dd, '01/01/2005', '01/10/2005')
```

The code in Example 3 will return the number 9. What went wrong? Nothing… it did exactly what we asked. It subtracted the start date from the end date, kind of like 10 -1 in this case, and came up with the number 9, as expected. The lesson here is that to include both the start date and the end date in the count of days, you have to add 1 to the result. Another way of thinking of it is to ask how many whole days are in the date range from one day to the same day? The answer is, of course, is 1, not 0. We have to add 1 to the answer to calculate the correct number of days

So, **the final formula for counting the whole number of days in a given date range** is as follows (for clarity, the variable definitions and SELECT are not included)

Example 4: Using DATEDIFF to calculate total number of days

```
DATEDIFF(dd, @StartDate, @EndDate) + 1
```

What is a "Week"?

When I started to work on this algorithm, my initial inclination was to calculate the whole weeks using DATEDIFF and then to multiply by 5 to get most of the workdays. That turned out to be a problem because the WEEK datepart of DATEDIFF is very strange. Here's what I ran into… the week of 01/25/2005 through 01/31/2005 goes from a Sunday to a Saturday. How many weeks is that? Well, that's 7 days so one would expect DATEPART to return 1 for the number of weeks, right? And it does so correctly. But it also returns a 1 as the number of weeks for the date range of 12/11/2004 through 12/12/2004! That's only two days (Saturday and Sunday)!!! How is it that DATEDIFF thinks of that as a week? Then I tried it with a date range of 12/12/2004 through 12/24/2004, or 13 days and only 1 day short of two weeks. Did DATEDIFF return a 2? No, it returned a 1! And it didn't matter what DATEFIRST (a SQL Server function that identifies which day of the week has the number 1) was set to. Originally, my code got quite long trying to work around that little problem until I had an epiphany…

DATEDIFF for the WEEK datepart doesn't actually calculate weeks, it calculates the number of times a date range contains dates that represent pairs of Saturdays and Sundays. To think of it in more simple terms, it only counts WHOLE WEEKENDS! (It actually does the count a bit differently but it's helpful to think of it that way for this problem.) Now, *that's* useful!

So, let's write a formula that will **subtract whole weekends (2 days each weekend) from the total number of days** that we previously calculated ("wk" is the *datepart* name for "weeks" and must NOT be included in quotes)…

Example 5: Using DATEDIFF to subtract the total number of weekend days

```
-DATEDIFF(wk, @StartDate, @EndDate) * 2
```

Subtracting "partial" weekends

The only thing left to do is to subtract weekend days that aren't parts of a whole weekend. The only time that will occur is if the start date occurs on a Sunday (previous Saturday not included in the date range) or when the end date occurs on a Saturday (following Sunday not included in the date range).

The following formula **subtracts 1 if the start date occurs on a Sunday** ("dw" is the "day-of-week" datepart)…

Example 6: Using DATENAME to subtract a first Sunday

```
-(CASE WHEN DATENAME(dw, @StartDate) = 'Sunday' THEN 1 ELSE 0 END)
```

Likewise, the following formula **subtracts 1 if the end date occurs on a Saturday**…

Example 7: Using DATENAME to subtract a last Saturday

```
-CASE WHEN DATENAME(dw, @EndDate ) = 'Saturday THEN 1 ELSE 0 END)
```

Putting it all together

If you put all of the code together, you get what was shown at the beginning of this article (Example 1) and you could quit there. Instead, let's force a couple of things to always be what we expect, add some user-friendliness and commented documentation, and turn it into a UDF.

"One picture is worth a thousand words"

Rather than leading you through the development of all of the support functions and user-friendliness of the code, here's the rest of the code for a production UDF. I think you'll find the comments very explanatory...

Editor: The code is available at www.sqlservercentral.com

Capturing The Error Description In A Stored Procedure

By Amit Jethva

How do you accomplish error handling in a stored procedure? 99.99 % of people will answer **use @@ERROR**. How do you capture actual error message of the error raised by SQL Server within a stored procedure? Such as:

```
Server: Msg 547, Level 16, State 1, Line 1
DELETE statement conflicted with COLUMN REFERENCE constraint 'FK__titleauth__au_id__0519C6AF'.
The conflict occurred in database 'pubs', table 'titleauthor', column 'au_id'.

The statement has been terminated.
```

Again 99.99 % of people will answer not possible in TSQL. (or wait for Yukon/SQL 2005)

But, what do you do if you really want this error message to be available for your systems? Suppose you want to log this error message in to your own log tables, what do you do?

Well, I came across this situation in one of my recent projects. The requirement was to have a stored procedure running as a batch job. This procedure would collect and transform a large amount of data in a cursor. Results of transformations for each cursor fetch were to be logged into a SQL Table. In case of any errors during the transformation was also required to be logged. The cursor, the transformations, the logic and the data volume were not a big problem. The biggest question was how do I capture Error Description of error raised inside a stored procedure and assign it to a variable.

Some of other SQL professionals also have put up this question at various sites on the internet. On one of the site, somebody put up an idea and a script using DBCC OUTPUTBUFFER. Logic was to read DBCC OUTPUTBUFFER and then cleans it up for readability. However, this process is slightly unreliable as even PRINT messages fills DBCC OUTPUTBUFFER.

The second Idea that came to my mind was to use *sp_Oa* procedures and use dynamic SQL along with SQL-DMO to capture error messages. This was a good idea but It would have made entire SP logic far too complicated. The third idea was to use strings stored in *sysmessages* & replace the placeholders. This idea also got dropped very quickly.

So what do I do? While exploring *sysmessages* table, I remembered *sp_altermessage* stored procedure. The stored procedure allows DBA to configure the errors to be logged to "*SQL Server Error Log*". This suddenly gave me an idea, **Configure Most Likely Errors to be logged and then read them off the Error Log.** I configured Errors 515, 547, 2601, 2627, 3902 with sp_altermessage to be self logging. So every time there is a Constraint Viuolation (PK, FK, NOT NULL, UNIQUE), the error was logged inside SQL Error log, like this:

```
2004-04-05 12:39:37.68 spid61 Error: 515, Severity: 16, State: 2
2004-04-05 12:39:37.68 spid61 Cannot insert the value NULL into column 'PkId',
table 'TESTDB.dbo.testtable'; column does not allow nulls. INSERT fails..
```

I wrote a stored procedure, which requires a number (Error number captured with @@ERRROR). It reads the SQL Error log and finds out the last error with the error number passed for current spid. A Quick SQL programming allows me to select Error Description lines and join it and send it back as an output parameter.

I EXECUTED FOLLOWING

```
Set xact_abort off  -- required !

Declare @intError INT
Declare @VcDescr VARCHAR(1000)

Insert testtable (PkId ) select null   -- expected error as above
Select @intError =  @@ERROR

If @intError <> 0
 Begin
        Exec GetErrorStringSP @intError, @VcDescr OUTPUT
        Print @VcDescr
 End
```

And bingo, it worked.

Now some downsides of this approach:

1. I needed to turn on SERVER WIDE settings to turn logging on, which might be slightly troublesome for SQL. Also, it increases the SQL Error log size quickly. I increased the total number of error logs for the system to 60 and put a job to cycle SQL Error logs daily at midnight.
2. I needed to give rights to a non sa login to be able to execute xp_readerrorlog.
3. A technical problem that I purposely kept open in my SP was to select the last error that might have occurred. Consider this situation, for SPID=50, Error = 515 has occurred and logging has been turned off after that error has occurred. After 2 hours, also, this error would continue to be in the SQL Error Log. But no new error descriptions will appear in SQL Error log (it is off now). Then this SP will still throw the error description same as the previous one. I could well have made it to look for errors in last 10 seconds, but it was not required in my case.

This effort has seen my project requirements through. I hope it will be useful for other SQL professionals.

Conditional Statements in WHERE Clauses

By Sotiris Filippidis

Conditional WHERE clauses in T-SQL using comparison operators

Ever had a query where you wished you could be able to specify the operator (equal, not equal, greater than, etc.) for each column contained in your WHERE clause, without having to use ugly string concatenations and the infamous EXEC keyword? Here we'll see an example of how this can be achieved with the use of a plain SQL query together with some CASE statements.

The Scenario

We will use the Customers table from the sample Northwind database for our example. Let's suppose you want to query the Customers table for the following:

1. All records that contain the word "the" in the company name
2. All records for companies located in Germany, excluding companies starting with the letter "A"

Normally, you could create a dynamic statement consisting of multiple IF statements and strings to be concatenated to a final variable which should be executed with the use of the EXEC keyword. But in some cases this is not desirable, and you would like something more versatile (although maybe slightly less efficient).

The code

Let's see how we can form a query to serve the above specs. Take a look at this code. Be sure to read the comments included in the code for an explanation of what is happening.

```
-- Declare some local variables. Actually, we are creating a pair of variables
-- for each column included in our WHERE clause.
-- The first variable represents the value we are filtering and the second
-- represents the "operator" for the filter.

declare @companyName varchar(255)
declare @companyNameOp varchar(2)
declare @country varchar(255)
declare @countryOp varchar(2)

-- Let's set some sample values now. The values you see here represent the second
-- of the two scenarios described above, i.e. all records for companies located in Germany,
-- excluding companies starting with the letter A

-- Operators are defined here with arbitrary, two-letter values.
-- Of course you could define your own set of operators, with different
-- naming conventions. For our example, here's the meaning of each possible
-- value:
-- ne = not equal
-- eq = equal
-- bg = begins with
-- ed = ends with
-- ct = contains
-- For our example, we are using only varchar fields in our WHERE clause.
-- It is very easy, though, to define operators for other data types as well.

set @companyname = 'A%'
set @companynameOp = 'ne'
set @country = 'Germany'
set @countryOp = 'eq'

-- Ok, now let's form our query.
select customerid, companyname, country
from customers
where case @companyNameOp
        when '' then 1 -- Operator not defined, get everything
        when 'eq' then -- Operator is "equals"
            case when companyname like @companyName then 1 else 0 end
        when 'bg' then -- Operator is "begins with"
            case when companyname like @companyName +'%' then 1 else 0 end
        when 'ed' then -- Operator is "ends with"
            case when companyname like '%' + @companyName  then 1 else 0 end
        when 'ct' then -- Operator is "contains"
            case when companyname like '%' + @companyName  +'%' then 1 else 0 end
        when 'ne' then -- Operator is "not equal"
            case when companyname not like @companyName then 1 else 0 end end =1
AND
-- Same approach for the second field
    case @countryOp
        when '' then 1
        when 'eq' then
            case when country like @country then 1 else 0 end
        when 'bg' then
            case when country like @country +'%' then 1 else 0 end
        when 'ed' then
            case when country like '%' + @country  then 1 else 0 end
        when 'ct' then
            case when country like '%' + @country  +'%' then 1 else 0 end
        when 'ne' then
            case when country not like @country then 1 else 0 end      end =1
```

Conclusion

The conditional WHERE clauses are based on the simple principle defined by the query "SELECT something FROM sometable WHERE 1=1" As you can see, all CASE statements evaluate to either 1 or 0, so the comparison with 1 can either be false or true for each row.

Of course, you can define your own set of operators (like operators for numeric values) and you can extend your queries to include more fields. The query, as defined here, lets you also NOT define an operator, meaning that nothing will be filtered by the specific field connected to the operator.

Please note that this article serves only as a starting point. You may need to put extra effort (and add extra functionality) in case something like this is required in a production environment, but in my personal opinion, this approach is particularly useful when dealing with customizable query wizards or similar stuff in applications, especially when some kind of custom reporting is involved. Such queries can be easily transformed to stored procedures with all parameters optional and, having some additional checks, return resultsets filtered only by the parameters (and operators) given each time.

Deleting Duplicate Records

By Sureshkumar Ramakrishnan

This article explains a solution which can be used for deleting non-unique duplicate records from a table. In Oracle, every row in a table has a unique identifier so deleting duplicate records can be done as each record is unique based on its rowid (rowid is the mechanism which Oracle uses to physically locate the records in a table). But as SQL Server 7.0/2000 does not have the concept of row identifier it's difficult to delete duplicate records from a table.

I have created a Script which I have found very useful when I am faced with such a problem. In the example below I have tried to explain how the script works. First let's create a non indexed table. The table below shows the data present in the 'Employee' table.

id	Name	Salary
1	Ram	1000
1	Ram	1000
2	Joe	2000
2	Joe	1000
3	Mary	1000
4	Julie	5000
2	Joe	1000
1	Ram	1000

The following script deletes the duplicates from 'Employee' table. If there are duplicate records then the script will get a count of the duplicate records and will then delete the records till the count is 1.

```
/**********************************************************************/
/* Script for deletion of Duplicate record from the Employee Table */
Declare @id int,
        @name varchar (50),
        @cnt int,
        @salary numeric

Declare getallrecords cursor local static For
 Select count (1), id, name, salary
    from employee (nolock)
    group by id, name,salary having count(1)>1

Open getallrecords

Fetch next from getallrecords into @cnt,@id,@name,@salary
--Cursor to check with all other records
While @@fetch_status=0
 Begin
  Set @cnt= @cnt-1
  Set rowcount @cnt

    -- Deleting the duplicate records. Observe that all fields are mentioned at the where condition
    Delete from employee where id=@id and name=@name
    and salary=@salary

  Set rowcount 0

  Fetch next from getallrecords into @cnt,@id,@name,@salary
 End

Close getallrecords
```

```
Deallocate getallrecords
*************************************************************
```

The logic of the script is pretty simple: the select query retrieves all the records that are duplicates; i.e., having Count greater than one. The result set is retrieved by opening a local cursor which fetches one row at a time.

Note here that the **Count** column is a part of the select query; this is used to identify the no. of duplicate rows in the result set.

The row count has been set to (Value obtained from the Count Column – 1). SQL Server uses rowcount to stop processing the query after the specified numbers of rows are returned. The delete statement is executed only to delete the rows set by the Set rowcount command. Once the records have been deleted, the rowcount of SQL server is reset to the default value of 0.

For more details on row count visit (http://msdn.microsoft.com/library/default.asp?url=/library/en-us/tsqlref/ts_set-set_0bjo.asp)

After the above script is executed, the data in the 'Employee' table is as shown below and note that there are no duplicates anymore:

id	Name	Salary
1	Ram	1000
2	Joe	1000
2	Joe	2000
3	Mary	1000
4	Julie	5000

In the above example duplicate records were deleted at a row level, as we had considered all the columns in the select query. By customizing the script you can also delete duplicate records at a column level. This Query can be extremely beneficial and time saving for data cleansing during Data Migration.

Extracting a String From Between Two Delimiting Characters

By Stephen Lasham

The problem

A table contains a column (*particulars*) consisting of a semi-colon-delimited string of text, for which the text between the first and second semi-colon needs to be extracted. The extracted text will be no longer than 99 characters.

The position of the first and second semi-colons is variable and the second semi-colon may not be present. Extract the text between the semi-colons.

Sample data

Table : Sample_table
Column : Particulars
LDR ; LUC20031026901 ; Vehicle
LDR ; Consolidated
LDR ; SUB35030172701 ; Building
LDRR ; LIQ200310121 ; Liquor

Solution

```
SELECT Particulars,
   CASE
         -- when no second semi-colon,
         WHEN CHARINDEX(';',(SUBSTRING(Particulars,CHARINDEX(';',Particulars,1)+1,99))) = 0
         -- then extract the full string from first semi-colon to the max length of 99
              THEN LTRIM(RTRIM(SUBSTRING(Particulars,CHARINDEX(';',Particulars,1)+1,99)))
         -- else extract the full string from the first semi-colon up to second semi-colon
         ELSE LTRIM(RTRIM(SUSTRING(
      /* <text>> */     particulars,
      /* <start > */    CHARINDEX(';',Particulars,1) + 1,
      /* <length> */    CHARINDEX(';', SUBSTRING(Particulars,
                                      CHARINDEX(';', Particulars, 1) + 1,
                                      99)) - 1
      ) ) )
         END    AS Result_string
FROM Sample_table
```

Resulting data

Particulars	Result_string
LDR ; LUC20031026901 ; Vehicle	LUC20031026901
LDR ; Consolidated	Consolidated
LDR ; SUB35030172701 ; Building	SUB35030172701
LDR ; LIQ200310121 ; Liquor	LIQ200310121

Method in Detail

SUBSTRING is used to extract the actual string value required.

```
    SUBSTRING(<text>, <start>, <length>)

    <text> = Particulars
```

CHARINDEX is used to identify the position of the semi-colons within the string.

```
CHARINDEX(, , )
```

The start position is easy, being the position of the first semi-colon plus 1 character.

```
    = CHARINDEX(';', Particulars, 1) + 1
```

The string length is the length of the text from <Start_pos> to the second semi-colon. This requires a second SUBSTRING to get a revised string of all text following the first semi-colon. A CHARINDEX over this revised text (less one character) gives the length.

```
<length> = CHARINDEX(';', <revised_text>, 1) - 1

<revised_text> = SUBSTRING(Particulars, <start>, <len>)

                        <start> = CHARINDEX(';',Particulars,1) + 1

                        <len> = 99 (maximum)
```

Substituting these back into the original SUBSTRING function gives

```
SUBSTRING(
/* <text> */     particulars,
/* <start > */   CHARINDEX(';', Particulars, 1) + 1,
/* <length> */   CHARINDEX(';', SUBSTRING(Particulars,
                                CHARINDEX(';', Particulars, 1) + 1,
                                99)) - 1
)
```

This now only needs to be wrapped in LTRIM and RTRIM functions to remove leading and trailing blanks. Additional code was also added to handle the condition where no second semi-colon was present.

Alternative Method

You can of course come up with other methods of doing this. For example, the ELSE statement above can be substituted with:

```
-- else extract the full string from the first semi-colon up to second semi-colon
ELSE RTRIM(LTRIM(LEFT(
        -- This is the text following the first semi-colon up to the max length of 99
        SUBSTRING(Particulars,CHARINDEX(';',Particulars,1)+1,99),
        -- This is the length, one character before the next semi-colon
        CHARINDEX(';',SUBSTRING(Particulars,CHARINDEX(';',Particulars,1)+1,99)) - 1
) ) )
```

Summary

You have seen demonstrated a method of extracting text from between two embedded delimiting characters. This has made use of the SUBSTRING, CHARINDEX, LTRIM and RTRIM functions. I have searched for simpler ways to do this without resorting to a cursor, but as yet have not found one. Any alternative suggestions would be most welcome.

Joins Clarified

By Sanket Naik

Normalization is an art; it is the best thing that can happen to databases .But it modularizes the data which means that we are not having all the data in the same table. This indirectly means that, suppose I want a receipt and for constructing that receipt I need data that is scattered across many tables. Then what do I do?

The answer to this is Joins. We will be briefly discussing the joins . Hopefully somebody finds this article helpful. This article is specific to T-SQL.

Joins

A join consolidates the data in two tables into a single result set. The tables aren't actually merged, they just appear to be in the rows returned by the query. You can even join more than one table at a time.

How do you join? Well, we perform join by merging two tables on the basis of one particular or maybe many columns having the same data respectively across the tables. It is really mandatory that for joins there be a common column with the same data type. Otherwise, join is not possible.

```
SELECT c.CustomerNumber, o.Amount FROM customers c, orders o WHERE c.CustomerNumber=o.CustomerNumber
```

The italicized part is the join condition or join criterion. When the join is successful, data in the second table is combined with the first to form a composite result set—a set of rows containing data from both tables. In short, the two tables have a child, but one bigger than them itself. There are basically two types of Joins:

1. Outer Joins
2. Inner Joins

The key difference between them is that outer joins include rows in the result set even when the join condition isn't met, while an inner join doesn't. When the join criteria in an outer join aren't met, columns in the first table are returned normally, but columns from the second table are returned with no value—as NULLs.

```
SELECT c.CustomerNumber, o.Amount FROM customers c JOIN orders o ON
(c.CustomerNumber=o.CustomerNumber)
```

This is the other way of writing the join, a multilevel T-SQL join statement:

```
SELECT c.CustomerNumber, o.Amount, i.Description FROM customers c, orders o, items i WHERE
c.CustomerNumber=o.CustomerNumber AND o.ItemNumber=i.ItemNumber
```

This query joins the composite of the customers table and the orders table with the items table. Note that the exact ordering of the WHERE clause is unimportant.

Note of Optimization

In order to allow servers to fully optimize queries, SQL requires that the ordering of the predicates (the join statements or conditions or the joins) in a WHERE clause must not affect the result set. They must be associative—the query must return the same result regardless of the order in which they're processed.

But, actually, the order of the terms in the WHERE clause is significant when constructing multilevel joins using the where clause syntax. That is why the SQL-92 standard moved join construction to the FROM clause. A multilevel syntax in the form of the "from clause":

```
SELECT c.CustomerNumber, o.Amount, i.Description FROM customers c LEFT OUTER JOIN orders o ON
(c.CustomerNumber=o.CustomerNumber) LEFT OUTER JOIN items i ON (o.ItemNumber=i.ItemNumber)
```

Now just don't worry about the LEFT OUTER JOIN . The explanation follows. In a LEFT OUTER JOIN the resultset contains the data as the following that columns in the first table are returned normally, but columns from the second table are returned with no value—as NULLs for the values corresponding to the ones returned in the columns of the first table.

The other types of Outer Joins are RIGHT OUTER Joins, CROSS Joins, and FULL OUTER Joins.

RIGHT OUTER Joins:

It isn't really that different from a LEFT OUTER JOIN. In fact, it's really just a LEFT OUTER JOIN with the tables reversed

Cross Joins:

A CROSS JOIN, by contrast, is an intentional Cartesian product. The size of a Cartesian product is the number of rows in one table multiplied by those in the other.

```
SELECT c.CustomerNumber, o.Amount FROM orders o CROSS JOIN customers c
```

Full Outer Joins :

A FULL OUTER JOIN returns rows from both tables regardless of whether the join condition succeeds. When a join column in the first table fails to find a match in the second, the values from the second table are returned as NULL, just as they are with a LEFT OUTER JOIN. When the join column in the second table fails to find a matching value in the first table, columns in the first table are returned as NULL, as they are in a RIGHT OUTER JOIN.

```
SELECT c.CustomerNumber, o.Amount FROM customers c FULL OUTER JOIN orders o ON
(c.CustomerNumber=o.CustomerNumber)
```

Conclusion

Hopefully, somebody will really find this article helpful . Comments are welcome!

Manipulating And Using DateTime Data

By Robert Marda

Introduction

Sooner or later someone will ask you to include dates and/or times in a query or two. Sometime after you start using dates and/or times you will notice that data stored with the datetime data type doesn't always react the way you expect in a query and that storing the date and time in non datetime data types creates other problems. In this article I plan to go over some of the things I have encountered when using dates and times.

Table Structure And Data For Examples

```
if exists (select * from dbo.sysobjects where id = object_id(N'[dbo].[tblDateTimes]')
        and OBJECTPROPERTY(id,N'IsUserTable') = 1)
    drop table [dbo].[tblDateTimes]
GO
CREATE TABLE [dbo].[tblDateTimes]
( [Row#] [int] NOT NULL ,
  [cDateTime] [datetime] NULL ,
  [cSmallDateTime] [smalldatetime] NULL ,
  [cVarChar] [varchar] (30) NULL ,
  [cChar] [char] (30) NULL
)
ON [PRIMARY]
GO

INSERT INTO tblDateTimes
   ([Row#], cDateTime, cSmallDateTime, cVarChar, cChar)
 SELECT 1, '2004-08-27 13:57:10.498', '2004-08-27 13:57:10.498'
             , '2004-08-27 13:57:10.498', '2004-08-27 13:57:10.498'
 UNION
 SELECT 2, getdate(), getdate(), getdate(), getdate()
 UNION
 SELECT 3, '3/1/1753 00:00:00.007', '3/1/1900 00:00:00.007'
             , '3/1/1753 00:00:00.007', '3/1/1753 00:00:00.007'
 UNION
 SELECT 4, '2004-08-27 13:57:10.494', '2004-08-27 13:57:10.494'
             , '2004-08-27 13:57:10.494', '2004-08-27 13:57:10.494'
 UNION
 SELECT 5, '2/1/1754', '2/1/1901', '2/1/1754', '2/1/1754'
```

Where Date/Times Can Be Stored

The datetime data type can store dates between 1 Jan 1753 and 31 Dec 9999. It can store times to the nearest 300th of a second such that you will always see the last digit stored as a 0, 3, or 7. One example would be 1:39:49.997. You will not be able to see the milliseconds in Enterprise Manager. Query Analyzer will display them.

The smalldatetime data type can hold dates between 1 Jan 1900 and 6 Jun 2079. It saves the time to the minute. Dates and times can be stored in columns with other data types including the char and varchar data types. To see how SQL Server stores data you can execute the sample code provided in the previous section. After you execute it run the following query:

```
SELECT *
 FROM tblDateTimes
```

You will get results similar to the below:

```
Row#  cDateTime               cSmallDateTime       cVarChar                  cChar
----  ---------------------   -----------------    ---------------------     ---------------------
1     2004-08-27 13:57:10.497 2004-08-27 13:57:00  2004-08-27 13:57:10.498   2004-08-27 13:57:10.498
2     2004-09-01 11:50:40.347 2004-09-01 11:51:00  Sep  1 2004 11:50AM       Sep  1 2004 11:50AM
3     1753-03-01 00:00:00.007 1900-03-01 00:00:00  3/1/1753 00:00:00.007     3/1/1753 00:00:00.007
4     2004-08-27 13:57:10.493 2004-08-27 13:57:00  2004-08-27 13:57:10.494   2004-08-27 13:57:10.494
5     1754-02-01 00:00:00.000 1901-02-01 00:00:00  2/1/1754                  2/1/1754
```

Now we can analyze how SQL Server handled each row inserted into tblDateTimes. For the 1st row cDateTime was rounded to the nearest 300th of a second, cSmallDateTime was rounded to the nearest minute, and the other two columns were stored as is. In the 2nd row we see that the date and time format is different for the columns cVarChar and cChar. For the 4th row we notice that the time for column cSmallDateTime is the same as the 1st row even though less milliseconds were specified. For the 5th row the dates for cDateTime and cSmallDateTime were reorganized so that the year is displayed first instead of the month and then a bunch of zeros were added to represent the time portion of those columns. cVarChar and cChar left the dates the way they were received.

Using Dates And Times

When you do comparisons using columns that contain dates and/or times you may get unexpected results. Make sure you understand how SQL Server handles dates and times to ensure you get the results you need.

Example 1

We want to see all rows that have a cDateTime greater than 27 Aug 04. When I began learning SQL I would have expected the below query to give me the results I wanted:

```
SELECT *
FROM tblDateTimes
WHERE cDateTime > '8/27/2004'
```

If you execute the above query you will see that the result set includes rows 1,2, and 4. I would have only expected row 2 to be in the result set. The reason the query didn't do what I expected is that SQL Server adds time to the end of the date I specified and so includes all dates of 27 Aug 04 as long as the time with them is not midnight. I can modify the query as follows to exclude 27 Aug 04:

```
SELECT *
FROM tblDateTimes
WHERE cDateTime >= '8/28/2004'
```

Now only row 2 comes out which is what I wanted.

Example 2

I want to sort dates using the dates I stored in column cChar. Execute the following query in Query Analyzer:

```
SELECT *
FROM tblDateTimes
ORDER BY cChar
```

You will notice that the dates are not sorted from the oldest to the newest. SQL Server does not treat dates as dates when not stored in a column of data type datetime or smalldatetime. It sorted them by comparing the first character in each column and then compared the second character and so on. This is one of the down sides of using the char and varchar data types to store dates. In the Manipulating Dates And Times section I will show you how to fix the above query so that it will sort properly.

Manipulating Dates And Times

Example 3 To fix the dates so the order by in a previous example will work empty the table called tblDateTimes and then run the code below to repopulate the table.

```
INSERT INTO tblDateTimes
    ([Row#], cDateTime, cSmallDateTime, cVarChar, cChar)
  SELECT 1, '2004-08-27 13:57:10.498', '2004-08-27 13:57:10.498'
    , '2004-08-27 13:57:10.498', '2004-08-27 13:57:10.498'
  UNION
  SELECT 2, getdate(), getdate(), CONVERT(varchar(23),getdate(), 21)
    , CONVERT(varchar(23),getdate(), 21)
  UNION
  SELECT 3, '3/1/1753 00:00:00.007', '3/1/1900 00:00:00.007',
      CONVERT(varchar(23),CAST('3/1/1753 00:00:00.007' as datetime),21),
      CONVERT(varchar(23),CAST('3/1/1753 00:00:00.007' as datetime), 21)
  UNION
  SELECT 4, '2004-08-27 13:57:10.494', '2004-08-27 13:57:10.494'
    , '2004-08-27 13:57:10.494', '2004-08-27 13:57:10.494'
  UNION
  SELECT 5, '2/1/1754', '2/1/1901', CONVERT(varchar(23)
      , CAST('2/1/1754' as datetime),21), CONVERT(varchar(23)
      , CAST('2/1/1754' as datetime),21)
```

Now execute this query:

```
SELECT *
 FROM tblDateTimes
 ORDER BY cChar
```

Now the order by sorted the rows in the order desired. It worked because all the dates in cChar are in the same order having the year first and then the month and the day last.

Example 4 One problem I have run into when manipulating dates is assuming that when I am at the end of a month and add one month to it that I will still be at the end of the month. When you execute the following query you will see that this assumption is not always true.

```
DECLARE @Date datetime

SET @Date = '9/30/2004'

SELECT DATEADD(m,1,@Date) AS [1 Month Added], DATEADD(m,2,@Date) AS [2 Months Added]
```

That query gives the following result set:

```
1 Month Added           2 Months Added
---------------------   ---------------------------------------------
2004-10-30 00:00:00.000 2004-11-30 00:00:00.000
```

You can see that I did not get October 31st. One way I have found to get the end of the month all the time is to go past the target month and set the day to the 1st and then subtract one day. This is a query that will do that:

```
DECLARE @Date datetime
SET @Date = '9/30/2004'
SELECT DATEADD(d,-1,DATEADD(m,2,STR(MONTH(@Date)) + '/1/' + STR(YEAR(@Date)))) AS [1 Month Added]
```

Now you get 31 October 2004. I used the STR function to avoid a syntax error. Without that function SQL Server tries to convert '/1/' to an integer.

Conclusion

When working with dates be sure you test your queries enough to ensure they do what you expect. Make sure the dates and times are stored the way you want them to be stored. These are not all the ways you can manipulate dates, simply a few that I have found useful. Your comments are welcome.

Null Functions (Aren't those Meetings?)

By Dinesh Priyankara

Definitely you must have read the article by James Travis's called =NULL AND IS NULL that is very informative. After reading the article, I really wanted to gather more related data that are used in day-to-day operation and ended up with a couple of things. Then, as usual, I decided to share with you because it may helpful to you, too.

About NULLs

Generally, null value is considered as unknown value that is not blank or not zero. Because they are unknown, operations like comparison adding may return UNKNOWN instead of expected result. Go through BOL and see-you can find enough information regarding this.

Now let's go through a couple of NULL-related functions. Before that we need to create two tables that need to see the functionalities. Run the below code.

```
CREATE TABLE Orders ([ID] int PRIMARY KEY NOT NULL, CompanyName varchar(100) NULL, DateToBeShipped
datetime NOT NULL,DateShipped datetime NULL)
GO
CREATE TABLE OrderDetails (OrderID int REFERENCES Orders([ID]) NOT NULL, Product varchar(20) NOT NULL,
Quantity int NOT NULL, Price money NOT NULL)
GO
CREATE TABLE OrderDetailsTemp (OrderID int REFERENCES Orders([ID]) NOT NULL, Product varchar(20) NOT
NULL, Quantity int NOT NULL, Price money NOT NULL)
GO
INSERT INTO Orders VALUES (245, 'Company 1', '02/10/2004', '02/10/2004')
INSERT INTO Orders VALUES (246, 'Company 1', '02/20/2004', '02/25/2004')
INSERT INTO Orders VALUES (247, 'Company 2', '04/02/2004', NULL)
```

```
GO
INSERT INTO OrderDetailsTemp VALUES (246, 'Product 2', 75, 80)
INSERT INTO OrderDetailsTemp VALUES (246, 'Product 2', 2, 1000)
INSERT INTO OrderDetails VALUES (245, 'Product 1', 5, 100)
INSERT INTO OrderDetails VALUES (245, 'Product 2', 2, 75)
GO
INSERT INTO OrderDetailsTemp VALUES (247, 'Product 2', 75, 80)
INSERT INTO OrderDetailsTemp VALUES (247, 'Product 2', 2, 1000)
```

ISNULL

ISNULL is used to validate the expression and replace it with specified value if it is null. Do not confuse with IS NULL that is used to make comparison with NULLs.
See given examples below.

```
--this query return hyphen for DateShipped if it not entered (null) yet.
SELECT [ID], CompanyName, ISNULL(CONVERT(varchar(8), DateShipped, 101), '-') AS DateShipped FROM
Orders

--this query returns number of items for order number 247. (
SELECT [ID], CompanyName, (SELECT SUM(Quantity) FROM OrderDetails WHERE OrderID = [ID]) AS NofItems
FROM Orders WHERE [ID] = 247

SELECT [ID], CompanyName, ISNULL((SELECT SUM(Quantity) FROM OrderDetails WHERE OrderID = [ID]),0) AS
NofItems FROM Orders WHERE [ID] = 247
SELECT [ID], CompanyName, ISNULL((ISNULL((SELECT SUM(Quantity) FROM OrderDetails WHERE OrderID =
[ID]),
                            (SELECT SUM(Quantity) FROM OrderDetailsTemp WHERE OrderID =
[ID]))),0) AS NofItems
FROM Orders WHERE [ID] = 247
```

The first query shows the basic functionality of ISNULL. It replaces the all null values with hyphen.
If you execute the second query, you will receive null for NofItems. The workaround is given with third query. There you can the usage of ISNULL with sub query.
The forth query has enhanced the third query that shows the NofItems from OrderDetailsTemp if record is not exists in OrderDetails.

NULLIF

With NULLIF, you can compare two expressions and it returns null if expressions are equal. If expressions are not equal, it will return the first expression. See the example below.

```
SELECT [ID], CompanyName FROM Orders WHERE NULLIF(DateToBeShipped, DateShipped) IS NULL

SELECT [ID], CompanyName FROM Orders
WHERE
        [ID] = 247
        AND
        NULLIF(         (ISNULL((SELECT SUM(Quantity) FROM OrderDetails WHERE OrderID = [ID]),0))
                        ,
                        ISNULL((SELECT SUM(Quantity) FROM OrderDetailsTemp WHERE OrderID =
[ID]),0)) IS NULL
```

The first query returns the orders that are shipped on time. Of course, you can get the same result by checking the equality of two values, but let's use this query to see the NULLIF functionality.
The second query returns all orders that have equal quantities in OrderDetails and OrderDetailsTemp tables.

COALESCE

This function allows you to get the first non-null expression from multiple expressions. Remember that all the expressions should be compatible data types and if all expressions are null, it returns null.

```
SELECT [ID], CompanyName, COALESCE(DateShipped, DateToBeShipped) AS ShippingDate FROM Orders
```

The above query returns all orders with shipping date that is taken from either DateShipped or DateToBeShipped.

= NULL and IS NULL

Read the James Travis's article: =NULL AND IS NULL

SET ANSI_NULL_DFLT_ON and SET ANSI_NULL_DFLT_OFF

This SET statement allows you to set the default nullability of new columns when create or alter tables. Remember, this is a run-time setting, not parse-time setting. By setting either ANSI_NULL_DFLT_ON to ON or ANSI_NULL_DFLT_OFF to OFF, all new columns will be allowed-null if the nullability is not explicitly specified and vice-versa. If both settings are set to OFF, the ANSI NULL default option of database is used. See the code below.

```
SET ANSI_NULL_DFLT_ON OFF
CREATE TABLE Test1 (col1 int)

SET ANSI_NULL_DFLT_ON ON
CREATE TABLE Test2 (col1 int)
```

The column in the first table will not be allowed null and the column in the second table will be allowed. Though some functions are rarely used, they are very useful. So, use them and enjoy.

Searching the File System

By Chris Cathers

Identifying the problem

I am in a unique situation where I work. I wear two hats. Of course I'm the local DBA doing everything SQL, from administration to development. But, I also wear the MCSE hat. As such, I often get asked various things from my CIO. Everything from, "Can you fix the email and give me reports on usage", to more recently, "Can you tell me how to best clear up the Home Drives folder, which is full?"

Identifying the solution

Interestingly enough, a solution to the first question spawned a solution for the second. I had already developed some code to read IMAP files into SQL, in order to produce Email Reports (A subject for another article). When he came to me with the problem of the Home Directory drive, I immediately thought of the IMAP solution as a tool to help me help him. The Home Directory was a 60Gb partition on our NT4.0 Cluster Server (Yes, I know, NT4 is going out of support at the end of the year, but "We're planning on having it upgraded by then…" Yeah, right). Anyway, This 60Gb partition was the home directory for over 300 employees and has been running virtually unmanaged for over 6 years. An attempt was made, at one point, to implement Disk Quotas, but it didn't work for various technical reasons. We knew that there were old files out there. We knew that much of the data could be archived to CD… but how to intelligently pick out that data? How can we tell what users have the oldest files? How can we tell what users have the largest? To answer these questions with Window Explorer would take 20 minutes each! Change one parameter and you have to invest another 20 minutes to find out that the parameter didn't give you what you wanted. Enter SQL.

Developing the solution

I quickly adapted the code, which I had written to read IMAP Email files from a hierarchical email folder structure, and adapted it to read all the files on the Home drives. In a nutshell, I used the DOS command 'DIR' to do a recursive search of the Home Drive. Luckily, I'm a Domain Administrator, so I had all the access permissions I needed. If you're not a Domain admin, you might try having your admin staff add the SQL Server Agent account to the Backup Operators group. That group usually has all the read permissions you'll need. Anyway, I captured the output of the recursive dir ("DIR \\FILESERVER\HOME$*.* /S") and then read the output into a SQL Temp Table. This, I then parsed into a SQL Table Variable. (Faster than writing to disk). Once my table was parsed, I was able to bulk insert the data into a permanent table and the script ended.

Implementing the solution

```
\\ccathers\
\\ccathers\dev folders\
\\ccathers\Articles\
\\ccathers\dev folders\project Autotime\
```

A sample of the folder structure on the Home Drive

Luckily for me, my admin staff had been very consistent with creating the home folders. Each users folder was also their network ID, and this 'user root' folder was placed in the root of the Home Drive. Hence, I was able to pattern search the output and look for the beginning of each tree path starting from the second character position to the first occurrence of a backslash '\' (See example above), and this was the user. The rest of the folder tree was user created, and was the various pathing information needed to find files. Thus, I would want to retain that as well.

Once I had pulled the data in, I was able to create some reports that the admins staff just ate up. I was able to tell them what were the largest 10 percent of files on the disk, who owned them, how old they were, and how much space could be reclaimed if they were deleted. Another report indicated what were the oldest files. I was able to create a report that indicated what oldest files needed to be deleted to reclaim 30 GB, or half, of drive space. (Try that one with a windows search) I was also able to provide a report, which ranked users by most files in their home folder, or largest home folder, or most oldest data in their home folders. The time savings were tremendous. It had taken me 27 minutes to gather the data on 276,933 files in 3,827 folders! The reports I was able to produce with the power of T-SQL saved over 2 hours when compared to using Windows Explorer.

Now I recognize that Active Directory, or SMS, or many other third party software packages could do the same thing. But, we are still a 4.0 shop. No SMS (Yet) and no interest from the CIO in spending more money on third party solutions. I ran the data gathering for this report Friday afternoon. On Monday, at 9:30 am, the home drive filled to capacity and users started having problems with applications like Outlook (Don't yell at me! I didn't put the PST files there!). I was able to produce the reports and give them to the admin staff, who in turn, were able to make informed decisions on what files to delete, and what users had to be notified to clean up their home drives. There is talk about using this on a weekly or monthly basis to monitor home drives, until we can implement 2000 or 2003 disk quotas. I have also entertained requests for collecting data on other drives. We have a SOX documentation folder that Admin wanted me to start tracking. There is also a Document Retrieval System our engineering department created that stores and prints PDF files. The Files and folders are constantly being added to the folder structure by an automated system, and the engineering staff has expressed interest in my solution. It takes them an hour and a half to gather data on 190,000 files in 30,000 folders. It had taken my system 13 minutes and 5 seconds to get the same data. That's when I realized that others might be interested in what I had done.

The Code…

The first statement after the title comments, which is bracketed by equal signs (===), is the location where you want to change the path to one that is relevant in your network. When I ran this script I did so from within the Northwind Database context. The script will automatically crate a permanent table, File_List, and dump the data into that. So, I wound up with a new table in the NorthWind Database called File_Lists. You, however, can run the script from any database you see fit. SQL 7.0 users, you will need to do a find and replace on @FILE_LIST TABLE to #FILE_LIST TABLE to make this script 7.0 compliant. Though, the benefits of a table variable are lost, and the savvy coder may want to reconfigure the script to use the permanent table instead…

Editor: This script is available at www.sqlservercentral.com

Here are some reporting scripts that can be quickly adapted to your individual needs. As it is posted here, the script will do nothing. You will need to read the header of each section to determine if it is the report you want. If so, uncomment the block of code in that section. (Highlight the block and CTL-SHIFT-R). The Table Variable at the beginning of the script is a common variable used by each block. So, don't comment or delete it. SQL 7.0 users, do a find and replace on @FILE_LIST to #FILE_LIST, to make this script 7.0 compliant.

Editor: This script is at www.sqlservercentral.com

This last bit of Code is a specialized report that will return data on multiple extensions. It will, however, require two custom functions that I have written, FN_PATCOUNT and FN_REPETITIVE_STR_PARSE. I've written a previous article about their functionality and use.

Make modifications in the section bracketed by (=========== MODIFY THIS STRING ONLY ========), right after the comments at the top. Format is '.ext1, ext2, extN...'

Editor: This script is available at www.sqlservercentral.com

Conclusions

As I have demonstrated here, SQL is a very powerful tool that can be adapted to many different situations. A little out-of-the-box thinking never hurts, and SQL is flexible enough to take you where you want to go. All you need to remember as a DBA is that computers excel at processing data, much of what is stored on a computer is data of one form or another, and SQL is one of the most powerful tools for gathering and processing data!

Sometimes the hardest part is determining how to get the data in to SQL so you can manipulate it. In this circumstance, I have used the DOS commands from a bygone era of computing and integrated them with one of the most powerful and modern tools, to allow me to solve a problem in a way that neither can do alone.

Any one who is looking to implement a Disk Quota on an existing drive could use these scripts. They can determine the Quota Threshold and use the scripts to find all users that exceed the threshold. Anyone who has an automated system storing files on a drive and wants to automatically gather data on that file system can use these scripts.

In short, if you have ever wished you could use a SQL query in a Window Search, then you can use these scripts!

Unique Identifier: Usage and Limitations

By Sharad Nandwani

GUID is a way to ensure uniqueness of the values. It finds use in various scenario's. GUID is produced by using a combination of Time and Network Address so there is no chance of getting a duplicate GUID. Microsoft guarantees GUIDs to be unique for the next century.

Some of the common scenarios are:

- Data is collected on many servers and merged in one single source.
- PDAs being used by Sales Representatives to store data while on move. They push the data back to CRM system when they have connectivity. SQL Server CE supports GUIDs and this makes it possible for GUIDs to be used extensively in applications made for PDAs.
- Editable Data is spread across many database Servers, a periodic replication is scheduled for same to update data on each of the servers.
- Companies trying to consolidate data on one single server after holding data on several servers.

Drawbacks of GUID

- GUID requires 16 bytes to be stored, which means four times the space required for an an auto increment integer, which is an alternate way of maintaining the uniqueness if the scope is limited to one server.
- Indexes, Primary Keys built on GUID degrade the performance of system due to more space requirements and hence more time required to update Indexes.
- GUID values are difficult to interpret so it becomes difficult to work with them directly.
- GUID does not follow a definite pattern so it cannot be used in any sort sequence.
- GUID cannot participate in queries involving Aggregate Function. GUID needs to be converted to Character to be used in aggregate function.
- It is not possible to convert the structure of the Table with Integer data type as Primary Key to

GUID directly as the two data types are not compatible. In such a scenario, It is required to change the structure of the table to Character(32). Populate the table with GUID values using NewId() function and then convert the structure to GUID.

Scripts to demonstrate this are available at www.sqlservercentral.com

There are a number of Database Applications in which the user has the right to add new rows, but there are some rows which are already existing and they need to have the same id across different installations. In such a scenario, one of the servers becomes the master and the same Id needs to be applied to the number of servers using scripts. In the table created above, we are assuming that all the rows with uservalue = 0 are the ones which should have the same id and the ones with uservalue = 1 can be added by the user so they don't need to have the same id. In such a scenario, a single script needs to be prepared to be applied across databases. This can be achieved by applying NewID() function on one of the master Databases and then the values generated on this Databases' corresponding to original Id be applied across on other Databases.

Demonstrating the same with scripts.

Run the following Script to get a set of Update Statements to be applied on other databases:

```
Select 'Update tblEntries Set Ivalue='''+convert(varchar(36),Ivalue)
    + '''' where Ivalue = '+convert(varchar(4),ivalueorig)
        +         ' and UserValue = 0' from tblEntries
```

A set of Update statements will be generated which can be used in Block A to apply to all other Databases to have the same IDs replicated across different installations. Hence, the script for the slave databases shall be as follows: (Editor: This script is at www.sqlservercentral.com)

Unique Identifiers should be used with caution as they impact performance of the Database. However, with WI-FI technology becoming more popular and usage of hand held devices increasing, GUID shall be used more extensively in many applications.

Versioning

By Andre Vigneau

The question is why do you want to know which version of Microsoft SQL Server you're running?

In my case it is for compatibility purposes. Applications or scripts might not always be compatible with older versions of SQL Server. Also, applications or scripts might not always be compatible with newer versions of SQL Server. I always have my applications check for compatibility first at startup before it's too late and some process or function does not complete properly or makes the application crash. It is so easy to have a message in place prompting the user to upgrade their application since the OS or SQL has been upgraded.

Another check is during installation when you should always check for other components' version compatibility to be sure it is the same as that which was tested with your application. This prevents other errors from occurring if you permit the application to continue.

I have developed an automated SQL Server administrative application that runs and uses many OS and SQL features that have a strong potential to change between versions. This makes sure the application gets upgraded to the appropriate version when the OS and/or SQL Server versions change.

```
-- DB & OS Version control START
DECLARE @VersionMaj dec(4,2), @OSVersionMaj dec(4,2)
DECLARE @VersionMin dec(4), @OSVersionMin dec(4)
CREATE TABLE #Version (IndexId int NOT NULL
                    ,Name varchar(60)
                    ,Internal_Value int
                    ,Character_Value varchar(255))
INSERT #Version exec master.dbo.xp_msver
SELECT @VersionMaj = CONVERT(dec(4,2),SUBSTRING(Character_Value,1,4))
, @VersionMin = CONVERT(dec(4),SUBSTRING(Character_Value,6,4))
FROM #Version
```

```
WHERE Name = 'ProductVersion'
SELECT @OSVersionMaj = CONVERT(dec(4,2),SUBSTRING(Character_Value,1,4))
, @OSVersionMin = CONVERT(dec(4),SUBSTRING(Character_Value,6,4))
FROM #Version
WHERE Name = 'WindowsVersion'

DROP TABLE #Version
-- DB & OS Version control END
```

From here you have all you need to compare your compatibility:

```
select @VersionMaj as VersionMaj,@VersionMin as VersionMin
, @OSVersionMaj as OSVersionMaj, @OSVersionMin as OSVersionMin
```

If you really need to know the service pack number you can do and maintain the following:(You can do the same for the OS Versions): (Editor: The version scipt is at www.sqlservercentral.com)

This is to get the Edition version, in case your application needs special features available only in some edition, or you really want to restrict it not to be installed on MSDE, for example. The edition is also available at startup as it is written into the SQL Server errolog,+ but there is no easy public way to get it.

The following will fail in Yukon. It seems Microsoft has forgotten to pad the information for the extra lines. You can use the above to bypass Yukon…

```
DECLARE @Edition varchar(255)
CREATE TABLE #ServerInfo
( ATTRIBUTE_ID int ,ATTRIBUTE_NAME varchar(60) ,ATTRIBUTE_VALUE varchar(255)
)

INSERT INTO #ServerInfo exec sp_server_info 2

SELECT @Edition = SUBSTRING(ATTRIBUTE_VALUE,CHARINDEX('Microsoft Corporation',ATTRIBUTE_VALUE)+23
,CHARINDEX('Edition',ATTRIBUTE_VALUE)-24-CHARINDEX('Microsoft Corporation',ATTRIBUTE_VALUE))
FROM #ServerInfo
DROP TABLE #ServerInfo

SELECT @Edition
```

This, however, should work correctly:

```
----------------------------------------------------
DECLARE @Edition varchar(255)
CREATE TABLE #ServerInfo
( ATTRIBUTE_ID int ,ATTRIBUTE_NAME varchar(60) ,ATTRIBUTE_VALUE varchar(255)
)

INSERT INTO #ServerInfo exec sp_server_info 2

SELECT @Edition = CASE WHEN CHARINDEX('Microsoft
Corporation',ATTRIBUTE_VALUE) = 0
            THEN 'Yukon' ELSE
SUBSTRING(ATTRIBUTE_VALUE,CHARINDEX('Microsoft
Corporation',ATTRIBUTE_VALUE)+23

,CHARINDEX('Edition',ATTRIBUTE_VALUE)-24-CHARINDEX('Microsoft
Corporation',ATTRIBUTE_VALUE))
            END
FROM #ServerInfo
DROP TABLE #ServerInfo

SELECT @Edition
----------------------------------------------------
```

Disaster Recovery

It's pretty rare that a major disaster actually strikes a company. With decades of experience between the SQLServerCentral.com staff, none of us has experienced a major disaster. We have, however, dealt with any number of minor ones, including many of our own making.

So we've added a section in this volume dealing with those disaster recovery issues. These articles are mostly looking at administrative issues and methods of dealing with management and situations. Most of these are more administrative, helping you look at disaster recovery from the standpoint of your manager and being organized in case one occurs. Paul Ibison has brought us a comparison of two strategies that you might employ when looking to setup a system that is resilient to a disaster situation.

From the soapbox: Does anyone know what disaster recovery is?

By James Luetkehoelter

Disclaimer: From the soapbox does not necessarily represent the views of SQLServerCentral.com, Microsoft, or the author himself.

So you have full backups, differential backups and transaction log backups enabled and functioning for your production databases. You have documented procedures for restoring databases, and you perform quarterly tests of the process. Is this disaster recovery for SQL Server?

No.

Disaster recovery is NOT the equivalent of a backup and restore plan; it encompasses much more than that. To be sure, this is an integral part of a DR plan, but it is still only a piece of that plan. Here are some common beliefs I've encountered; in fact, I've held some of them myself at one point or another in my career:

"Our server staff backs up all of the databases with product X -- I don't need to worry about it". I really hope there's no full-time DBA that would say this. I've run into this with "pseudo"-DBAs -- developers or systems staff that have the responsibility thrust upon them. While a centralized backup methodology in a large environment makes life much, much easier, you need to be certain that whoever manages that backup solution understands the specifics of how to properly backup a SQL Server database. More than once I've seen a DBA-less company use an open-file backup solution on a database; it's the easiest way to get introduced to dealing with a "suspect" database. Oh, it's so much fun.

"As long as my databases are backed up, my responsibility as a DBA ends". At one point earlier in my career, I actually believed this. At the time I was working with a company where IT was organized in "silos" -- all of the DBAs were in one group, the systems people in another, etc. This made cross team interaction difficult, both from a communication and logistical standpoint to a cultural one. Each group had very clearly defined areas of responsibility, and we all clung to them to ensure that we didn't get blamed for an issue that was beyond our control. I now fervently believe that it is irresponsible for a DBA to simply stop with the backups of databases. It doesn't do much good to have a solid database backup plan if there's no plan or process for recovering the server itself.

"As a DBA, I know the best way to set up a backup scheme for my databases". Of course, the DBA knows the best technical way to set up backups. The scheme, however, should **always** be dictated by business units. There are three questions that always need to be asked of any business unit:

1) What is an acceptable amount of data loss

2) What is an acceptable amount of downtime

3) How long do backups need to be retained

Initially, the answers will almost always be 1) "None", 2) "None", 3) "Forever". When that happens, simply explain the costs of co-location, data archival services, SAN implementation, clustering, etc. At that point you'll get a reasonable answer. Your legal department should also be involved, because there may be legal ramifications of data loss unknown to the business unit. From there you can build a technical backup scheme -- how often you backup up, do you need to use differentials, how long do you retain transaction logs, etc. This plan and its ramifications should then be reviewed with the business unit, legal, etc. Having them sign off on it is also an advisable thing. :)

"Disaster recovery is the responsibility of IT". While IT plays an integral role in the development of the plan, it is ultimately the responsibility of the business itself. Executives and management need to understand the impact of each disaster scenario, as well as what's required to get up and running again. Business units must have some sort of contingency to continue operating without access to an application. Facilities staff must be ready to correct power, HVAC and environment problems (such as water leaking into the server room -- has anyone else had the joy of dealing with a soggy server?). Again, I believe it is irresponsible for a DBA not to raise awareness of the company's entire responsibility towards disaster recovery.

"I'm just a DBA -- I can't make a company-wide disaster recovery plan happen". Ah, the sweet smell of despair -- I've been there myself. It is true that you can't make a company-wide DR plan, but you **can** make it happen. Talk to your manager about concerns you have. Talk to business units and their managers. Pound on the CEO's door as if you're storming a castle. As long as you are tactful and professional in your approach to driving change (avoid wandering around the halls beating a drum and shouting "We're doomed!!" – take it from experience, it doesn't go over too well), chances are someone will eventually listen, and your efforts **will** be appreciated.

"I have a full backup scheme in place – I can recover to any point in time. I have redundant hardware, off-site backups, transaction logging, etc. We could lose this entire facility in an earthquake, and I can still restore the database to another server up to the latest committed transaction. The database can be recovered in the event of any disaster." Any disaster? Are you sure? What about the data entry clerk who's been inconsistently entering incorrect data? Sure, you can recover to a point in time, but when is that point in time? And how disruptive will it be to the use of the application to attempt this type of restore? User error is the most frustrating and difficult disaster scenario to deal with. When the CEO is standing in front of you demanding that you "fix it", you still have to deal with it, **whomever** is responsible.

"Our company understands the true needs of a disaster recovery process – we just don't have the time or resources to undertake a project of this size." Creating a DR plan doesn't have to be a major project – in fact, it's less likely to be successful or useful if it is undertaken as a single, all-encompassing project. Take things in small steps and create the DR plan as you go. You could start by simply writing down the names and phone numbers of anyone that needs to be contacted, from internal staff to outside vendors (power, plumbing, HVAC, etc). Document restore procedures. Store backup information off-site. The point is, take it slow. Disaster recovery planning should be viewed as an ongoing process, not a single task to be completed.

If any of these scenarios sound familiar, you could be heading for trouble. At least that's what the view looks like from up on the soapbox.

Am I wrong? Am I right? Am I just plain crazy? Just because the rant is over, it doesn't mean the debate is resolved.

Incident Response - The Framework

By Steve Jones

Introduction

Disaster Recovery is something that's on my mind lately. With hurricane Charlie rolling through Florida recently (it's August 2004 as I write this), and my partner Andy without power for nearly a week in central Florida, we've had some discussions about how to prepare for a disaster and the value of doing so. I'm not big on getting too detailed in a recovery plan, but I do agree that there are some good reasons for setting up a framework under which to work. This article looks at some ideas for such a framework based on my experiences.

Incident Response

One of the neat things that I saw setup at J.D. Edwards when I worked there was an Incident Response Team. This was a group of people in the IT group that were designated as those who would be called in to triage any type of incident and determine the course of action. There were similar groups in the business side of things, but I didn't really work with them at all. These people all had 2 way pagers and cell phones and would get called in for any type of incident.

So what's an incident? Well, a disaster or any sort certainly qualifies. A natural disaster, fire, tornado; etc., could initiate an incident. As could a virus, major network outage, pretty much anything that interrupts a large set of users. These people were from different areas and there were two people in each area, a primary and a backup. This was to ensure that there would always be someone available and both the primary and secondary were not supposed to both be on vacation, out of town, unavailable at the same time. In practice this wasn't always the case, but by having a good sized group, it tended to work well and it was always likely that any qualified person might be "drafted" if need be.

The team included people from different disciplines, as you might have guessed. A sampling of job functions from which people would be drawn includes:

- Network (NOC, physical network infrastructure people)
- Windows - General AD and Windows domain infrastructure people
- Email - Server side, Exchange people
- Desktop - both desktop support (help desk) and engineering, anti virus, scripting, etc. people
- Unix - General Unix infrastructure people
- Database - Can't forget the DBAs can we?
- Application Engineering - Those who know how the internal applications work.
- Director level managers - Someone needs to lead the group and have the appropriate level of authority to ensure things get done.
-

There may be different groupings or areas that you want represented depending on your organization, but it should be fairly easy to identify the major areas for your company. You might include voice specialists if that's needed, or you might need a representative from your change management group. You will want a primary and secondary person from each area and be sure they are equipped with some sort of technology to enable you to get in touch with them-quickly!

Preparation

Now that you've assembled a team, there are a few things that should be pre-staged in your environment, the first of which is documentation. Now I'm not talking about how you restore a failed database server, I'm talking about more basic documentation. Here are a few things you should have available in both electronic AND paper form:

- Contact information for all team members
- Management contact information
- Vendor Contact Information
- Other IT Employee Contacts
- Procedures
- Food/Beverage Companies and Menus
- Nearby Accommodations
- Client Contacts

Below I've provided a little more detail on each of these items and what the purpose is or what it should consist of.

Team Contact Information

This is basic stuff, but includes home, work, cell, pager, etc. contact information for each person on the team. They should be designated as primary or secondary and logically ordered in some fashion. I use alphabetical by first name since most of us work with each other by first name. Be sure their specialty is listed prominently as well. You never know who will be charged with contacting the "primary network guy" and they might not know who that is, so be sure all the information is listed. I've seen nearby relatives' contact information for key employees listed as well for people that may move to a different place in an emergency. For example, Andy's mother and sister live nearby and it would make sense to list their numbers. After hurricane Charlie, he didn't have power, but his mother did, so it made sense to be able to contact him there.

Management Contact Information

The biggest part of successfully managing and getting through an incident is communicating successfully with those affected. Usually this means upper management. More important than fixing the problem is letting people know you are working on it, the status, major issues or possible support that might be needed and estimates for when things will be accomplished. Even if you have to change your estimate, calling your VP every couple hours to update him goes a long way; much further than telling him 4 hours, being out of contact for 3:55 and then calling and saying nothing worked, it's another 4 hours.

However you handle it, you definitely want to be able to contact any of the senior management you need to, which means not fumbling for their contact information. This should be nearly as detailed as the Team contact information.

Vendor Contact Information

Face it; things break and you have to fix them. Without a doubt sometime in your IT career, some piece of vendor supplied hardware or software will break and you'll need to contact them. It makes it much easier if you have a central list of vendors, your customer numbers, phone numbers, sales people's names, keys, etc. Having a list of this stuff at 3am is handy when you call Cisco and they're asking you for it because you need support for the firewall that's DOS'd and the CTO has asked you to call them. Figuring out this information is a pain, so take some time and assemble it so it's available. Buy something new? As part of the receiving process, jot down the relevant information in your Incident Response documentation.

Other IT Employee Information

Similar to the contact info for the team. You never know when you might need the one application developer that worked on the one project that just blew up.

Procedures

Again, these aren't the "To Restore The Exchange Server, you need to.." documents. These are the ones that spell out how to handle the incident. They should be fairly short, but make a few decisions up front so there is no grey area. A few of the things that I've seen put in here:

- Who's in charge - List clearly that the directors are in charge and if they can't be reached, it's person A, then B, then C, etc. You want to be sure that you pick people who can take charge of the group and ensure that procedures are followed. Not many people can do this well.
- Updates - Spell out how updates will be given and received. I've seen a dedicated voice mailbox in some companies, dedicated bridge (conference call) lines, posted at some external web site, etc. for the updates. Communication is critical and you don't want each person on your team being called individually by different people all trying to get updates. Spell out the method and frequency of updates as well as a method for people to get their own updates from the team without bothering them.
- Notes - You want to be sure that notes are taken regarding the assessment and courses of action, including what works and what doesn't. It helps to designate someone to be responsible for this during the incident, but set up a place to keep these notes. Be sure you allow for non-electronic note storage.
- What's not allowed - Have a list of actions that are not allowed, like ordering new hardware, spending above $xx; etc., things that you don't want done without some additional approval. Usually this number was US$1,000, though it could be spent if the VP or CIO was called.

Food/Beverage Companies and Menus

My favorite part. And this is the area of documentation that will get used the most!

Everyone needs to eat. And while they're working on a problem, the last thing you want them worrying about is how they are going to get their next meal. Do they need money from the ATM, who's open?, etc. Do yourself a favor and compile a list of local, nearby restaurants, their hours, what they serve, phone numbers, directions, and menus and have them available. It will greatly ease the process of getting your people fed when you need to. And it will generate lots of goodwill when you provide them with dinner.

A few hints: try to pick places that deliver so you don't have to send someone out. Get a variety of food to appeal to different tastes, but don't go overboard. Picking 20 places when 6 will do only increases the confusion as too many people have differing opinions. Try to find someplace that is open all night. Not always possible, but it does seem that things like to break at night. You might also stock up on some snacks in the office for emergencies, perhaps replacing them monthly and just giving away the old stuff.

Nearby Accommodations

Hopefully you won't need this section, but if you do, it's handy to have ready. Get a few hotels approved by management ahead of time in case you need them. I've often worked with people who had long commutes and having them drive home after working 22 hours or asking them to drive an hour each way home and back and be back in 4 hours isn't very respectful or smart. If you need them, get a couple rooms and have people take shifts sleeping. Most people will want to go home, but it isn't always an option, so be prepared.

Client Contacts

Not applicable to everyone, but I have worked in some companies where I might need to notify clients of a major issue, or get in contact with them to change something. Whatever the reason, if you think you might need it, include it just in case. Be sure you have multiple ways to contact people wherever possible.

Conclusions

This is the first part of the Incident Response Framework. In the next article, I'll look at how the group should function in an incident and some of the things I've seen done well and not so well in handling things. Unfortunately, I've a bit more experience with this sort of thing than I would like.

It seems like this might be overkill at some companies, but even in my little 30-person company, having some of these ideas in place would have helped us in quite a few situations. It makes things run a little smoother and definitely helps to keep people working together. I'll admit that the team might have been 4 people total out of 30, but it still would have helped.

Give me some feedback and perhaps we can come up with a framework that many people will agree with.

Steve Jones - ©dkRanch.net August 2004

Incident Response - Responding to an Incident

By Steve Jones

Introduction

Disaster Recovery planning is something that everyone says you should do. Everyone wants a detailed plan that spells out exactly what you will do, especially those Sarbannes-Oxley auditors. But in reality, a detailed plan won't work and if you expect a detailed plan to succeed, you'll be in trouble. People need to be able to think on their feet, react, and make up for documents that aren't up to date or don't cover the situation.

In my first article on the Incident Response - The Framework , I looked at the outline of things that you need to get the framework in place. This one will look at the actual things that should happen when an incident occurs.

Declaration

The number of people that can declare an incident should be pretty large. You should have good people in place, doing their jobs, and they should be able to react. When a network technician realizes that there is probably something major going on, they should be able to invoke an incident. Their manager might be at lunch, and you don't want to wait an hour to get things moving. Trust your people to make good decisions and if they don't, work with them after to explain why it wasn't the appropriate time. But don't berate them or revoke their ability to declare an incident in the future. Teach them what needs to be done.

Communication

From your framework, you should have a contact list as well and a way for this to be invoked. In a smaller organization it could be as simple as having the person invoking the incident call everyone. In larger companies the task has usually been handed off to some group that always has people on call, like the help desk or the NOC. It's then this group's responsibility to first contact a leader (see below) and determine the meeting place (also below) before starting to call the people on the contact list.

For this list, there are a few things you should have. For primary people, those in various areas that are important to solving problems like the senior network engineer, mail engineer, DBA, etc., you should have multiple methods of contacting them. Home phone, work, cell, friends, etc. Be aware that if this is a larger disaster, cell phones might not work, so prepare for that. You might even have people call into some landline if they suspect a problem. If you cannot contact a primary Subject Matter Expert then a secondary person should be contacted.

I have also seen the "on call" person for each area being contacted. In smaller companies, you might only have one person on call, but in larger organizations, more than a 1000 people, you likely have 3, 4 or more people on call at any given time. At Peoplesoft, with 12,000+ employees, we had 10 people on call at anytime for the various areas.

Leadership

As I mentioned in the last article, not everyone is suited to manage a crisis. At Peoplesoft there were 4 designated people who had a little training and were allowed to lead an incident response. It's a skill that's hard, being able to remain calm under pressure, inspire as well as ensure that people get things done, not blame anyone or get too upset when more things go wrong or solutions aren't working. It takes a cool, calm, collected person that can easily communicate with both technical people and senior management. Typically it is someone at a director level, not so high up that everyone is afraid of making a mistake, but not so low as to not have enough respect and power to make things happen or to be allowed to make decisions.

You should designate a few people that can assume leadership in a crisis and have the authority to make decisions. Typically this person is in charge of ALL actions and is the only person. At least two people should be chosen so you can work in shifts if need be.

In a crisis, this person should be called first and they can lead the initial crisis meeting. From there, this person is in charge of assigning actions, receiving status reports, and giving the updates to management and other groups on how the incident response is proceeding.

Scribe

It's a little thing, but someone should be responsible for taking notes; either electronically, on a whiteboard, somewhere. In one of my larger employers there was a secretary pool that was on call just as others were in case they were needed for a crisis. In smaller groups the leader designates someone, even one of the techies, but be sure someone documents the problem, the plan, the action items and who they are assigned to. Be sure that you update and post these notes regularly.

Meeting Place

There should be a designated meeting place and meeting phone for most companies. If you're truly a small company, then you might just meet in someone's office and use regular phone lines and 3 way calling, but if you've gotten IT above 10 people, you probably should designate some predetermined setup.

The meeting room should be a room large enough to hold the group of people who will be working on the problem. Not for the actual work, though I've seen that done, but large enough for meetings of everyone that might have input. There should be equipment pre-staged and always available since one never knows when an incident will occur. You might consider having the following available:

- speaker phones for remote attendees
- preferably whiteboards for diagramming or making notes, but if this is not possible, a large notepad that can be written on and the pages taped or stuck to the walls. Be sure writing utensils are available.
- Computer projector - For displaying something from a laptop for everyone to see.
- Extra power cords, power strips, network cables, etc.
- A clock. This will be the authoritative clock by which everyone will work. Individual computer clocks, watches, etc. can be managed by each person once they know how this clock relates to their own watch or computer clock.

This can be a normal conference room, which it was in a few companies I've worked for. Larger companies also tend to have extra laptop power supplies, multiple hubs/switches; etc, setup in the room.

You also want to plan for remote attendees. For whatever reason, people will not always be able to be in the crisis room in person, so having conference capabilities is a must. Whether you permanently assign a number or not, there should be some conference facility setup for the initial meetings and updates. If it is not a permanent number, then the temporary number should be assigned by someone and given to the central point of contact for the group (help desk, NOC, etc.) The same number should be used for the duration of the crisis if possible.

At one company, a permanent line was setup and once an incident was declared, the line was permanently left open on speaker phone for the duration of the event. It was nice to be able to just call into the number and ask for some status item, but it could also be distracting to those working.

However you do it, be sure that you allow for more than one person to call in for meetings and updates. Chances are that an incident will occur when you have at least one person on vacation, out sick; etc., so plan for it in advance.

Initial Meeting

An incident has been declared and you've convened a meeting-now what? As silly or redundant as it might seem, the first thing you want to do is have someone give an update on what the incident is. People will have an idea, but it may only be a partial idea or they may not be aware of the scope or impact of the incident. It helps to have someone, preferably the person who initiated the incident response, to give the firsthand impressions of what is occurring to be sure everyone is on the same page. This should be documented so anyone coming in late or joining the group knows what is being focused on.

Others should add information that is relevant and ask questions to determine the scope of the incident, both in assessing what needs to be done as well as the impact to the business. It is important to note that no one should be getting blamed for this. Let management deal with issues like this later. The incident response is the time to determine what is wrong and its impact to the business, not to fix things that you don't like, not to test someone's competence. You are here to deal with a specific issue-virus attack, network outage, etc. Work on that issue and don't expand the scope of things that need to get done. The goal is to respond to an incident, get it fixed, and get back to your normal routine.

Once the scope of the problem is determined, the group should come to some consensus on how to proceed. Decide upon an action plan that will start to resolve the incident. Whether that is someone reconfiguring something, an order placed with a vendor for equipment, or something else, invite arguments, discussions, disagreements, etc. You want people to poke holes in the plan, to find potential problems. Everything should be laid on the table so that the risks are understood by all. Most things will be a tradeoff and the incident was declared because there isn't an easy answer or quick fix.

Once you feel that the plan is solid enough to proceed, assign tasks to people, give a summary, and decide when the next update will occur before sending people to complete their tasks.

Updates

Update are crucial to ensure that the system runs smoothly and people trust it. Even though you are in the "work as fast as I can to get things working" mode, not everyone knows that, especially management. And people will have questions and planning their future activities based on the information you give them. So give them regular updates. Even if you cannot solve the problem, give an update on what is being done.

At the least, updates should be every couple of hours. The only exception would be when there is a very small group, 2-3 people working on something overnight. You might defer an update for 6 hours then, but in general they should come more often. I've seen then as often as every 30 minutes, which I think was overkill. I'd say do them once an hour unless there is some overriding reason to change that.

Be sure that everyone with an action item returns to update the leader between 45-55 minutes after the last update. This ensures the leader is aware of what is going on and can have those updating him go back to work or remain in case there are questions. Even if your task will take 3 hours, give an update on what has been accomplished in the last hour and any revised estimate.

When giving the update, summarize the situation quickly for those that may be new, outline the plan and give updates on what has occurred to date and what is occurring in the future. Allow for questions and then schedule the next update. You want this to go quickly, so try and keep it under 10 minutes.

One more thing to think about is that the updates should not be limited to just the update meeting (including remote attendees). People that want or need to know what is happening are still leading their lives. They might be commuting, eating dinner, putting their kids to bed, etc. and not be able to attend or call in for the scheduled update. They still need to be informed, but you certainly don't want 25 people calling the incident response leader for an update.

At one company, a trouble ticket was used to track incidents, along with all other issues, and updates were required on the ticket every 30 minutes. At another company, a voicemail box was available and updated regularly for people to call into and get the latest status. Neither method is preferable, but having some sort of non-real time update is important if you don't want to be saying the same thing over and over.

Work the Plan

After the plan is decided, each person should either have something to do, or may have a short downtime. In either case, if any person is leaving the meeting room, they should be sure that the leader knows where they are going, when they will be back, and how they can be contacted. There have been many times where someone leaves for a smoke or some other break and they are needed 5 minutes later. This should remain in effect for the duration of the incident. At any time the leader should be able to contact anyone.

You should also work only the action items you have been assigned. Getting creative, trying to "fix" something else while you're handling an incident is a great way to cause more problems, delay the closure of the event, and make more work for yourself down the road. Deviations from the plan, if necessary, should be approved by the leader.

You also should keep track of what you are doing so you can report back at the update meetings what occurred. These don't need to be detailed step-by-step instructions, but if things were successful, what was done, and if there was any side effect or failures.

Little Things

There are a few other little things that you want to be aware of, or make your manager aware of when dealing with a crisis. These are fairly obvious, but they mean a lot to keeping people cool and working efficiently.

The first is that you should prepare for things to take longer than expected. I've been in this business for over a decade and absolutely everything takes longer than expected. That being said, there are two things that I always look out for when scheduling people. The first is that when an incident is declared I go into shift work mode. That means that if it's during business hours I send someone home with the expectation that I might call them to work overnight sometime. If it's overnight, the unlucky person that got stuck with it is immediately reprieved from coming in for some or all of the next day. I want people to be sure that their interests are being looked at and since I'm asking for above and beyond normal duty help, I'll reward them in some way. Also, that I'm not going to work them on some 48-hour death march. Shift work is hard, but it enables us to keep working; and more importantly, keep people rested. You may have to force people to leave at some point and be sure you watch them. I've seen people push for 24 hours, then not want to leave because they're sure the answer is an hour away. It isn't and when you need them in 12 hours, they're not rested, focused, etc. You can't usually make huge rewards for people, so be respectful of the fact you're having them work over and above.

The other half of this is that whoever is managing needs to keep resources handy in case they are needed. But if they are not, or not anticipated, cut them loose. I've seen crisis situations run for 24 hours and people kept on for 8 or 10 hours more than they were needed because no one thought to let them go. Once this is over you want to get back to normal business and have people working as soon as you can. That won't happen if you burn everyone out. Keep it on your mind at every status meeting that you want to be looking for people to send home. The group will run smoother and you'll have more rested people if you need them. Lots of people will be afraid to ask to go and others won't want to go. The leader needs to be strong enough to handle both situations and send people home as soon as possible.

Food is the other big item that people worry about. If it's 11:00am and a crisis is declared, lunch plans may be cancelled. If it's 4:00pm, people immediately start thinking of dinner. The leader should do everyone a favor once the scope of the problem is determined and you have an estimate to resolution. If it's anywhere close to a meal, let people know that you'll be providing a meal at xx time. Take a few suggestions and then decide what the meal is and ensure that someone gets it at the proper time. Usually between updates the leader or scribe can take orders, contact some vendor and arrange delivery or go to pick up food. This will go a very long way to keeping people happy. If you have a 4 or 6am update meeting, be sure you bring breakfast of some sort. Spending $100 isn't going to impact the cost of the crisis and you will get a great return on the investment from your people.

Conclusion

Handling a crisis is a huge pain in the rear. It's hard, it stresses people, and it may push some of your people over the edge or make them quit if it happens too often. You should be ensuring that your daily procedures and practices are geared towards preventing incidents. Virus protection, patches, etc. should be part of your IT group to be sure that the number of incidents is a minimum.

You also should try to reward people that work on the incident. Maybe not everyone, but for sure the people that have shined under pressure, worked extra hard, whatever. Even a $10 movie pass (get two so they can take their significant other) goes a long way after you're been working all night to solve something. I wouldn't setup a standard, but depending on the situation, reward people. It's an easy and inexpensive way to help retain them.

Lastly, while I hate responding to incidents after doing so for over a decade, I do know these are the times that you grow. You learn the most, you grow your skills, and you bond with your teammates. These times are important to building a winning and effective team, so try to make them go smoothly. There will be enough things that go horribly wrong without worrying about some of the items I've mentioned above.

Steve Jones - ©dkranch.net 2004

Log Shipping vs. Replication

By Paul Ibison

Many previous articles on log-shipping and replication have concentrated on solving set-up and configuration issues. This article outlines the differences between them, for the purposes of maintaining a standby server. To put this in context, log-shipping and replication are two methods which are often compared to clustering; however, clustering is really a technology created to solve a different business requirement - that of *automatic* fail-over. In solving this requirement it has some intrinsic restrictions: the distance between nodes is extremely limited, meaning the entire system must be in the same geographic location, and the data itself physically resides in one place. This latter point sounds obvious, but consequently there is no possibility of using the topology to distribute query load; e.g., to have a reporting server. On the more prosaic side it also has a reputation as being relatively difficult to set up and maintain and the licenses required are not cheap. So, many DBAs take advantage of their existing skill set to implement a methodology which maintains a standby server, accept that fail-over will be a manual process but hope to gain the bonus of having standalone reporting capability. Commonly the choice is between log-shipping and replication, but one needs a clear understanding of which methodology is the more appropriate. The table below outlines some of the key differences, which are then explained further.

	Log-Shipping	Replication
What is the latency?	>1min	Potentially as low as a few seconds
Is the schema altered at the publisher?	No	Snapshot - no Transactional - no Updating subscribers or merge - yes
Is the schema altered at the subscriber?	No	Possibly (see text)
Are there schema requirements?	None	Primary keys required for transactional table articles
Can we select individual articles?	No	Yes

Is the subscriber/standby database 'protected'?	Yes	No
Is system data transferred?	Mostly	No
Is the subscriber/standby server useable as reporting server?	Unlikely (see text)	Yes

What is the latency?

Log-shipping can backup once every minute and the copy and load frequency can also be every minute. If you use transactional replication or merge replication, the latency can be as low as a few seconds, assuming the relevant -POLLINGINTERVAL agent parameters are minimized. Snapshot replication will have a much higher latency as it requires an exclusive lock on the publisher's replicated tables - consequently it is often considered an offline solution.

Is the schema altered at the publisher?

Log-shipping and snapshot replication do not alter the publisher's schema. Updating subscribers (transactional and snapshot) and merge replication will add a guid column if there isn't one there already with the rowguid property. This may cause some queries on the publisher to fail, e.g. if you had TSQL inside a stored procedure which did the following:

```
INSERT INTO ExistingTable
SELECT * FROM ReplicatedTable
```

Is the schema altered at the subscriber?

Log-shipping makes no alterations to the schema. Snapshot and transactional replication may make subtle schema changes; standard transactional and snapshot will not transfer identity attributes - they become normal numerical columns (int, smallint, numeric...) on the subscriber. Some DBAs try to get around this by doing a nosync initialization and ensuring the table on the subscriber has the Identity 'Yes (Not for Replication)' attribute, which essentially allows the replication process to do identity inserts. However, on use of the fail-over server this methodology fails as the internal identity counter has not been incremented, and use of DBCC CHECKIDENT to reseed will not work on columns created with this attribute. This problem is not apparent if merge or queued updating subscribers are selected.

Are there schema requirements?

There are no requirements for log-shipping whereas all forms of transactional replication require primary keys on table articles.

Can we select individual articles?

Log-shipping takes the whole set of tables, stored procedures, triggers; etc, existing in the published database, while replication has the granularity to select articles individually.

Is the Standby database 'protected'?

Log-shipping restores the logs to the standby server with NoRecovery or with Standby - both options disallow edits to be made to the data. Replication doesn't enforce such a restriction so explicit permissions would be required to prevent changes to subscriber data.

Is system data transferred?

A front-end application usually requires the presence of some system data. What I am referring to here is data in the system catalog or the database catalog: logins, messages, users, permissions, etc. In the case of log-shipping, the database catalog is transferred but not the system catalog, while replication transfers neither.

Is the subscriber/standby server useable as reporting server?

Log-shipping can't usually allow the standby server to be used for reporting as it requires an exclusive lock on the database to restore the log; i.e., during the restore users will be forcibly removed, or the log-shipping job will fail. Replication can allow reporting queries to be run, and as typically concurrent replication is not a big resource drain, such queries usually run quickly.

Conclusions

Hopefully this article provides enough info to make a more informative choice. Although this is a little simplistic, generally I recommend log-shipping for fail-over, followed by transactional replication with queued updating subscribers. The order is reversed if there is a possibility of needing to go back to the production server once it is repaired (in which case one can simply run the queue reader agent) or if there is a requirement for a standby server to function additionally as a reporting server.

Paul Ibison

June 2004

Business Intelligence, Reporting Services, and ETL

Supposedly the hot new area for DBAs. That's been the talk for a few years now, but the BI world of Analysis Services, cubes, and MDX hasn't really taken off. That has now stopped Microsoft from continuing to develop in this area and one of the hot new technologies during the time these articles were written was Reporting Services.

We're bringing you a few articles in each area, designed to help you get started and understand a bit more about the BI world. A short look at DTS along with a couple on Analysis Services, a part of SQL Server that many DBAs have not worked with.

Lastly we have 4 articles on Reporting Services, the newest add-on to SQL Server that Microsoft has given us. A true reporting engine and development tool that competes nicely with Crystal Reports and other report writers at a great price. Free.

Analysis About Analysis Services

By Ramunas Balukonis

In this article I'll demonstrate how one can learn more about the queries that are sent to analysis services.

Every analysis services administrator should know about the table named "QueryLog". This table contains information about the queries, which are submitted to analysis services. By default this table is placed in an Access file, in the \Bin directory of the Microsoft analysis services path. I would recommend that this table will be moved to a SQL Server database. Simply use the import / export wizard to copy this table to your OLAP repository database. Do not use the default msdb database!

After exporting this table to SQL Server database, you need to tell the Microsoft OLAP server that queries will be logged into that table. To do so, open the registry editor, seek the key "hkey_local_machine -> software -> Microsoft -> OLAP server -> CurrentVersion " QueryLogConnectionString and RemoteQueryLogConnectionString. Replace the text with the connection string to your SQL Server database, something like "Provider=SQLOLEDB.1;Integrated Security=SSPI;Persist Security Info=False;Initial Catalog=yours_olap_database;Data Source=your_sql_server".

Note, after moving the table from Access to SQL Server, the SQL Server service should always be started to ensure that this information can be logged.

Now all new information about queries will be written to this SQL Server table. Remember that after a cube is changed, query information about that cube is deleted from the table. To save information about all user queries I created new table named QueryLog_history, the same as QueryLog. The script for the QueryLog_history is:

```
--Ramunas Balukonis 2004.04.15
CREATE TABLE [dbo].[QueryLog_history] (
   [MSOLAP_Database] [nvarchar] (255) NULL ,   [MSOLAP_Cube] [nvarchar] (255) NULL ,
   [MSOLAP_User] [nvarchar] (255) NULL ,       [Dataset] [nvarchar] (64) NULL ,
   [Slice] [nvarchar] (64) NULL ,              [StartTime] [datetime] NULL ,
   [Duration] [int] NULL ,                     [MOLAPPartitions] [smallint] NULL ,
   [ROLAPPartitions] [smallint] NULL ,         [SamplingRate] [int] NULL
) ON [PRIMARY]
GO
CREATE  CLUSTERED  INDEX [IX_StartTime] ON
[dbo].[QueryLog_history]([StartTime] DESC ) ON [PRIMARY]
GO
```

My QueryLog_history has a start time ordered descending, so "select * from dbo].[QueryLog_history]", and "select * from [dbo].[QueryLog_history] order by starttime DESC" will return result in the data being returned in the same order.

Information to QueryLog_history should append when a new record is added to QueryLog, i.e. query was executed. So, QueryLog_history is populating using a trigger. The text for this trigger is :

```
--Ramunas Balukonis 2004.04.15
create trigger dbo.trg_QueryLog_I_history
on dbo.QueryLog
for insert
as
insert into querylog_history
  (MSOLAP_Database, MSOLAP_Cube, MSOLAP_User, Dataset, Slice, StartTime
  , Duration, MOLAPPartitions, ROLAPPartitions, SamplingRate)
 select MSOLAP_Database, MSOLAP_Cube, MSOLAP_User, Dataset, Slice, StartTime
     , Duration, MOLAPPartitions, ROLAPPartitions, SamplingRate
from inserted
```

After creating this trigger, in querylog_history, I find all the queries that are sent to my olap server. My table, querylog_history, was created in April, and in July it has ~2 million records.

From this table querylog_history, I created new OLAP db "Admin" and the cube "OLAP queries". The script for this cube is attached in file admin.vbs.txt. Just change server name at 43 line and run the vbs. This script will creates a new olap database "Admin", and then creates 2 cubes. This file was generated using MetaDataScripter from sql server resource kit.

You will need to change the connection parameters in the data sources folder olap_repository connection. To do so, open analysis manager, find your new database named "Admin", expand database, expand folder "Data Sources", right click on "olap_repository" data source, and choose edit. in the "1. Select or enter a server name" box, write your sql server name, in the "3. Select the database on the server" select your olap repository database (See Figure 1).

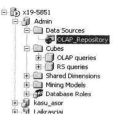

Figure 1

In the olap database there exist 2 databases: olap queries (queries, sent to analysis services) and rs queries (queries sent to reporting services). The Fact table for "rs queries" is the view from your reporting services database, ExecutionLog table. You can create the view in the same olap repository database.

```
--Ramunas Balukonis 2004.04.15
create view dbo.querylog_rep
as
select username, timestart
        , (TimeDataRetrieval + TimeProcessing + TimeRendering ) / 1000 as duration
        , status, bytecount, [RowCount], parameters
from reportserver.dbo.ExecutionLog
```

In my cube olap queries I have measures: "duration", "number of queries" and "Time to execute query, avg" . Dimensions are: "users", "cube" and "time" dimensions. Cube "rs queries" has similar dimensions and measures. You can create new calculated members like "number of queries / hour, avg" etc. I created my package to make a full process of admin database and scheduled to run them every day 2 times a day (See Figure 2).

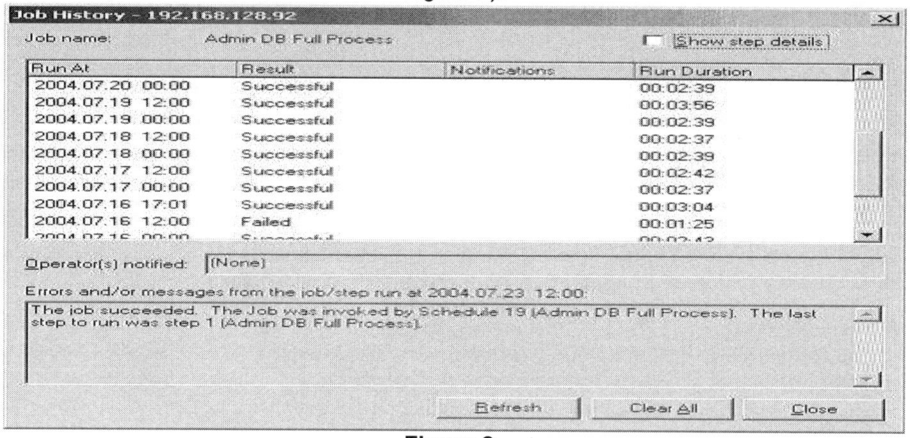

Figure 2

Conclusions

After implementing the cube from querylog table, I can answer these questions:
1. How much queries are send per day/month/year.
2. Which users queries takes the most time to execute, which cube is the most popular in the database?

After that, you can create aggregations only for certain users or those queries that take more than 3 sec. See Figure 3 for long running queries or Figure 4 for the most popular.

Msolap User	Data	
	Number of queries	Time to execute query, avg
X19-5851\RemigijusPl	4	94.25
X19-5851\ingami	613	8.050570962
X19-5851\JurgitaRub	128	5.9609375
X19-5851\MantasD	6	4.166666667
X19-5851\AndriusVi	99	4.050505051
X19-5851\TomasJa	13	3.307692308
X19-5851\VilmaPr	3572	3.298712206
X19-5851\remigijuspe	1752	2.594178082
X19-5851\DonatasMi	2584	2.345975232
X19-5851\modestakl	700	2.24
X19-5851\IngaSt	668	2.196107784
X19-5851\gytist	57	2.035087719
X19-5851\DaleKr	1315	1.759695817
X19-5851\eglelu	337	1.620178042
X19-5851\LauraAd	2282	1.606047327
X19-5851\gintas	6885	1.584894699
X19-5851\nomedasa	9658	1.492959205
X19-5851\EgleKl	763	1.49017038
X19-5851\gerdajo	9614	1.468483462
X19-5851\ligitace	498	1.401606426
X19-5851\gintaras	1625	1.349538462
X19-5851\dainam	691	1.228654124
X19-5851\mariusga	1221	1.198198198
X19-5851\aleksandras	6262	1.192111147
X19-5851\AstaJ	1777	1.166010129
X19-5851\VaidaPe	1364	1.151026393
X19-5851\VitalijaSi	507	1.136094675
X19-5851\kristinavr	620	1.117741935
X19-5851\Rolandasp	1834	1.095419847

Figure 3

Msolap Database	Msolap Cube	Data	
		Number of queries	Time to execute query, avg
Sales_Stock_LT	Sales_Stock_LT	194598	0.963637859
	Cash_register_sales	151354	0.191557541
	Procurement	21197	0.012124357
	Procurement_Fin	16286	0.000184207
	Known_customer_sales	5824	0.003777473
	p2p	155	0.548387097
Sales_Stock_LT Total		389414	0.556944537
Grand Total		389414	0.556944537

Figure 4

3. How much time the queries take now after I designed my aggregations? Was the designing of the aggregations successful? What is the different of time spending answer a query before and after aggregations design.

So, after creating the cube "olap queries", I can more effectively support my olap databases: create aggregations, plan the process time, find the longest queries and analyze, why they take so much time?

A DTS Data Store

By Bruce Szabo

Data Transformation Services (DTS) is extremely useful in solving a number of problems. In some cases I have used it to solve data problems, and in other cases I have used it to solve some tasks that have nothing to do with SQL. One difficulty I found with DTS was managing the different packages that exist on servers. For example, I may have packages A, B and C on Server 1 and packages D, E and F on Server 2, although the packages can be made generic and abstracted so they use common data sets too often I find subtle differences between packages on different servers. For this reason it is nice to have a backup of each package from each server. As you should know, backing up packages is important and can be a relatively trivial task, but to gather up a group of packages from a variety of servers and store them in one location can be more involved.

At the heart of DTS packages is the MSDB database. All the information pertaining to DTS packages resides in the MSDB database. The table that contains the packages is SYSDTSPACKAGES. This table contains the current version of the DTS package and also the previous versions of the package.

To see this for yourself right click on a DTS package in Enterprise Manager. One of the options in the context menu is versions.   Selecting versions will list all the versions of the package stored in the MSDB..SYSDTSPACKAGES table. This is one way to access steps in a package that may have been deleted as the package was modified.

Any time a package is saved and a server is specified, the package is stored in the MSDB database of that server. When there are multiple servers and workstations in an organization containing DTS packages, the packages can be difficult to manage and backup.   If the MSDB database is backed up on each server and workstation in the organization the DTS packages can be recovered if needed.

In order to simplify backing up the packages for my company I created a DTS package to gather all the packages from various servers and store them in a single database. The packages are gathered by querying MSDB on all the servers and using a Data Pump to load them in a central database.   I then created a small extraction package so I could output a package from the DTS store to a SQL server.

As an aside, it should be noted that one key to working with MSDB and the SYSDTSPACKAGES table is in order to access the table within DTS packages one may need to do a disconnected edit to access it.   I found this information on the site www.sqldts.com. The disconnected edit is avoided here by specifying a query to access the data we need. If, however, you wanted to access the SYSDTSPACKAGES table you would need to use a disconnected edit because it is not possible to access the table via the drop down list in the data pump.

The tasks involved in moving the DTS packages to a central location are as follows. First, a database and table need to be created to hold the packages. The packages are transfered via a data pump. A query is used as a source for the data pump so that only the most recent version of the DTS package is extracted. Once the server name is appended to the source query the data can be pumped from the MSDB database on a selected server to the DTS Store.

In order to implement the DTS Store, the first step is to create a database and table to hold the desired information. The name of the database I created was DTSStore. In this database I created a table using the following SQL Script:

```
if exists (select * from dbo.sysobjects where id = object_id(N'[dbo].[DTSStore]') and OBJECTPROPERTY
(id, N'IsUserTable') = 1) drop table [dbo].[DTSStore]
GO

CREATE TABLE [dbo].[DTSStore] (
[SourceServer] [nvarchar] (128) COLLATE SQL_Latin1_General_CP1_CI_AS NULL ,
[name] [nvarchar] (128) COLLATE SQL_Latin1_General_CP1_CI_AS NOT NULL ,
[id] [uniqueidentifier] NOT NULL ,
[versionid] [uniqueidentifier] NOT NULL ,
[description] [nvarchar] (1024) COLLATE SQL_Latin1_General_CP1_CI_AS NULL ,
[categoryid] [uniqueidentifier] NOT NULL ,
[createdate] [datetime] NULL ,
[owner] [nvarchar] (128) COLLATE SQL_Latin1_General_CP1_CI_AS NOT NULL ,
[packagedata] [image] NULL ,
[owner_sid] [varbinary] (85) NOT NULL ,
[packagetype] [int] NOT NULL ,
[datecreated] [datetime] NULL
) ON [PRIMARY] TEXTIMAGE_ON [PRIMARY]
GO
ALTER TABLE [dbo].[DTSStore] ADD
CONSTRAINT [DF_DTSStore_datecreated] DEFAULT (getdate()) FOR [datecreated]
GO
```

NOTE: The database and table storing our DTS packages have the same name (DTSStore) because of the author's inability to come up with creative names.

This table has almost the same structure as the MSDB..SYSDTSPACKAGES table.   There are two additional fields in the DTSStore table: SourceServer and DateCreated. These two fields help identify packages that may have the same name but exist on different servers and also identify the date when a package was extracted from a server. Notice that the DateCreated has a constraint so that the date defaults to the current date and time.

The DTS Package to do the work of acquiring the packages is straightforward. In this case it is nothing more than a data pump between a source server (DTSPackageSource) and a destination server (DTSStore). The destination server is the server that contains the DTSStore database created above.   The **Get Packages** DTS package is shown below.

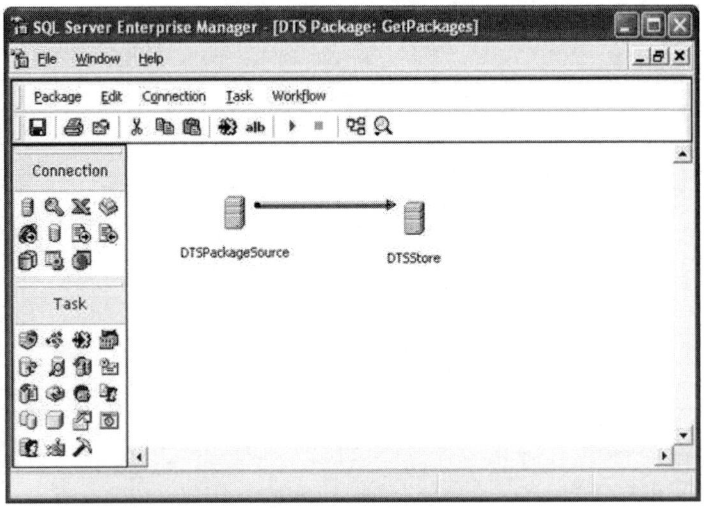

If we look at the properties of the data pump we will see the following on the source tab.

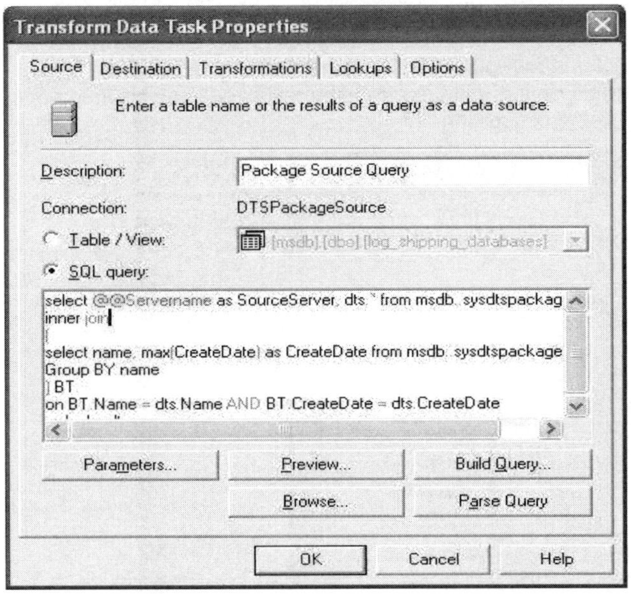

The source is an SQL query. I have listed the query below because the query cannot be read in the above image.

```
select @@Servername as SourceServer, dts.*
from msdb..sysdtspackages dts inner join
(select name, max(CreateDate) as CreateDate from msdb..sysdtspackages
Group BY name) BT on
BT.Name = dts.Name
AND BT.CreateDate = dts.CreateDate
order by dts.name
```

Only the most recent version of each package is collected from the source server.   The most recent version is selected by specifying the package with the greatest creation date. I have also added the @@Servername to the select statement so the source server name can be added to the DTSStore for each package.

The destination tab contains the DTSStore as our destination table.

If the store was created using the query above the DTSStore can be used directly, it simply needs to be selected on the destination tab of the data pump.

The source query and the destination match up column for column except for the datecreated. The transformation tab can then map each column directly from the source to the destination. Datecreated does not need to be specified because it has a default value constraint.

At this point everything is complete to copy packages from a source server to the DTS store. By changing the server name properties of the DTSPackageSource object the DTS packages from a variety of servers can be copied to the store. With a little extra work this package could be designed to query a variety of servers and acquire the packages in an automated manner. The package could then be scheduled so the packages would be backed up on a regular basis by backing up a single database.

Using a simlar process it is possible to move the packages from the destination server back to a source server. It is also possible to create a package that will extract a single package. These topics will be covered in a future article or can be explored by the reader.

Data Migration : Step by Step

By Chris Kempster

This article covers a wide variety of areas concerned with data migration. Primarily, it focuses on process, standards and some of the many issues to consider when undertaking this role.

Example Scenario

Throughout this article I will mention an example data migration project with the following characteristics. The system is a complete re-write of existing client server applications to a single integrated data model spanning 3 core systems. The system is intranet/internet based using VB 6, Active Directory Services (Win2k AS), SS2k EE, XML, DTS, IIS 5, COM+.

System Summary

Source Name	Tables	Summary
NEWSYS	286	New corporate data model
APP_A	60	Application A to be migrated to NEWSYS 1:1 mapping with some system code changes (remapping) and data merging with other applications.
APP_B	80	Application B to be migrated to NEWSYS 60% of all tables require complete remapping and merging 40% of tables need to merge with APP_A data (ie. shared data needs to be merged together to form a unified source of data).
Other	90	Reference Data from APP_A, APP_B, spreadsheets.

Overall Team Dynamics

1 x Project Manager

1 x DBA

2 x Systems/Business Analysts

      (representing APP_A, APP_D and APP_B)

6 x Programmers

1 x Application Architect

Migration Team (made up of people from above list)

1 x DBA

2 x Systems/Business Analysts

2 x Programmers

Broad Summary - Drill Down on Migration and Processes

The following summary does not include the initial planning phases and standard definitions; this is discussed later in the article.

Source data; determine load/connectivity strategy, liase with DBA in building the staging databases (MIG_<name>) and preparing DTS routine to load data on a regular basis. Document the refresh strategy and test; deal with performance issues as required.

Development of data cleansing scripts and other data migration routines, focusing on reference data first and if the resources are available, working on other scripts in parallel. Discuss with DBA indexing strategies for staging databases, rules for data cleaning if more than one "group" of programmers require the same data sets.

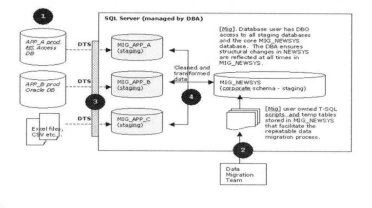

Data cleansing routines run, typically, only once. Reports developed and communication managed between business owners and analyst to resolve issues as required. All documented in detail and decision processes tracked.

Migration begins - primary and foreign keys are always enabled (typically via T-SQL). Concurrency issues discussed and planned for with migrations teams. Migration "may" occur in multiple (and identical) MIG_NEWSYS databases if 1 migration team has different requirements to another in terms of performance and time to load. Even so, the DBA must have strict control of common reference data, schema configuration to ensure no issues arise when the teams meet to on common grounds.

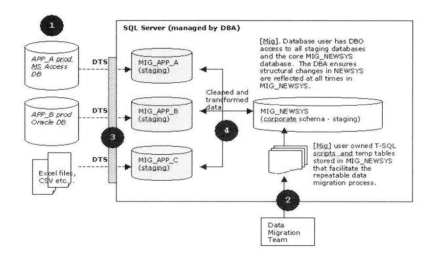

General Definitions

NEWSYS   is the name of our new application database.

MIG_NEWSYS   is our dedicated migration database for the app.

<sub-app>   represents an applications database to be merged.

Migration Team & Responsibilities

Data Migration Role	Data Migration Responsibilies
Business Owners (users)	Data cleansing. Migration testing. Data mapping and migration business rule approval. Final approval and signoff Sourcing and management of additional staff to assist migration data cleansing.
Analyst(s)	Data model. Adherence and champion to migration standards. Mapping of data from source to destination systems. Requirements Analysis and ongoing user liaison. Inter-system mapping and merging of data documentation, management and liaison. Supply migration team with all associated documentation to complete/change migration scripts and associated reporting. Reports to users in all cases with migration progress. Liase with project managers.

Database Administrator	Physical data model schema ownership.
	Migration document QA and naming standard checks.
	Ownership of all staging databases and final "migration" databases (schema image of corporate data model).
	Communicate schema changes to all key analysts and programmers and get approval before any change is made.
	Own the database security model.
	Ongoing standard DBA tasks.
Application Architect	Architecture and methodology
	Common libraries
	Configuration Management
	Standards and QA (not so much migration)
	Technical Support/Special Projects
Senior Application Programmer	Allocation of programming tasks to programmers.
	Provide high level of technical expertise and assistance to programmers.
	Ensure adherence to architecture and programming standards.
	Code walkthrough's.
	Verifies all data merging tasks.
	Verifies all migration reports send to end-users via Analysts.
	Liase closely with analysts with migration tasks, reporting, impact analysis.
Programmer	Develops all migration code based on documentation allocated my senior programmer.

End User Management (CRITICAL SUCCESS FACTOR)

It is very important that the business owners actually do "own" the data and the associated application redevelopment, and I mean this actually does extend from the steering committee and executive meetings out into user land and is not something born from your imagination. In them doing so, it is important that you provide your clients with effective reporting mechanisms throughout the data migration effort. You must be consistent and firm, as a slip up in a row count from one month's data cleansing/migration effort to another can result in a flurry of sarcastic emails and calls from your managers. The client will invest a significant amount of their time with cleansing and merging of data, and therefore, will require ongoing statistical reports on their progress, and possible views into your system for the more advanced user to check up on data merging results.

Reference Data (CRITICAL SUCCESS FACTOR)

It is not unusual to find that over one third of all tables are reference data tables. It is very important to get this right early in the migration, as all systems will depend on it. It is not uncommon for programmers to embed specific lookups (ie. to *address type, relationship type* columns for example) in their code, and as such, changing it 4 to 6+ weeks into the project will not be a pleasurable experience for you and the programming staff. Even so, strictly speaking, the impact should be measurable so long as well managed programming standards are employed.

Reference data will be sourced from:

a)   external data files

b) incoming staging databases (ie. one system has the definitive set of data)

c) one off hard coded inserts/updates in t-sql code

The standards section of this paper will discuss naming conventions, but where possible keep t-sql routines that manipulate reference data to a minimum. Look as using a series of generic scripts that allows you to quickly reload all reference data at any time. For example:

```
sp_msforeachtable "ALTER TABLE ? NOCHECK CONSTRAINT all
sp_msforeachtable "ALTER TABLE ? DISABLE TRIGGER  all"
exec MIG_REFDATA_LoadAll_sp
sp_msforeachtable "ALTER TABLE ? CHECK CONSTRAINT all"
sp_msforeachtable "ALTER TABLE ? ENABLE TRIGGER  all"
```

Use the following DBCC command for validating foreign keys after each re-load.

```
DBCC CHECKCONSTRAINTS WITH ALL_CONSTRAINTS
```

As a final note, take careful consideration of reference data that changes regularly to meeting external (and possibly internal) reporting requirements. You need to decide how the mapping strategy with work, namely:

a) will the table cater for the versioning of reference data?

b) will the table cater for the enabling/disabling of reference data items?

c) will all reference data remapping take place via views or within the application ?

d) does your scheme for reference data versioning apply to all applications using it?

Migration Step 0 – Define Standards and Process

The DBA should clearly define the standards to be used for all objects created in the MIG_NEWSYS database. I have successfully used the following:

[MIG] database user

All migration "users" will be connecting as the [MIG] user. This user has DBO access to the MIG_NEWSYS database and all associated MIG_<sub-app> databases. Why?

- simple to move scripts between servers and DB's as required

- simple to identify migration scripts over other users

- easier to maintain security and control over mig users

- do not have to give SA access or other higher privs

- can quickly revoke access without any impact

Database do's and don'ts for the MIG user:

- Don't – create any objects in the MIG_<sub-app> (staging databases) or remote databases.

- Do – always login as the MIG user

- Do – always follow the standards listed below

- Do – manage your own script change control (including t-sql stored procedures, UDF's, views, tables).

- Don't – remove data on shared tables

- Don't – edit stored t-sql code without adding comments as to the purpose of the change.

- Do – carefully document your changes to all migration code

- Do – complete code headers and dependency maps

File System Layout and Process Documentation

All migration team members work off a generic file structure. This is very important for DTS routines and obviously for ease of administration during the migration process. The directory structure may vary significantly between projects, but a based set may be:

Note: myApp = source system name to be merged into corporate data model.

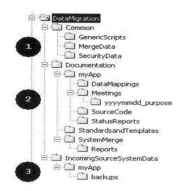

NOTE: Make sure this is a common drive map for all developers (ie. same drive/path)

1. Common directory

i.   Generic script – all common utility scripts and command line tools.

ii.   Merge data – includes all spreadsheets, Access DB's or CSV files etc that have manually merged data for the corporate database to link two or more applications together. This area is critical and must be updated at a minimum. It will be used my a variety if people to approved the merging of records for subsequent data loads via DTS.

iii. Security data – optional and depends of your security framework within your application. Includes data files listing base security privileges and system parameters to be loaded into the corporate data model for the migrated applications.

2. Documentation directory

i.   MyApp – documentation specific to the application. Base documentation templates will come from the directory below it and have created and managed by the DBA or analyst. This document has the step my step processes to load and report on a data migration for the application.

ii.   Standards and Templates - includes code templates, migration document templates, naming conventions and associated standards.

iii. System Merge - information about the merging of data from one application to another, and the rules associated with the merge. Typically these are signed off my data owners and are pivotal for the merge process.

3. IncomingSourceSystemData directory

i.   MyApp – copies of production databases (optional) ready for loading via DTA into the staging database(s). Multiple backup copies may be required.

General Naming Standards

Standards are critical for a successful migration as the amount of code can grow dramatically over time. In all cases the purpose of an object (see below) should be short, to the point, and documented.

DTS packages

```
<newsys> - MIG - <purpose>            loading reference data, staging databases etc.

Generic Utility T-SQL Code
```

mig.UTILITY_<purpose>_sp   generic utility t-sql code, ie. stip <cr> etc

```
T-SQL Code
```

mig.MIG_REFDATA_<name>_sp   single to many procs to load reference data,
may utilise remapping tables or call other remapping stored procedures.
mig.MIG_LOAD_<sub-app>_<purpose>_sp   migration code specific to the sub-app
mig.MIG_REMAP_<name>_sp   remapping specific stored procs (optional)

```
Tables
```

```
mig.MIG_REFDATA_<name>            staging reference data
```
mig.MIG_REMAP_<purpose>   remapping data tables, optionally add <sub-app>
mig.MIG_<sub-app>_<purpose>   staging and other tables specific to app mig
mig.MIG_System_Log   logging of all errors etc during running of stored
procs
mig.MIG_Conversion_Matrix   to map old p.keys to the new p.keys (where
applic.)

```
Views
```

mig.MIG_sub-app>_<purpose>   custom views

Tracking, Error handling and Transactions

The MIG_SYSTEM_LOG table should be used to track long running jobs; alternatively, the programmer may choose text files (especially if they are writing code in VB). This is not mandatory but available for use. The developer must take responsibility with:

a)   clearing data from the table (and not affecting other users), this can be cater for the with the columns `SystemLogIntendedFor or SystemLogByWhom` and of course the date column for the table (see table structure below). The DBA may need to setup indexing and of course monitor space usage. Ideally, the DBA should set physical database limits to manage disk space or proactive monitoring scripts.

With T-SQL, the developer must determine:

a)   what constitutes a transaction and a valid record or set of records. Take care with transaction management and ensure all transactions are counted for, you don't want the DBA killing off an apparently stalled job only to find SQL Server rolls it back.

b)   whether the first set of steps in the script is the remove all previously inserted data (in key order) in case then script is being run for a second, third of more times (typically due to error).

c)   When to break out of the code and how? (do you need to cascade errors up the chain of code calls?)

Here are some examples code snippets:

```
<...>
    <mysql statement>
set @v_error_count = @v_error_count + @@ERROR
<...>
    if @v_error_count > 0 begin
        print 'Error @ employer# '
        print @emp_id
        raiserror('Error in - MIG_MYAPP_Load_Employers_sp', 16,1)
        while @@TRANCOUNT > 0
```

```
                    ROLLBACK TRAN
        RETURN 1
    end
    <...>
```

In the data models I have worked with, all tables had these columns (or similar to):

last_update_count	integer	default 0	not null
last_update_on	datetime	default getdate() not null	
last_update_by	varchar(50)	<no default, app user>	not null

Therefore, standards were defined for record marking as they came to in easily remove records that belonged to your particular migration script. If you do not have this, look at using the matrix table (see next) to identify your rows verses existing data.

Core Migration Tables and Stored Procedures

The migration effort will result in data being remapped, requirements to track the progress of long running stored procedures, and operate simultaneously with other migration tasks underway in other areas of the corporate data model. As such, we require some pre-defined and documented tables to ensure based migration concurrency and auditing:

Conversion Matrix

This table tracks all new/old value remapping during data migration (where appropriate).

```
CREATE TABLE [mig].[MIG_CONVERSION_MATRIX] (
    [table]         [varchar] (50)  NOT NULL ,
    [typeof]        [varchar] (80)  NOT NULL ,
[newkey1]    [varchar] (50)  NULL ,
    [newkey2]       [varchar] (50)  NULL ,
    [newkey3]       [varchar] (50)  NULL ,
    [newkey4]       [varchar] (50)  NULL ,
    [oldkey1]       [varchar] (50)  NULL ,
    [oldkey2]       [varchar] (50)  NULL ,
    [oldkey3]       [varchar] (50)  NULL ,
    [oldkey4]       [varchar] (50)  NULL ,
    [notes]         [varchar] (100) NULL ,
    [lastupdated]       [datetime]      NOT NULL ,
    [lastupdatedby] [varchar] (50) NOT NULL
) ON [PRIMARY]
GO
```

System Logging / Tracking

Used to tracks data migration activity and progress.

```
CREATE TABLE [mig].[MIG_System_Log] (
    [SystemLogId]            [decimal](18, 0)       IDENTITY (1, 1) NOT NULL ,
    [SystemLogDetails]    [varchar] (2000)    NOT NULL ,
    [SystemLogTypeCode] [varchar] (25)       NOT NULL ,
    [SystemObjectAffected] [varchar] (50)     NULL ,
    [SystemLogDate]       [datetime]           NOT NULL ,
    [SystemLogByWhom]     [varchar] (50)       NULL ,
    [SystemLogIntendedFor] [varchar] (20)     NULL
) ON [PRIMARY]
GO
```

Migration Step 1 – Staging Database(s) and Sourcing Data

The first step is to establish the MIG_ databases. If the temporary MIG_ databases are not possible then read-only linked servers may be used. Even so, never link to production databases for whatever reason. The MIG_ databases will be loaded often from their production system counterparts, and as such, must be repeatable and quick to run. I use DTS for a majority of the work here.

The major advantages to creating the MIG_ databases are:

- can run "pre-migration data fix" scripts against the data before we begin the major load
- once in SQL Server, its very easily to transform and query data rather than dealing with flat files or other database formats and syntax
- we have complete CRUD control

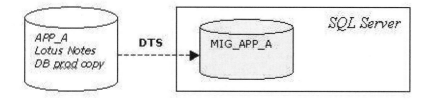

In the end it's the DBA's call. Very large data sources may be a problem and the time to load and build the MIG_ databases may be unacceptable. Even so look at a staged approach to the migration to resolve.

The regularity of the load will increase near the end of the data migration process and during initial testing. The DBA may choose to script the databases to easy of restoration. Be careful that replacing databases may impact multiple migration team members and can result in complete reloads of reference data etc associated with the staged data. Also be aware that a *support* server may also need to be refreshed in order for users to compare their production database snapshot with the *migrated* data set.

Look at indexing the MIG_ database tables to speed your extraction and querying of migration data, and always use a fill factor of 95% (you will never insert new data and the updates will be minimal).

Migration Step 2 – Load Core Reference Data

Up next we have the T-SQL stored procedure and DTS routines to load in the core application reference data. You will be surprised how many tables are reference data tables, at times being over 1/3 of the total tables.

Reference data is critical. I cannot highlight the importance of well-defined, accurate reference data as early as humanly possible. Why? For these fundamental reasons:

impact the developers – who hard code ID lookups, eg. 1 = Postal Address type and 2 = Guardian, if you swapped these two months into the project then be prepared to wear a helmet.

change of codes or addition of missing codes can mean complete UAT and/or testing of coded logic to ensure the program still works.

can delay development as no data means no code cutting.

Reference data is not too difficult to source and most codes will be retained from the incoming systems. There will be a small percentage of tables that require code remapping. To mange reference data and remapping, I set-up the following spreadsheets:

> refdata.xls – 1 sheet per incoming table

> remap.xls – 1 sheet per table for remapping.

This maps to a single MIG_REMAP_<purpose> table within the MIG_NEWSYS database.

Not all reference data is kept in the spreadsheet; data may be transformed within a single t-sql routine to complete the load from the staging databases based on general agreement from all business owners.

This can cause issues with managing the reference data loads:

Spreadsheets are an easy way to maintain lists of reference data outside of the scope of other incoming migrated data sources. A single stored procedure should be developed to process all reference data. Use staging tables for reference data within MIG_NEWSYS, eg. mig.MIG_REFDATA_<name>.

Migration Step 3 – Ongoing Scripting and Loading of Core Data

It is very important that the migration database schema is kept fully in-sync with the other development database. The only trick here to watch out for is scripting changes from Enterprise Manager and running them in development may work fine, but in the migration database you have thousands of extra rows; etc, so timing a change may require a little more timing. I have always kept a strict control of DDL in all database environments to better manage change. If this is a problem for you, then look at schema comparison tools such as those available from red-gate software.

The DBA should also consider scripting the databases once per week for safety sake more than anything. This is, of course, on top of your daily backups. It is very rare that your staging and migration databases require anything more than full backups once per day, and possible twice if you consider a possible one-day loss too great. Don't forget, though, that databases are one thing, but your file system with merge data and associated documentation is also critical.

The timing of staging database reloads needs to be planned with end-users and all affected migration team members. A reload of a staging database may coincide with the refresh of the production database on your staging server, for example, so end-users can report on the staging database to compare data with the migration effort.

Migration Step 4 – Merge and Remapping Data

Data merging is one of the most difficult tasks in the migration progress. You must be very careful here simply because people will be investing large amounts of their time and money mapping one data value to another and do not want to be told days or even weeks down the track that what they have been doing is no longer relevant. This can happen for a variety of reasons, but change of key is a typical gotcha.

As an example of data merging, I had two key systems that worked with *traineeship* data (a traineeship being a 2,3 or 4 yr contract between an employer and a student to undertaking on the job training in their chosen field; i.e., plumber). The problem here is one system had the apparent "definitive and fully accredited" set of traineeships, but is wasn't their core buss to manage students doing them, versus the other system whose job it was to track, manage and maintain traineeship contracts. Therefore, both had lists of "valid" traineeship codes and the associated qualification for the traineeship, and both business areas wanted *their* data.

In order to do this, we:

a)   Load System A in first – this had the formally "approved" set of traineeships and qualification data. Identity value were fixed on a set range for these particular tables to cater for ensure expansion (yes – the systems still work as per normal while you are migrating).

b)   Load in remapping tables

c)   Load System B based on mapping table data.

The merge spreadsheets (remapping data) can be difficult to produce. Ours consisted of a series of sheets. The first has the 1:1 mapping to date of System A data with System B data (and their p.keys). The last column was an *approved* flag (Y or N) to denote a merge approval. Other spreadsheets includes all data values from System A and other sheet for System B, then a final sheet that had both systems data ordered by the description of the traineeship to assist users in locating "similar" records. Of course, this sounds all fine and dandy, but producing the sheets is tough. Look for a common ground for merging data over (id fields, descriptions, combinations of field, etc). The critical part here is making sure that you have all the data necessary to map back to System A and B to complete the merge as stated in the spreadsheet. Don't forget also to run scripts over the mapping tables from time to time to locate missing or new codes from the systems when new snapshots are taken.

Migration Step 5 – Core Data Migration

When I say "core data migration", I am talking about the series of scripts that are run after staging databases are refreshed and cleansed and reference data has been loaded and validated. Once done, we begin the series of scripts that will populate the migration database (whose schema as previously mentioned is identical to what will eventually go into production).

The migration documentation for your system will clearly outline of pre-and-post scripts to be run for each stored procedure. The developers may choose to write a single t-sql routine that calls a series of others in step to make life a little easier. When using t-sql, use SET NO COUNT and take care with error handling. The developers should also be making using of the matrix and system tables. As a minimum, use the matrix table whenever keys are altered and data is to be remapped, this table should also go into production for future reference if need be.

Introduction to MDX

By Keith Henry

This article is intended to get you started on Multi-Dimensional eXpressions, the Microsoft OLAP query language. MDX allows you to do complex reports quickly on Very Large Databases. We have reports that run on many millions of records with over 20 fields in under a second! OLAP is a powerful technology.

OLAP is a way of looking at data that has been totaled up, but allowing any report on that data you require.

```
Suppose you were logging sales in SQL server, you could have a table [sales] which had [value],
[customer], [product], [timeofsale], [salesrep], [store], [county] etc.  If you wanted to know how
many sales each sales rep had made you might use:

select s.[salesrep], count (*) as 'total' from [sales] s group by s.[salesrep]
```

If you had a lot of sales this report would take a long time. Suppose you wanted to report on something else at the same time? You might want to see a cross-tab report of [salesrep] by [product]. This is messy to write in SQL as you have to use case statements for each value of whichever field you want on the columns.

What we may need to do is build all these totals at a time of low load and then make them easily accessible for reporting all the time. This is what analysis services does. In OLAP we would build a cube of this [sales] table. We call them cubes because they can be visualized as such for simpler reports. As a cube can have up to 128 dimensions, however, this metaphor quickly breaks down. Supposing that we only want to report on 3 fields ([timeofsale], [salesrep] and [product]); we could think of all the reports you could want on those fields as a cube. Each edge of the cube would have all the values of a field along it, and each face would be a cross tab of two of the fields.

An introduction to the rest of the terminology may be useful at this point:

Dimension - A dimension is one of the fields that you want to report on. Dimensions have a tree structure, allowing complicated data to be reported on at different levels. For instance, [timeofsale] could be a dimension if you wanted to report on it

Measure - What we are actually reporting on, be it sum, count or average.

Level - A level is a step along a dimension. In [timeofsale] we could have [Year], [Month], [Day] and [Hour] allowing us to report on sales per hour or products year on year.

Member - A member is a value of a level. In [timeofsale].[Year] we might have [2001], [2002], [2003], or in [timeofsale].[Month] we have [March], [April], [May] etc

Axis - This is what you set to put [product] across the columns, [timeofsale] down the rows or report on a [salesrep] to a page. An MDX statement can have up to 128 axis, although it is rare to use more than 2. The first 5 have names:
0 Columns
1 Rows
2 Pages
3 Chapters
4 Sections

Dimensionality - This is an attribute of a collection of members or levels which describes what dimensions they are from and what order those dimensions are in.

Tuple - A tuple is a collection of members which all have **different** dimensionality (so each is from a different dimension). Tuples have () brackets around them, but don't need them when there is only one member. For instance
([timeofsale].[Year].[2001], [product].[all products] **)**

Set - A set is a collection of tuples which all have **the same** dimensionality (so all have the same dimensions in the same order). Sets have {} brackets around them, and always need them. For instance:
{ ([timeofsale].[Year].[2001], [product].[all products]) , ([timeofsale].[Year].[2002], [product].[all products]) **}**

Function - Functions can return Sets, Tupels, Members, Levels, Dimensions or values. We'll come across some of the more useful ones later.

Slice - We may want to cross tab by two fields for some specific value of a third; for instance, [timeofsale] by [product] for a particular [salesrep].
When we picture the report as a cube we think of this filter as a slice into the cube, to show the values on a new face.

So now that the lexicon is done, how do we use it? Well, here is the structure of a statement:

```
select
{set 0} on axis(0) , /* this would be a block comment */
{set 1} on axis(1) , // this is a line comment
...
{set n} on axis(n)
from [cube]
where (tupel)
```

No axis or the where statement can share any of the same dimensions.

So if we wanted a report of [product] on columns by [salesrep] on rows we would execute:

```
select
{ ( [product].[productname].[product1] ) ,
  ( [product].[productname].[product2] ) } on columns ,
{ [salesrep].[repname]. members } on rows
from [sales]
```

Note that I've used on columns and on rows rather than on axis(n) , because it is more clear.

On the columns I have a set with two tupels from the same dimension. The () brackets are not required in this case because each tupel contains just one member. The {} are required.
The rows has a function . members , which returns a set with all the member of that level it. As . members returns a set we don't need the {} brackets but again I've put them in.

Here is another one:

```
select
{ [product].[productname].[product1] : [product].[productname].[product20] } on columns ,
{ [timeofsale].[Year].[2002]. children } on rows
from [sales]
```

In this example I've used a **range** to give me a set of all the products inclusive between [product1] and [product20] on columns. On rows I've used another function called . children to give me all the months in [timeofsale].[Year].[2002]

. members works on a level to give all the members at that level.
. children works on a member to give all the members below it (assuming there are any).

Two more useful features before we look at slices:

```
select
non empty { [product].[productname]. members } on columns ,
{ { [timeofsale].[Year].[2002]. children }
    *
  { [salesrep].[repname]. members } } on rows
from [sales]
```

First of all the keyword non empty excludes any values from that axis where no values are returned.
The * operator does a cross join between the two sets, and works in a similar way to a cross join in sql. The final set will be made up of every possible combination of the tuples in the two sets.

Now we will add a slice:

```
select
{ [product].[productname]. members } on columns ,
{ [timeofsale].[Year].[2002]. children } on rows
from [sales]
where ( [salesrep].[repname].[Mr Sales Rep1] )
```

Note that the where criteria requires a tuple rather than a slice and that tuple cannot contain any of the same dimensions as the sets on the axis

And to finish off this introduction a list of all the MDX functions along with a brief summary of what they do. For more detail look them up in SQL Books Online or MDSN:

Returns a set

AddCalculatedMembers	Adds calculated members to a set.
AllMembers	Returns a set containing all members of a specified dimension or level, including calculated members.
Ancestors	Returns all the ancestors of a member at a specified distance.
Ascendants	Returns the set of the ascendants of the member, including the member itself.
Axis	Returns the set associated with the main axis.
BottomCount	Returns a specified number of items from the bottom of a set, optionally ordering the set first.
BottomPercent	Sorts a set and returns the bottom n elements whose cumulative total is at least a specified percentage.
BottomSum	Sorts a set and returns the bottom n elements whose cumulative total is at least a specified value.
Children	Returns the children of a member.
Correlation	Returns the correlation of two series evaluated over a set.
Crossjoin	Returns the cross product of two sets.
Descendants	Returns the set of descendants of a member at a specified level or at a specified distance from a member, optionally including or excluding descendants in other levels.
Distinct	Eliminates duplicate tuples from a set.
DistinctCount	Returns the count of tuples in a set, excluding duplicate tuples.
DrilldownLevel	Drills down the members of a set, at a specified level, to one level below. Alternatively, drills down on a specified dimension in the set.
DrilldownLevelBottom	Drills down the bottom n members of a set, at a specified level, to one level below.
DrilldownLevelTop	Drills down the top n members of a set, at a specified level, to one level below.
DrilldownMember	Drills down the members in a set that are present in a second specified set.
DrilldownMemberBottom	Similar to DrilldownMember, except that it includes only the bottom n children.
DrilldownMemberTop	Similar to DrilldownMember, except that it includes only the top n children.
DrillupLevel	Drills up the members of a set that are below a specified level.
DrillupMember	Drills up the members in a set that are present in a second specified set.
Except	Finds the difference between two sets, optionally retaining duplicates.
Extract	Returns a set of tuples from extracted dimension elements. The opposite of Crossjoin.
Filter	Returns the set resulting from filtering a set based on a search condition.

Generate	Applies a set to each member of another set and joins the resulting sets by union.
Head	Returns the first specified number of elements in a set.
Hierarchize	Orders the members of a set in a hierarchy.
Intersect	Returns the intersection of two input sets, optionally retaining duplicates.
LastPeriods	Returns a set of members prior to and including a specified member.
Members	Returns the set of all members in a dimension, hierarchy, or level.
Mtd	A shortcut function for the PeriodsToDate function that specifies the level to be Month.
NameToSet	Returns a set containing a single member based on a string expression containing a member name.
NonEmptyCrossjoin	Returns the cross product of two or more sets, excluding empty members.
Order	Arranges members of a set, optionally preserving or breaking the hierarchy.
ParallelPeriod	Returns a member from a prior period in the same relative position as a specified member.
PeriodsToDate	Returns a set of periods (members) from a specified level starting with the first period and ending with a specified member.
Qtd	A shortcut function for the PeriodsToDate function that specifies the level to be Quarter.
Siblings	Returns the siblings of a member, including the member itself.
StripCalculatedMembers	Removes calculated members from a set.
StrToSet	Constructs a set from a string expression.
Subset	Returns a subset of elements from a set.
Tail	Returns a subset from the end of a set.
ToggleDrillState	Toggles the drill state of members. This function is a combination of DrillupMember and DrilldownMember.
TopCount	Returns a specified number of items from the top of a set, optionally ordering the set first.
TopPercent	Sorts a set and returns the top n elements whose cumulative total is at least a specified percentage.
TopSum	Sorts a set and returns the top n elements whose cumulative total is at least a specified value.
Union	Returns the union of two sets, optionally retaining duplicates.
VisualTotals	Dynamically totals child members specified in a set using a pattern for the total label in the result set.
Wtd	A shortcut function for the PeriodsToDate function that specifies the level to be Week.
Ytd	A shortcut function for the PeriodsToDate function that specifies the level to be Year.

Returns a tupel

Current	Returns the current tuple from a set during an iteration.
ItemItem	Returns a member from a tuple or a tuple from a set.
StrToTuple	Constructs a tuple from a string.
ValidMeasure	Returns a valid measure in a virtual cube by forcing inapplicable dimensions to their top level.

Returns a member

Ancestor	Returns the ancestor of a member at a specified level or at a specified distance from the member.
ClosingPeriod	Returns the last sibling among the descendants of a member at a level.
Cousin	Returns the member with the same relative position under a member as the member specified.
CurrentMember	Returns the current member along a dimension during an iteration.
DataMember	Returns the system-generated data member associated with a nonleaf member.
DefaultMember	Returns the default member of a dimension or hierarchy.
FirstChild	Returns the first child of a member.
FirstSibling	Returns the first child of the parent of a member.
Ignore	Prevents further recursion along the dimension
Lag	Returns a member prior to the specified member along the member's dimension.
LastChild	Returns the last child of a member.
LastSibling	Returns the last child of the parent of a member.
Lead	Returns a member further along the specified member's dimension.

LinkMember	Returns a hierarchized member.
Members	Returns the member represented by the string expression
NextMember	Returns the next member in the level that contains a specified member.
OpeningPeriod	Returns the first sibling among the descendants of a member at a level.
Parent	Returns the parent of a member.
PrevMember	Returns the previous member in the level that contains a specified member.
StrToMember	Returns a member based on a string expression.

Returns a value or something else

Aggregate	Returns a calculated value using the appropriate aggregate function, based on the context of the query.
Avg	Returns the average value of a numeric expression evaluated over a set.
CalculationCurrentPass	Returns the current calculation pass of a cube for the current query context.
CalculationPassValueCalculationPassValue	Returns the value of an MDX expression evaluated over the specified calculation pass of a cube.
Call UDF (args)	Executes the string expression containing a user-defined function.
CoalesceEmptyCoalesceEmpty	Coalesces an empty cell value to a string or number.
Count	Returns the number of dimensions in a cube, the number of levels in a dimension, the number of cells in a set, or the number of dimensions in a tuple.
Covariance	Returns the population covariance of two series evaluated over a set, using the biased population formula.
CovarianceN	Returns the sample covariance of two series evaluated over a set, using the unbiased population formula.
Generate	Evaluate a string expression for each member of a set
Iif	Returns one of two numeric or string values determined by a logical test.
LinRegIntercept	Calculates the linear regression of a set and returns the value of b in the regression line y = ax + b.
LinRegPoint	Calculates the linear regression of a set and returns the value of y in the regression line y = ax + b.
LinRegR2	Calculates the linear regression of a set and returns R2 (the coefficient of determination).
LinRegSlope	Calculates the linear regression of a set and returns the value of a in the regression line y = ax + b.
LinRegVariance	Calculates the linear regression of a set and returns the variance associated with the regression line y = ax + b.
LookupCubeLookupCube	Returns the value of an MDX expression evaluated over another specified cube in the same database.
Max	Returns the maximum value of a numeric expression evaluated over a set.
Median	Returns the median value of a numeric expression evaluated over a set.
MemberToStr	Constructs a string from a member.
Min	Returns the minimum value of a numeric expression evaluated over a set.
Name	Returns the name of a dimension, hierarchy, level, or member.
Ordinal	Returns the zero-based ordinal value associated with a level.
Predict	Evaluates the string expression within the data mining model specified within the current coordinates.
Properties	Returns a string containing a member property value.
Rank	Returns the one-based rank of a tuple in a set.
RollupChildren	Scans the children of the member parameter and applies the string expression operator to their evaluated value.
SetToArray	Converts one or more sets to an array for use in a user-defined function.
SetToStr	Constructs a string from a set.
Stddev	Alias for Stdev.
StddevP	Alias for StdevP.
Stdev	Returns the sample standard deviation of a numeric expression evaluated over a set, using the unbiased population formula.

StdevP	Returns the population standard deviation of a numeric expression evaluated over a set, using the biased population formula.
StrToValueStrToValue	Returns a value based on a string expression.
Sum	Returns the sum of a numeric expression evaluated over a set.
TupleToStr	Constructs a string from a tuple.
UniqueName	Returns the unique name of a dimension, level, or member.
UserName	Returns the domain name and user name of the current connection.
ValueValue	Returns the value of a measure.
Var	Returns the sample variance of a numeric expression evaluated over a set, using the unbiased population formula.
Variance	Alias for Var.
VarianceP	Alias for VarP.
VarP	Returns the population variance of a numeric expression evaluated over a set, using the biased population formula.

A good place to go start trying the ideas in this article is the Foodmart 2000 database that comes as a sample when you install Analysis services.

Reporting Services Part I: Overview, Architecture and Installation

By James Luetkehoelter

So it's here. Finally. For those of you who haven't had a chance to work with the beta, it's probably a good idea to download the evaluation version and start. This add-on should be widely adopted in a relatively short time. It doesn't matter if you're primarily a developer or primarily a DBA -- there's a great deal to know in both arenas.

In this article we're going to discuss Reporting Services in general, its architecture and how it's installed. We'll be focusing more on *gotchas* and related information rather than duplicating BOL documentation. Later articles will discuss report design, reporting extensibility, automating administration, and enterprise-level design and deployment.

Overview

Unless you're living under the proverbial SQL Server rock, you've heard of SQL Server Reporting Services. You probably already know that it is an add-on to SQL Server that allows you to create and distribute reports. You may not be aware of some of the more useful features:

- You can create role-based security to allow users access to specific reports.
- Users can "subscribe" to reports without the intervention of an administrator.
- You can schedule off-line execution of reports to minimize processing time.
- You can embed Reporting Services functionality within other applications.
- You can maintain a history of executed reports (useful when existing data is changed frequently).

Reporting Services (RS) is often described as a "free" add-on to SQL Server. It isn't free. It follows the existing SQL Server licensing structure. If you're using CALs, you need a SQL Server CAL to use reporting services. If you want to provide anonymous access to reports (say, from a public website), you'll need to have processor licensing. If you want to deploy RS to a web-farm, you need SQL Server Enterprise edition licenses. In a number of scenarios, effective use of the product will require additional SQL Server licensing.

An additional cost could be Visual Studio 2003. The Report Designer provided by RS only works within VS 2003. Now you can design the reports by writing the XML-based report definition file manually. I'm sure some of you read that and say "Yay!" -- I say "Ugh". You can also write your own designer. I still say "Ugh". I would imagine that most reporting vendors will support Microsoft's report format in the near future. The exception might be Crystal Reports; it doesn't appear that version 10 will have an export to Microsoft's format. This makes sense for them since they have a competing report distribution product (Crystal Enterprise). I don't have Crystal 10 yet, so I can't say for certain. I also know of no existing utilities to convert Crystal to RS reports. I'm sure someone will do this, but there should be licensing considerations for Crystal.

Another thing to note is RS's role in business intelligence. At the moment, working with Analysis Services requires writing MDX queries and provides only basic drill-down functionality. I attended an early partner-focused training session, and this was a particular point of disappointment for many of the attendees. Their opinion was that business intelligence *is* multi-dimensional analysis, so labeling RS as a business intelligence tool is misleading. I disagree. Any method of representing information that helps a company understand itself should be considered business intelligence. This includes static, relational database reporting. Not every data consumer needs to slice and dice.

Architecture

Reporting Services is comprised of a number of technologies and environments. So what exactly does that entail? I see it as four major logical components:

A report development environment -- A standard report definition language is defined, and a report designer is made accessible through Visual Studio 2003.

A centralized report repository -- A SQL Server database is created to house not only the report definitions but also snapshots of executed reports.

A report processing and distribution system -- A Windows service manages rendering reports, scheduling execution, and distributing via email or file share.

A webservice-based management and report viewing tool -- An ASP.NET application provides an interface for scheduling, defining security, managing connectivity, etc.

I'm making a point of separating these components to stress that the entire RS package spans many areas of IT. In a production environment it would be crucial to involve not only developers, but DBAs, systems staff, network staff, and email administrators. These four logical components are implemented by:

- *Report Definition Language* -- This is the report itself. Microsoft has provided an open, documented XML format for report definition (.RDL). As I mentioned before, this means you can either write reports by hand or build your own interface to do so.
- *Report Designer* -- Right now, this is Visual Studio 2003. Two new project types appear under "Business Intelligence" when starting a new project in VS 2003 -- Report Project and Report Project Wizard. The interface for building reports is very Access-like; you can actually upgrade Access reports to RS .RDL formats. The designer also lets you easily deploy projects or individual reports.
- *Report Manager/Viewer* -- "Report Manager" is an ASP.NET application that comes with RS. It's a solid tool that not only lets you manage security, scheduling, etc., but also acts as a report viewing interface.
- *Web Service* -- Accessing the core RS functions is done by way of web services. This provides an easy way to extend RS functionality into other applications. They expose the real "guts" of the engine, the Report Service.
- *ReportServer Service* -- This Windows service is the real engine behind everything. It handles everything -- report rendering, data retrieval, etc.
- *ReportServer database* -- This SQL Server database holds all of the report definitions, schedules, subscriptions, etc. It also holds snapshots of reports, which are stored in an intermediate, unrendered format. This keeps the overall size of the database down to a minimum. I'm in the middle of running stress testing, so at this point I can't give any sizing guidelines. I'll discuss this in detail in a later article.
- *ReportServerTempDB database* -- This database has only two tables, "ChunkData" and "ExecutionCache". It's primarily used for rendered report caching purposes. Again, I have no sizing or management guildlines yet, but they will be in a later article.
- *Reporting Data Sources* -- Of course, there has to be some data source to report on. This can be

any OLE DB datasource. Since there is an OLE DB driver for ODBC, this means practically anything.

- *SQL Agent* -- Subscriptions are set up as SQL Agent jobs so you obviously need to have this running.
- *IIS server with the .NET framework installed* -- Report Manager is an ASP.NET application so it needs an environment to run in.
- *SMTP* -- If you plan on distributing reports via email, you need to have an SMTP server available. Currently there's no other email option than SMTP (Dear MAPI: Your services are no longer required). One thing to be aware of is that the SMTP server must be used on the local network.
- *File Share* -- If you plan on distributing reports by writing them to a central file location, you'll need to have a share setup with the appropriate permissions defined.

After writing out this list, it really struck me how complex the product is. There are numerous technologies involved: IIS, ASP.NET, Windows Services, Web Services, SQL Server, etc. Given that complexity, it's amazing how easy the product is to work with after you it is properly installed.

The basic workflow is as follows:

1) A report definition (.RDL file) is created by VS 2003.

2) This report is stored in the ReportServer database by the ReportServer service, which is then exposed by the ReportingServices webservice.

3) When executed, the ReportServer service retrieves the necessary information from the specified databases and creates an intermediate report.

4) This intermediate report is stored either in the ReportServer or ReportServerTempDB, depending on whether it is executed by means of a subscription or on demand.

5) The ReportServer service then renders a formatted report using the intermediate definition, presenting it to the Report Manager application, sending it contained in an email via SMTP, or writing it to a pre-defined file share.

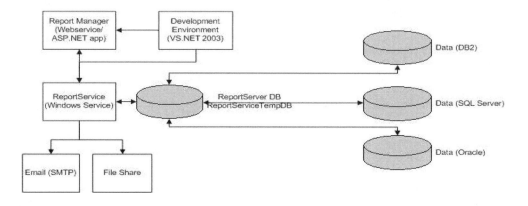

Looking at the workflow diagram, the critical piece that I see are the number of access points to be secured. The Windows Report Server needs security rights to the operating system. It also needs SQL Server security defined to connect to the ReportServer database. The ReportServer database stores security information for source data connectivity. If you're pushing reports to a file share, that share should be configured with the appropriate NTFS and share permissions.

Installation

The installation process we'll be examining follows the developer edition. The evaluation edition available on Microsoft's website does have a few differences between the developer and enterprise editions, primarily in deployment. There is also a command-line syntax for installing RS, as well as the ability to create unattended install scripts. For the purposes of this article, we are going to focus solely on the installation wizard.

If you select all of the components, the following items will be installed:
- The ReportService Windows service
- The ReportServer and ReportServerTempDB database
- A new database role called RSExecRole within the ReportServer database
- The AdventureWorks sample database
- A ReportService and Report virtual directory on an IIS server
- A ReportServer webservice is registered
- New project types are created within Visual Studio 2003
- An ASP.NET Report Manager application
- Command-line administration tools (under %SQLroot%/80/Binn by default)
- Application coding samples (under %SQLroot%/MSSQL/ReportingServices by default)

The installation has a number of *gotchas* that can be extremely frustrating. The single biggest piece of advice I can give is: read the documentation. I tend to be the kind of person that dives into a new product without studying all of the accompanying documentation. When the production version was released, I wasted significant time troubleshooting installation issues that were clearly identified in the readme. I'm not going to simply rehash all of the documented prerequisites and issues, but rather focus on the major items:

- The software platform requires SQL 2000 SP3, Windows 2000 SP4, Windows XP SP1 or Windows 2003 server. MDAC must be at 2.6 or higher. The 1.1 .NET framework is required, as is ASP.NET version 1.1.4322.
- If you aren't already running the Distributed Transaction Coordinator (DTC), it will need to be started and should be set to start automatically. You can do this either through Enterprise Manager (Server Properties|General) or under Services under Administration Tools.
- If you're a DBA and haven't configured a IIS server for ASP.NET, you may need to run the ASP.NET IIS registration tool (ASPNET_REGIIS.EXE). There are a number of command-line options for that utility, but for the most part you can just run "aspnet_regiis -i". Visit http://msdn.microsoft.com/library/en-us/cptools/html/cpgrfASPNETIISRegistrationToolAspnet_regiisexe.asp?frame=true for more information.
- The Reporting Services BOL suggests that a minimum of 256 RAM be available to the Windows ReportServer service; that's an awfully high minimum requirement for a single service, approaching a service like SQL Server or Exchange. I haven't done any real stress testing, but it does look as if the ReportService could have a heavy memory load. Just starting the service consumes around 35-40MB of memory on my test server. In a real deployment, you'll probably want to have the ReportServer service on a dedicated machine.
- Installing Reporting Services on a domain controller requires manual configuration. See the installation readme.htm for details. This scenario should only occur in a single-server, small office environment.
- Be aware of the difference between NT Authority/System and Local Service. Since NT Authority/System is often referred to as the local system account, I sometimes mistake it with Local Service, which is only available under XP or 2003 Server.

Before you begin the installation, verify the following:

- The IIS server is available.
- The Distributed Transaction Coordinator service is started.
- The proper version of .NET framework is installed on that web server.
- The proper version of ASP.NET is enabled on that web server.
- No ReportServer or ReportServerTempDb database exists.
- No ReportServer or Reports virtual directory exists.

The actual installation process has some screens that are less than intuitive:

One of the first steps in the installation process is to check to see if you have the necessary software requirements. What frustrates me with this screen is that *if* you're missing a component, you can't easily go back to re-run the system check. No "Back" button is supplied. This is why I can't stress enough the need to have everything needed in place before starting the install.

Another item that confused me briefly was the missing directory location for some of the installation components. After going through the install, it was clear why there was no installation path available; the location of those items are determined later during the install. I still would like some sort of message here.

The Best of SQLServerCentral.com – Vol. 3

Microsoft SQL Server 2000 Reporting Services Developer Edition Se...

Service Account
Provides the accounts under which report server services will run.

Select the account under which the ReportServer Windows service will run.

○ Use a built-in account: NT AUTHORITY\SYSTEM

◉ Use a domain user account

    User name:

    Password:

    Domain:

    ☑ Auto-start the service

The Report Server Web service will run under the following account:

    Account:

[Help]   [< Back] [Next >]   [Cancel]

Next we're asked to setup the ReportServer Windows service. It is installed locally on the machine that runs the installation. By default, it assumes that you will provide a domain user account; however, BOL recommends using a built-in account. If you aren't installing on Windows Server 2003, NT Authority\SYSTEM is really your only choice (2003 allows you to use a Local Service or Network Service account). The Report Server Web service will default to running under the local ASPNET user account.

Microsoft SQL Server 2000 Reporting Services Developer Edition Se...

Reporting Services Virtual Directories
Specify the virtual directories on which Report Server and Report Manager are accessible.

Virtual Directories

Report Server Virtual Directory:

ReportServer

For example by specifying "ReportServer", report server can be accessed as:
http://<servername>/ReportServer

Report Manager Virtual Directory:

Reports

For example by specifying "Reports", Report Manager can be accessed as:
http://<servername>/Reports

☐ Redirect the default Web site home page on this computer to the local Report Manager virtual directory.

☑ Use SSL (Secure Sockets Layer) connections when retrieving data on these virtual directories.

[Help]   [< Back] [Next >]   [Cancel]

Microsoft SQL Server 2000 Reporting Services Setup

⚠ Report Server Virtual root already exists and can't be used for installation.

[OK]

When selecting virtual directories, it defaulted to these names during my installation. As I mentioned before, I had previously installed beta 2, and uninstalling did not remove the existing virtual directories. The installation will not automatically overwrite or use these directories, so you'll need to drop them from the IIS management tool. Chances are you aren't going to want to select the "Redirect the default Web site..." option unless the IIS server is going to be dedicated to RS, and you want to make it as easy as possible for your end-users to reach the Report Manager site.

This screen asks for the location of the ReportServer database and the credentials that the Report Service (the Windows service) will use to connect to that database. Again, if the database already exists, the install will *not* overwrite it on a local SQL Server instance. It does say that if the database is on a remote SQL Server, it will be used. I have yet to verify this. More info on distributed deployments will be included in a later article. In addition to the ReportServer databases, the ReportServerTempDB database will be created.

This screen is asking where to set up the *sample* database. In case you didn't already know, Microsoft is moving away from Pubs and Northwind as sample databases. The new database is called AdventureWorks and will also be used in Yukon.

Remember, this licensing scheme should be exactly the same as the licensing scheme for your existing SQL Servers. Unless you have less than 25 users, processor licensing is generally the most cost-effective and manageable method; it allows for unlimited and anonymous connections to the database (no need to count up CALs!).

So my installation was nearly finished when I got this message. I was starting the ReportService under the LocalSystem account and I was logged in with administrator privileges while I was installing. There was no way that I didn't have privileges to start the service. The wonderful thing is when you hit Cancel, it rolls back the entire installation! Well, that isn't quite true. It didn't drop the SQL databases or remove the IIS virtual directory--they needed to be cleaned out by hand.

There is a hotfix referenced in the readme that sounded like it might be the source of my problem. I received the same results after applying it. And again, the installation was rolled back. After numerous attempts, a serious amount of caffeine, and a few obscenities, I discovered that the original beta 2 Reporting Services application files were still there, even though I uninstalled the beta before attempting the production install. After deleting those, the installation completed without a hitch.

Now you're ready to explore Reporting Services. It's finally here, and it's definitely here to stay. It doesn't matter how you work with SQL Server; you need to get to know it -- well. Stay tuned for Reporting Services Part II: Report Design.

Links

Reporting Services Website -- http://www.microsoft.com/sql/reporting/default.asp

Trial software -- http://www.microsoft.com/sql/reporting/productinfo/trial.asp

Licensing info -- http://www.microsoft.com/sql/reporting/howtobuy/faq.asp

ASP.NET registration tool -- http://msdn.microsoft.com/library/en-us/cptools/html/cpgrfASPNETIISRegistrationToolAspnet_regiisexe.asp?frame=true

Tutorial: Designing Your First Report in SQL Server Reporting Services

By Brian Knight

Trying to get past the Microsoft SQL Server Reporting Services learning curve? Well never fret, this article is a first in a series of tutorials to walk you through creating a practical report for your company to monitor your SQL Server's databases. In this sample report, we're going to create a job monitoring system. Specifically, we're going to connect to our SQL Server and report if the jobs succeeded or failed the last time they ran.

Easy enough right? This article assumes you already have Reporting Services installed on the servers and the client installed on your side. If you haven't installed these components yet, please go out to this link and download and install the client and server. http://www.microsoft.com/sql/reporting/productinfo/trial.asp#download. For your development PC, you should only have to install the client component unless it is also acting as your server. Also, for the purpose of this report, we're going to steal a query written by another SQLServerCentral.com member and can be downloaded in clear text here: http://www.sqlservercentral.com/scripts/contributions/916.asp.

With the installation complete and the housekeeping complete, let's open up Visual Studio and begin designing our report. Visual Studio 2003 will act as my design interface.

1. Open Visual Studio and go to File | New | Project

2. Select Business Intelligence Projects under the Project Types box. If you do not see this project type, then the Reporting Services client is not installed on your machine. Once you've selected Business Intelligence Projects, click Report Project Wizard. Then, type the name of the project. For the purpose of this example, I typed SQLMonitor as my project data. Click OK once you have those steps completed.

3. In the Select Data Source screen, type a logical name for the connection you're going to make in the Name field under New Data Source. I named mine msdb. You may also see the Shared Data Source drop-down box populated if you have created one in the past. Next, click Edit to set the connection properties. I'm connecting to a server called REPORTS and connecting to the msdb database. Alter enter your login credentials and whether you'd like to connect with Windows or SQL authentication. You can also specify that you'd like the user to be prompted for login credentials when viewing the report under the Credentials area. I also checked Make this a Shared Data Source. This means other reports that we create later will be able to use this same connection information. It's important to note here that this connection may or may not be your

reporting services server. Instead, this is the SQL Server whose jobs you'd like to monitor. After entering my data, the Connection String looked like this:
data source=REPORTS;initial catalog=msdb

4. The next screen allows you to enter the query manually that you'd like to run against the data source. My query was taken from the earlier mentioned script by one of our users, but I have modified it so we're prepared for another part in this article series. So, please use this script in the Query String text box instead of the one in the link:

```
select distinct j.Name as "Job Name",j.enabled, j.category_id, j.description as "Job Description",
h.run_date as LastStatusDate, case h.run_status
when 0 then 'Failed'
when 1 then 'Successful'
when 3 then 'Cancelled'
when 4 then 'In Progress'
end as JobStatus
from sysJobHistory h, sysJobs j
where j.job_id = h.job_id and h.run_date =
(select max(hi.run_date) from sysJobHistory hi where h.job_id = hi.job_id)
order by j.Name
```

5. Notice that you can also click the Edit button to write the query in a GUI design fashion. Fancy and familiar interface for those like me who hate writing queries!

6. By clicking the Next button, you will be taken to the Report Type screen. For most reports including this one, you'll want to do a Tabular report and click Next.

7. You must then design the table by highlighting the SQL Server column that you'd like in the page, group or details and select the corresponding button as shown in the below screenshot. The Page selection will create a new page any time that the column's row changes. The Group selection will group the data by that column. The Details selection is the column that we're concerned with and we want to use all the columns except for the CategoryID column as shown below.

8. Once you click Next, you'll be taken to the Table Style screen in the wizard, which may look very familiar to many of you. Later, I'll show you how you can modify the templates that are presented here to reflect your corporate style. For the time being, though, let's just select the Casual template.

9. Next, choose your deployment server. This is the SQL Server Reporting Services server that you're going to send the reports to after they're complete. This can be altered later once you're ready to deploy to a different environment or server. The default is http://localhost/ReportServer so all you'll have to do is change the localhost entry to your server name. Mine is http://REPORTS/ReportServer. You can also specify here what folder you'd like Visual Studio to

create once you deploy your reports. A report helps you subdivide the tons of reports you may have and secure them at different levels. My folder name is SQLMonitor.

10. After clicking next, the last screen is the confirmation screen where you type the report name. Spaces are allowed if you'd like. I called mine Job Monitor and clicked Finish.

Congratulations, you've finished your first report. Well, almost. Let's explore some of the features now that you have your report essentially complete. If you haven't already done so, click on the Preview tab above to view the report. The report is a pretty useful report for administrators but it's very unattractive. As you can see, the columns need widening and the Enabled column is pretty useless in its Boolean form for a novice user.

First let's widen the first two columns, deploy the solution, and then call it a day. To do this, go back to the Layout tab in Visual Studio. To adjust column width, select the column's header you'd like to widen by left-clicking. You'll then notice an extra row with no data will be presented to you above the column. Left-click and hold between the two columns and drag them to the appropriate size, much like you do in Excel or SQL Server. An alternate way is to select the column, then change the column width in the Properties pane on the right of the design interface. Click the preview again and see your progress. It may take a few hundred times before you have configured it to the perfect width for your viewers. You may also want to adjust the report header width as well to make it look nicer. Here's a sample of what my report looks like in Preview mode. I've shrunken it down a bit so it would fit in HTML cleanly.

Now that your report is ready for primetime, you can deploy it to the development server for others to view it. To do this, click Deploy Solution or Deploy SQLMonitor (if you only want to deploy the individual report project) under the Build menu in Visual Studio.

With your report deployed, users can now go to Internet Explorer (if they have permission to) and go to your deployment directory to view the report. There are other methods to view the report as well. Primarily, users could view it through your application or through a web service. Here's how mine looks:

You probably don't want users seeing the msdb data source in the default view. To remove that, you can click on the msdb data shared data source and check Hide in List View.

In future articles in this tutorial series, we'll explore bite-sized chucks of Reporting Services, from administrating the server to more complex design components. Please save the report you've just created, though! We'll use it in each part of this series as we progressively become more complex.

Tutorial: Adding Conditional Formatting into Reporting Services

By Brian Knight

Last week, we discussed how to create your first report in Microsoft SQL Server Reporting Services. The report we created was a status report on SQL Server Agent jobs. That article can be found here: http://www.sqlservercentral.com/columnists/bknight/designingyourfirstreportinreportingservices.asp. The report we created was from the template and was very crude looking because of it. In this short article, we're going to look at improving that report and answer a common newsgroup question I see. This week, we're going to set the rows of the report to alternate colors. In other words, row 1 will have a grey background and row 2 will have a white background. This makes your report much more readable. We'll also change the color of data based on jobs failing or succeeding. Let's start by first opening the report we worked on in the last tutorial. If you don't have a copy of it, click on the earlier mentioned link. If you download the RDL file, you'll only have to copy and paste it into the Solution Explorer side of Visual Studio. Now that you're caught up on the report, let's jump into solving the following goals: 1) alternate row colors and 2) change the data to red on jobs that have failed.

Tutorial 1 – Alternating Colors Between Rows

To make our report more readable, your viewers probably want to have each row an alternate color. To do this, pull open your report and follow these steps:

1. Select one of the fields in the report. Once you select the field, you'll see a grid surrounding the row. Left-click on the grey column to the left of the data as shown in the below figure. By left-clicking on this row, you can now set the properties for the entire row and not a single column in the table.

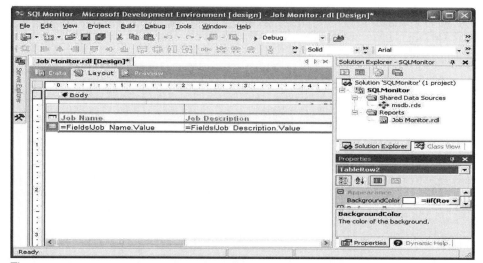

2. The property you want to set in the right-pane is the BackgroundColor property. If you don't see the Properties window on the right as seen in the above screenshot, select Properties Window under View. The default background color is Transparent. To change this to our dynamic property, click the drop-down box and select <Expression…>.

3. You should not be in the Edit Expression dialog box as shown in the below screenshot. In the Expression box to the right you can type the following syntax to alternate colors (make sure you remove what was there before):

=iif(RowNumber(Nothing) Mod 2, "WhiteSmoke", "White")

Essentially, this variant of .NET code above means that the first row will be a slightly grey color and the second will be white. Then, the rows will alternate between the colors. If you'd like to change the colors, just type the new color name where WhiteSmoke is in my example. The list of color names can be found where you clicked the drop-down box to select <Expression…> earlier. If you wanted something to occur every 3rd row, change the 2 in the above code to 3.

After you have typed in the expression, click OK and you're done! Almost anything can be set dynamically like this in Reporting Services. For example, if you'd like the report to look different based on the UserID that generated the report, you can do that by using the global variable.

Tutorial 2 – Changing the Color of Text Dynamically

Next, we want to make bad numbers in our report jump out. To do this, we're going to dynamically look at the data in the Job Status column and if it says "Failed", turn it red so it stands out for a casual viewer. To do this, follow these simple steps in Visual Studio:

1. Left-click the row and column that you'd like use dynamic formatting on.

2. You will again want to go to the Properties Window and select the drop-down box under Color in the Appearance group. Select <Expression...> to open the Expression Editor.

3. Replace the word Black (which is the default) with the following text and click OK.

   =iif(Fields!JobStatus.Value = "Failed", "Red", "Black")

Now, you can preview the data and see if can see any failed jobs. Essentially, the syntax above says that if the value of the JobStatus field is equal to the word Failed then turn the color to Red. Otherwise, keep it black. Likewise, you could change the color based on profits not being met with the following syntax.

=iif(Fields!Profit.Value < 0 , "Red", "Black")

You can also make the word Failed really stand out by making the font style a bit more dynamic. If you want the text bolded dynamically, then you can change the Normal default in the FontWeight property (under font) to the following syntax:

=iif(Fields!JobStatus.Value = "Failed", "Bold", " Normal ")

Well, hopefully this showed you a bit about how to make two simple but necessary changes to your report to make them more readable. In the next articles in this tutorial series, we'll begin securing our report that we've just created so you'll need special rights to see the job status.

Tutorial: Changing the Visibility of Objects in Reporting Services

By Brian Knight

In the last tutorial in this series of Reporting Services tutorials we added conditional formatting to the report. Now that we've created our first report and have added a bit of flare to it, let's go ahead and make it even cleaner. In this very quick demonstration, we'll go ahead and change the visibility of rows or columns based on given conditions.

Other articles in this series (in order):

- Tutorial: Designing Your First Report in SQL Server Reporting Services
- Tutorial: Adding Conditional Formatting into Reporting Services

In our example, we're going to continue with our SQL Server job monitor report. This tutorial will filter out jobs that are not enabled. In our scenario we don't care about jobs that are disabled and we're assuming they were disabled with good reason. To do this, follow these steps:

1. Select one of the fields in the report in the Visual Studio report design interface. Once you select the field, you'll see a grid surrounding the row. Left-click on the grey column to the left of the data as shown in the below figure. By left-clicking on this row, you can now set the properties for the entire row and not a single column in the table.

2. The property you want to set in the right-pane is the Hidden property under the Visibility group. If you don't see the Properties window on the right as seen in the above screenshot, select Properties Window under View. The default visibility property is True. To change this to our dynamic property, click the drop-down box and select <Expression...>.

3. You should now be in the Edit Expression dialog box as shown in the below screenshot. In the Expression box to the right you can type the following syntax to change the visibility (make sure you remove what was there before):

   =iif (Fields!enabled.Value = 0 OR Fields!enabled.Value IS Nothing, True, False)

   Essentially, this will change the Hidden property to True if the value of the enabled column is 0 or NULL. Otherwise, the Hidden property will be set to false.

4. Click OK and preview the report. If you have any jobs that are disabled, they will not show in the

report any more.

If you want to change the properties of an individual group, column, or header you can follow the same logic. Even graphics can be hidden or shown with this technique. In those cases you would just select the individual object and go to the Hidden property again. That's all there is to it! Sorry, I couldn't stretch it out further. Currently, I'm taking this series from common newsgroup posts. If you have any areas that you'd like to see documented, please click on Opinion below to post a message to me.

Database Design and Strategy

Spending a few more minutes in design can pay off in a big way when building a system. This is the mantra that we hear and what most people would like to strive for, but it seems that we can never find the time to do detailed design. We don't get what Andy Warren calls "thinking time". So what can you do?

The only real thing that you can do to get better at design is to learn and practice it more. Just as an experienced developer can build things quicker, having that intuition on typing code, an architect of a database system can get better by learning what works and what doesn't.

Below we have a few articles for you that can help with your education and give you some additional insight into design and strategy.

Lookup Table Madness

By Don Peterson

Over the years I have had a number of "discussions" about the practice of creating generalized "lookup" tables for storing multiple code types in a single table. I won't keep you in suspense about my view of this practice; the idea stems from a failure to learn and appreciate the fundamentals of good database design. Accordingly, I developed an appropriate name for these tables: Massively Unified Code-Key tables, or MUCK tables.

Let's take a look at the reasons why some are tempted to use this approach, but more importantly I hope to explain why you shouldn't. Many "lookup" tables tend to look something like these examples:

```
CREATE TABLE EmployeeStatusCode ( EmployeeStatusCode int IDENTITY(1,1) , Description varchar(50))

CREATE TABLE CustomerStatusCode ( CustomerStatusCode int IDENTITY(1,1) , Description varchar(50))

CREATE TABLE FacilityStatusCode ( FacilityStatusCode int IDENTITY(1,1) , Description varchar(50))
```

For the record, I don't like the term "Lookup" tables, nor any of its cousins (Code Table, Domain Table, Reference Table, etc...) the term is far too ambiguous to be useful. Exactly how do you define them? Is it just any table that is referenced by a foreign key? Obviously not. How about any table that is referenced by a FK and doesn't reference any other table? Nope... Even though I use the term in this article, I want to point out that these tables are fundamentally no different than any other tables in your database and should therefore receive no special treatment.

** While I'm clarifying things..., I am not advocating the across-the-board use of IDENTITY columns (or of surrogate keys in general); that subject would require much more detail than I am prepared to go into in this article. I use the example only because it is so common.**

Since the Employee, Customer, and Facility status codes look the same, it is argued that when viewed from a "certain perspective" they are of the same type and should therefore be in the same table. This seems sensible enough until you realize that sharing a set of common attributes is only **one** of the criterion that should be used to determine such things. Unfortunately, that "certain perspective" in which your code tables can appropriately be combined also makes them ineffective for use in their original purpose--ensuring data integrity. Even a cursory examination should tell us that EmployeeStatusCode is not the SAME thing as CustomerStatusCode no matter how SIMILAR they are in appearance.We would never want a Customer status to be "Fired", or an Employee status to be "Vacant" regardless of how appropriate that description might be for some. ;-)There are several alternatives available to prevent this from happening, but as I will show, they each have major problems.

Basically, during the process of normalization (and no, normalization is not a dirty word) these codes are removed from the Employee, Customer, and Facility tables and appropriately placed in their own tables. Then, someone notices the similarity among the code tables and decides that the database would be simpler if they were combined into a single table. Normalization eliminates redundant data, thus making the task of enforcing data integrity vastly simpler, but the process of creating a MUCK is something else entirely. MUCKs do not eliminate redundant data; rather they are an elimination of what are PERCEIVED to be redundant tables, but as I will demonstrate, fewer tables does not equal simplicity.

You may be saying, "This guy doesn't know what he's talking about! MUCKs do help eliminate redundant data in those cases where an EmployeeStatusCode shares the same description as a CustomerStatusCode and so on." Nice try, but this just further serves to illustrate why you shouldn't treat these codes as the same type of thing. It shouldn't take too much contemplation to realize that this logic quickly leads us right back into the ugly world of update anomalies and other non-relational ugliness; i.e., what if the business decision is made to change that particular description but only for Employees? Can it be done? Sure, but what a pain.

As mentioned above, once you have a MUCK, the problem that presents itself is: just how do you constrain your data to ensure that codes of type X are only applied to X? The first option that many people think of is triggers. Add a CodeType column to the MUCK and write your triggers appropriately. Simple!,...but before you settle on this approach, read on. If you don't want to use triggers to enforce integrity you could try including a CodeType column in the Employee table with a column constraint that prevents any status codes that are not of the employee type.

Let's look at an example:

```
CREATE TABLE Code ( CodeID int IDENTITY(1,1) , CodeType int, Description varchar(255))

ALTER TABLE Code ADD CONSTRAINT PK_Code PRIMARY KEY (CodeID, CodeType)
```

Obviously, we would have a CodeType table...but then again, why not just shove that into our Code table too? After all, it looks the same as all our other codes! There's room for everyone aboard this recursive roller-coaster ride!

Our Employee table would look something like this:

```
CREATE TABLE Employee ( EmployeeID int IDENTITY(1,1) , FirstName varchar(50)
, LastName varchar(50) , CodeType int , CodeID int , etc... )

ALTER TABLE Employee ADD CONSTRAINT FK_Code FOREIGN KEY (CodeID, CodeType)
 REFERENCES Code (CodeID, CodeType)

ALTER TABLE Employee ADD CONSTRAINT CHK_CodeType CHECK(CodeType = 1)
```

It should work, right? Yes, but you have to be willing to ignore the elephant in the living room; our employee table is not properly normalized because CodeID is partially dependent on CodeType which is not part of the key. (and no, you can't just make CodeType part of the key because FirstName, LastName etc... would not be dependent on the whole key).Then think of what a mess this becomes if an employee can have more than one Code/CodeType combination. Further, what if one of those multiple Code/CodeType pairs is dependent on another one? Before you go running back to the "simplicity" of the trigger option you should realize that it has exactly the same problem, but it's hidden and likely hard-coded in the logic of the trigger. In fact, it could be argued that trigger option is worse because CodeID has a functional dependency on a column that isn't even there!The picture just gets uglier if you consider the performance overhead of triggers vs. DRI.

The reasoning that leads to MUCK tables, if taken to its logical conclusion, would have every entity in the database reduced or "generalized" down to a "Thing." The Thing table would have a key (it would naturally be an IDENTITY column) and a few other generalized attributes like Name, Type, and Description etc...:

```
CREATE TABLE Thing (
  PKey bigint IDENTITY(1,1) --We better use a bigint since there will be a lot of rows in this baby...
  , ThingType int
  , Attribute1 varchar(8000)
    -- We can't provide any domain integrity so we have to go with what I call the "Garbage Heap"
approach.
  , Attribute1Type int
  , Attribute2 varchar(8000)
  , Attribute2Type int
, etc...)
```

Congratulations, we have now worked our way right back to managing data in a spreadsheet, albeit one with a handy query language. Oh, wait...better still would be to just use an IDENTITY column and an XML string. That way we don't need to define more than a single table with two columns in the database, and we just won't bother with the whole data integrity thing; "isn't that stuff best handled by the application anyway?" Now that's what I call a flexible database design! (OK, I apologize for the sarcasm, sort of...but those who were thinking "Yeah!" might want to cut your losses and stop reading now.) And, yes I have personally dealt with people who thought that those options were not only viable, but superior to a normalized database.

Some might say that these examples are far-fetched and that no reasonable person would go that far. But that is exactly the point: how do you know when you have gone too far? When you abandon the fundamental principles upon which good database design is predicated, what principles **are** you using to guide your efforts? The difference between a MUCK and the "Thing" table is one of degree, not of kind, and they are both wrong. Now, before you say "there is no 'right' way to design a database", it is true that given a set of fairly complex requirements, two **competent** individuals might arrive at superficially different database designs, but rest assured; the variety of incorrect designs that the ignorant will pull out of their hats is virtually limitless!

Generalization is a good thing in the right context, but it is a tool and should not be used indiscriminately. Generalization is something that can be very useful in the Object Oriented (OO) programming world where you are concerned with what things **do**, or how they **act**. If two things act the same way they can be brought together under a single class. Even if they differ significantly, they might be able to inherit their common characteristics from a parent class, relying on subclasses to provide their unique behaviors. In the world of relational database design we really don't care so much about how things act, we care about what they **are**. In that context, generalization is very seldom useful. In the world of OO programming generalization helps improve code reuse, modularity, and maintainability. By contrast, generalization in a database leads to ambiguity or loss of meaning. I suspect that this practice got its start with those OO programmers who mistakenly think that a table is analogous to a Class when in reality a table is a variable. Astute readers will recognize this mistake as what C.J. Date called "The First Great Blunder", but that is yet another subject for another day...

Be careful that you don't generalize your database into irrelevance, building in so much flexibility that your system degenerates into chaos (chaos being the ultimate in flexibility). Remember that the primary reason to use a database is not to "persist data"; that can be done more efficiently with file-based systems. The purpose of a relational database is to enforce the rules that govern how data is to be created, maintained and used; in other words, the database enforces the rules that give the data meaning.Without those rules your data becomes a meaningless tangle of 1's and 0's. In database design, the first and foremost consideration should always be logical correctness; all other concerns are secondary. After all, just what is a database? Hugh Darwen provided the most useful definition of a database that I have come across:

"A database is a set of axioms. The response to a query is a theorem. The process of deriving the theorem from the axioms is a proof. The proof is made by manipulating symbols according to agreed mathematical rules. The proof (that is, the query result) is as sound and consistent as the rule are."

In other words you need only concern yourself with the logical correctness of your database design if you want **correct** answers to your database queries. If you just want answers you don't have to bother with all this "theoretical" stuff.

By Don Peterson Wednesday, July 28, 2004

How To Be a Good DBA – Strategy and Tactics

By Jeffrey Yao

Introduction

Having been a DBA for about 9 years, I am frequently asked by some programmers, "I am tired of coding, now I want to switch my career to be a DBA, so where should I start?" I promised that I would write an article to answer these questions based on my experience, so this article is mainly based on my experience as a SQL Server and DB2 DBA, and I welcome other DBAs to share their experiences on this topic.

Strategies for Junior DBAs

Focusing on the basic DBA tasks: first thing first.

The quickest way to be a qualified junior DBA is to understand the scope of daily DBA tasks and grasp the necessary skills to do these tasks. I figure that a junior DBAs work accounts for at least 40% of daily DBA tasks. The following is a list of tasks essential to every DBA.

- SQL Server installation. Knowledge needed: SQL Server components (EM, Profiler, Query Analyzer, other tools etc), edition of SQL Server and its environment requirements (hardware, OS, network protocols etc), remote / automatic / manual installation
- Backup/Restore. Knowledge needed: recovery models, backup / restore tools and SQL statements for backup / restore, and how to adapt your recovery plan to your business needs.
- Security: roles/login/user accounts. Knowledge needed: authentication modes, types of roles, how to manage security accounts, grant /revoke permission to access data and how to make a security

plan matching your business needs.
- Database Maintenance. Knowledge needed: some DBCC commands (dbcc checkdb / dbreindex / checkcatalog / inputbuffer are among my favorites), sp_who, sp_kill and all the SQL task wizards.

Focusing on programming with SQL: foundation for future growth

T-SQL is a powerful tool that enables DBAs to personate their database management styles by scripting their daily tasks such as auditing, backups / restores, performance tuning, etc. Most of application performance issues in real world are related to bad SQL statements. I cannot overemphasize the importance of writing good SQL scripts.

The following are the essential SQL statements to me:

a) CRUD (Create, Read, Update, Delete) statements about database, table, view, UDF, triggers, stored procedures.
b) T-SQL programming control statements, such as if…else…, begin…end, while…break…continue and case statement and use of cursor.
c) SQL Server internal functions, such as @@identity, @@spid, substring(), covert/cast(), etc.

Strategies for intermediate DBAs

- Focusing on data modeling: beyond data and into business. Knowledge needed: knowledge of business for which the database is going to be built; knowledge of logical / physical model (3rd norm); expertise in the modeling tools, like ERWin, Visio etc. A good data model will not only improve an application performances, but also reduce the database maintenance. For example, I once reviewed a data model of a government agency which stores all employees' salary information in several tables. The original idea was to facilitate the quick summary reports needed by different departments but later is found too costly to synchronize all the information in terms of time and speed. (Some tables have triggers, which increase delays during synchronizations.)
- Focusing on performance tuning: fun and challenges. Knowledge/Skills: table/index architecture, Index choice/building; server / database /session options; execution plan; use of profiler to optimize and audit SQL statements, dbcc statements. Performance tuning is where a DBA can shine. Challenges always hide somewhere for a DBA to tackle so that a query can run within 2 seconds instead of two minutes. Believe me, it is fun to do performance tuning!
- Focusing on advanced management: key to being an expert. Knowledge / Skills: VBScript, DTS, SQL-DMO, replication. I always believe that a DBA who does not know VBScript cannot be creative in managing SQL Server system. Because Microsoft has made VBScript so powerful that it can be used to facilitate the administration of most Window-based applications, SQL Server is no exception. When combining VBScript with DTS and SQL-DMO, I bet almost all administration work can be scripted and automatically run under a schedule.

Strategies for senior DBAs

- Focusing on soft skills: key to career. As a senior DBA, you spend most time in doing requirements analysis with clients and providing guidance to other team members; here soft skills such as time management, communication, negotiation and leadership, etc, play more important roles than the technical skills. Without soft skills, you can hardly be a valuable DBA. I learned the lesson the hard way. I still remember my experience that happened a long time ago. I was assigned as a database architect for a project and had to discuss with clients in different departments regarding their requirements. From time to time, I would release a new version of data model. However, during this process, there were a few columns that I made constant changes by either adding them to different tables or simply getting them removed or renamed. The problem was I forgot to document why I made the change based on my talk with whom. When I was challenged with the differences between version 1.0.04 (four weeks ago) and version 1.0.06 on a specific column, I could not tell why the column appeared in 10.04 but disappeared in 1.0.05 and then reappeared in 1.0.06. I was accused of being incapable of my role even though my project manager was assured of my technical capability. Later, I was removed from my role because the project manager had to satisfy the client's concern. How stupid I was! From then on, I formed the habit to record each reason behind every change I made to my base line project document.
- Focusing on innovations: the last step to glory. Innovation is to use the current technology and

resources to create new processes / methods that can make better solutions in terms of time or economic efficiency. As a senior DBA, one needs to have a broader view and interests in contributing to your employer's business bottom line. In the e-business era, more businesses are relying on data for decision and operation, and this gives all DBAs, especially the senior DBAs, more opportunities to creatively manipulate the data at each stage of the data value chain, from data collecting, processing, mining, to reporting, distributing and storing.

Conclusion

To be a qualified DBA, you have to master the right skills at the right time. You do not have to know everything to start your career as a DBA, but you have to know where to start. There is no distinct line between a junior DBA and an intermediate DBA, or an intermediate DBA and a senior DBA. But my personal feeling is that when your rank goes higher, you need more than technical skills to demonstrate your values. My final word to those who are interested in DBA career:
"Do not think of database management as a routine job, but think of it as an art work that you can demonstrate your imagination and creativity."

An Introduction to Database Models

By Frank Kalis

Consider this article **a very basic** introduction to an area in which countless multi-hundred page books have been written during the last four decades. This article cannot and does not intend to compete with any of these books, but rather tries to explain different database models in a non-academic style. I will discuss the following database models:

- Flat Files
- Hierarchical Model
- Network Model
- Relational Model
- Object-Relational Model
- Object-Oriented Model
- Other Models

Flat Files

Simply put, one can imagine a flat file database as one single large table. A good way to visualize this is to think of a spreadsheet. A spreadsheet can only have one meaningful table structure at a time. Data access happens only sequentially; random access is not supported. Queries are usually slow, because the whole file always has to be scanned to locate the data. Although data access could be sped up by sorting the data, in doing so the data becomes more vulnerable to errors in sorting. In addition, you'll face following problems.

1. Data Redundancy. Imagine a spreadsheet where you collect information about bonds to manage a fixed income portfolio. One column might contain the information about the issuer of that bond. Now when you buy a second bond from this issuer you again have to enter that information.
2. Data Maintenance. Given the above example consider what happens when the information of this issuer changes. This change has to be applied to every single bond (row) of that issuer.
3. Data integrity. Following 2; what happens when you have a typo when changing the information? Inconsistencies are the outcome.

As a result one concludes that Flat File Databases are only suitable for small, self-evident amounts of data.

Hierarchical Database Model

Hierarchical databases (and network databases) were the predecessors of the relational database model. Today these models are hardly used in commercial applications. IBM's IMS (Information Management System) is the most prominent representative of the hierarchical model. It is mostly run on older mainframe systems.

This model can be described as a set of flat files that are linked together in a tree structure. It is typically diagrammed as an inverted tree.

The original concept for this model represents the data as a hierarchical set of Parent/Child relations. Data is basically organized in a tree of one or more groups of fields that are called segments. Segments make up every single node of the tree. Each child segment can only be related to just one parent segment and access to the child segment could only happen via its parent segment. This means that 1:n relations result in data redundancy. To solve this problem, the data is stored in only one place and is referenced through links or physical pointers. When a user accesses data he starts at the root level and works down his way through the tree to the desired target data. That's the reason a user must be very familiar with the data structure of the whole database. But once he knows the structure, data retrieval could become very fast. Another advantage is built-in referential integrity, which is automatically enforced. However, because links between the segments are hard-coded into the database, this model becomes inflexible to changes in the data structure. Any change requires substantial programming effort, which in most cases comes along with substantial changes not only in the database, but also in the application.

Network Database Model

The network database model is an improvement to the hierarchical model. In fact, it was developed to address some of the weaknesses of the hierarchical model. It was formally standardized as CODASYL DBTG (Conference On Data System Languages, Data Base Task Group) model in 1971 and is based on mathematical set theory.

At its core the very basic modeling construct is the set construct. This set consists of an owner record, the set name, and the member record. Now, this 'member' can play this role in more than one set at the same time; therefore, this member can have multiple parents. Also, an owner type can be owner or member in one or more other set constructs. This means the network model allows multiple paths between segments. This is a valuable improvement on relationships, but could make a database structure very complex.

Now how does data access happen? Actually, by working through the relevant set structures. A user need not work his way down through root tables, but can retrieve data by starting at any node and working through the related sets. This provides fast data access and allows the creation of more complex queries than could be created with the hierarchical model. But once again, the disadvantage is that the user must be familiar with the physical data structure. Also, it is not easy to change the database structure without affecting the application, because if you change a set structure you need to change all references to that structure within the application.

Although an improvement to the hierarchical model, this model was not believed to be the end of the line. Today the network database model is obsolete for practical purposes.

Relational Database Model

The theory behind the relational database model will not be discussed in this article; only the differences to the other models will be pointed out. I will discuss the relational model along with some set theory and relational algebra basics in a different set of articles in the near future, if they let me :).

In the relational model the logical design is separated from the physical. Queries against a Relational Database Management System (RDBMS) are solely based on these logical relations. Execution of a query doesn't require the use of predefined paths like pointers. Changes to the database structure are fairly simple and easy to implement.

The core concept of this model is a two-dimensional table, comprising of rows and columns. Because the data is organized in tables, the structure can be changed without changing the accessing application. This is different than its predecessors, where the application usually had to be changed when the data structure changed.

The relational database model knows no hierarchies within its tables. Each table can be directly accessed and can potentially be linked to each other table. There are no hard-coded, predefined paths in the data. The Primary Key - Foreign Key construct of relational databases is based on logical, not on physical, links.

Another advantage of the relational model is that it is based on a solid house of theory. The inventor, E.F.Codd, a mathematician by profession, has defined what a relational database is and what a system needs to call itself a relational database [1], [2]. This model is firmly based on the mathematical theories of sets and first order predicate logic. Even the name is derived from the term relation which is commonly used in set theory. The name is not derived from the ability to establish relations among the table of a relational database.

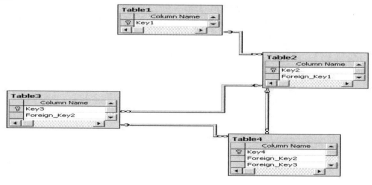

Object-Relational Model

This is also called post-relational model or extended relational model. This model addresses several weaknesses of the relational model, the most significant of which is the inability to handle BLOB's. BLOBs, LOBs or Binary Large Objects are complex data types like time series, geospatial data, video files, audio files, emails, or directory structures. An object-relational database system encapsulates methods with data structures and can therefore execute analytical or complex data manipulation operations.

In its most simple definition data is a chain of 0's and 1's that are ordered in a certain manner. Traditional DBMSs have been developed for and are therefore optimized for accessing small data elements like numbers or short strings. These data are atomic; that is, they could be not further cut down into smaller pieces. In contrast are BLOB's large, non-atomic data. They could have several parts and subparts. That is why they are difficult to represent in an RDBMS.

Many relational databases systems do offer support to store BLOBs. But in fact, they store these data outside the database and reference it via pointers. These pointers allow the DBMS to search for BLOBs, but the manipulation itself happens through conventional IO operations.

Object-Oriented Model

According to Rao (1994), "The object-oriented database (OODB) paradigm is the combination of object-oriented programming language (OOPL) systems and persistent systems. The power of the OODB comes from the seamless treatment of both persistent data, as found in databases, and transient data, as found in executing programs."

To a certain degree, one might think that the object-oriented model is a step forward into the past, because their design is like that of hierarchical databases. In general, anything is called an object which can be manipulated. Like in OO programming, objects inherit characteristics of their class and can have custom properties and methods. The hierarchical structure of classes and subclasses replaces the relational concept of atomic data types. As with OO programming, the object-oriented approach tries to bring OO characteristics like classes, inheritance, and encapsulation to database systems, making a database in fact a data store.

The developer of such a system is responsible for implementing methods and properties to handle the data in the database from within his object-oriented application.

There is no longer a strict distinction between application and database.

This approach makes Object DBMS an interesting and sometimes superior alternative to RDBMS when complex relationships between data are essential. An example of such an application might be current portfolio risk management systems.

However, these systems lack a common, solid base of theory that Codd provided for relational databases. There is a model proposed by the Object Management Group (OMG) which could be viewed as de facto standard, but the OMG can only advise and is not a standards body like ANSI.

Other Models

For the sake of "completeness", what now follows is a list of other models without further detailed explanation:

- Semistructured Model
- Associative Model [3]
- Entity-Attribute-Value (EAV) data model [4]
- Context Model

Conclusion

Well, no real conclusion. I hope you are with me so far and have seen that there (still) is a world outside the relational model which can be pretty exciting to discover. If you are interested in more details, you might want to follow the links provided in the reference.

References

[1]Codd, E.F. "Is Your DBMS Really Relational?" and "Does Your DBMS Run By the Rules?" ComputerWorld, October 14 1985 and October 21 1985.
[2]Codd, E.F. The Relational Model for Database Management, Version 2; Addison-Wesley; 1990.
3) http://www.lazysoft.com/docs/other_docs/amd_whitepaper.pdf
4) http://ycmi.med.yale.edu/nadkarni/eav_cr_contents.htm

Speed up Development on Backend and Middle Tier with SQL Scripts

By Ameet Phadnis

Introduction

Many projects do access data through Stored Procedures. There are 5 standard stored procedures for tables in the database. The standard procedures are for:

1. Get: Getting a list from the table.
2. GetSingle: Getting single record from the table.
3. Add: Adding record to the table.
4. Update: Updating the edited record
5. Delete: Deleting single record.

Before I wrote my first Stored Procedure generator, I used to create all these procedures manually. So, in case of 10 tables database I had to write 50 stored procedures manually. This used to take time and I was getting tired doing the same job over and over again. Also, in case of complicated/large tables it used to leave room for ID10T (IDIOT) errors or typing errors. So, I started thinking of designing a SQL procedure which will generate all these procedures for me. The first Stored Procedure Generator I wrote was using System tables. But System tables can change in future versions of SQL Server. That's when I found out that SQL Server provides Information Schema views on most of the information on the data. So, I started writing another Stored Procedure generator which is well organized and uses information schema views. In this article, I will explain different ways of accessing meta data and also I will give an example of Insert procedure generator.

This article will initially explain the System Tables and System Stored Procedures, then I will explain the recommended Information Schema Views. I have structured it in this fashion to explain the complexity of System Tables and how easy it is with Information Schema Views. Readers can jump directly to Information Schema Views section.

The same principle of building Stored Procedures do apply for Business functions or building Data Access Layer functions that do access Stored Procedures. This article will provide some examples on building Stored Procedure Generator, and also building VB function Generator.

Free Download of complete Stored Procedure Generator and DNN VB Function Generator is available at www.etekgloballnc.com

Accessing Meta Data - System Tables

SQL Server stores information about data in system tables. It also provides system stored procedures to access this information or Information Schema Views to access this information. Using the system tables needs to have in depth knowledge on columns in these tables.

System Tables: Most common or used system tables are:

SysObjects: This table keeps information on all objects in the database. The objects are identified by the xtype column. Some of xtypes are U User Table, P Stored Procedures, C Check Constraint, F Foreign Key Constraint etc So, for example, to get all tables in the database you can write select statement as:

```
SELECT * FROM sysObjects where xtype = 'U'
```

SysColumns: This system table stores information on all columns for tables. The column identifying the relationship between columns and tables is the id column in sysColumns table. Also, the data type for columns is stored in xtype column. It relates to the sysTypes table. For example, assume you have a table called tblUsers. You would like to list all columns, their data types, and data size from this table. Your SQL would look like:

```
SELECT syscolumns.name columnname, systypes.name datatype, syscolumns.length, syscolumns.prec from
SysObjects JOIN syscolumns ON SysObjects.id = SysColumns.id JOIN systypes ON syscolumns.xtype =
sysTypes.xtype Where SysObjects.name = 'Users'
```

SysTypes: This can be considered as lookup table to get all the Data types in the database. To get all the data type names in the database your SQL will look like this:

```
SELECT name from Systypes
```

SysForeignKeys: This keeps information regarding foreign key relationships in the database. The way it is stored needs some explaination. SysForeignkeys table has 4 important columns. The columns are:

Fkeyid: This stores the ID related to SysObjects table. The ID stored is for the table which contains the foreign key.

rkeyID: The ID stored is for the referenced table that has the primary key.

Fkey: This actually references to the column that is the foreign key in the table. It is related to the colid column in the sysColumns table.

Rkey: References the primary key in the primary table. It is related to the colid column in the sysColumns table.

To select all tables that depend on Users table your select statement will look like:

```
SELECT ChildTable.tablename, ChildTable.columnname
FROM sysforeignkeys JOIN (Select SysObjects.Name tablename, sysObjects.id, sysColumns.name columnname,
sysColumns.colid FROM SysObjects JOIN sysColumns ON SysObjects.id = sysColumns.id Where
sysobjects.xtype = 'U') PrimaryTable ON sysforeignkeys.rkeyID = PrimaryTable.ID AND
sysforeignkeys.rkey = PrimaryTable.colid JOIN (Select SysObjects.Name tablename, sysObjects.id,
sysColumns.name columnname, sysColumns.colid FROM SysObjects JOIN sysColumns ON SysObjects.id =
sysColumns.id Where sysobjects.xtype = 'U') ChildTable ON sysforeignkeys.fkeyID = ChildTable.ID AND
sysforeignkeys.fkey = ChildTable.colid WHERE PrimaryTable.tablename = 'Users'
```

Accessing Meta Data - System Stored Procedures

Another way of accessing data about data is system stored procedures. I will explain the system stored procedures for the above context except for foreign keys as it is a bit complex. Also, while researching the foreign keys system stored procedure I came across the Schema views.

Sp_Tables: This stored procedure returns back all the table names. For example, to get all user defined tables from XYZ database, your SQL will look like:

```
EXEC sp_tables NULL, dbo, XYZ, "'TABLE'"
```

Sp_columns: This stored procedure returns back all the columns for specified table. Let's consider the example above. The best part about this stored procedure is it hides the complexity of joins to get the data types and column names as shown in system tables section. To get all columns in the Users table you will call this procedure as:

```
Exec sp_columns 'Users'
```

sp_datatype_info: This stored procedure returns back information on all data types. Syntax is going to be:

```
EXEC sp_datatype_info
```

Accessing Meta Data - Information Schema Views

All the above ways do allow us to get the data about data. But the recommended way is Information Schema views. The reasons are next versions of System tables might change but the information schemas would remain the same. It also hides the complexity. If you look back at the System Tables section you will realize that you need to do some research or need to have in depth knowledge of System Tables. But with information schema views it hides all the join information etc. In this section, I will explain commonly used views.

Information_schema.Tables: Returns information about Tables. To return all user defined table names in the database you can write select as:

```
SELECT TABLE_NAME from Information_schema.Tables WHERE TABLE_TYPE = 'BASE TABLE'
```

Information_schema.Columns: Returns information about columns in the table. To get column name, data types and sizes for Users table, you can write SQL as:

```
SELECT COLUMN_NAME, DATA_TYPE, CHARACTER_MAXIMUM_LENGTH FROM INFORMATION_SCHEMA.COLUMNS Where
TABLE_NAME = 'Users'
```

For data types that have fixed size like int, datetime, the CHARACTER_MAXIMUM_LENGTH will return null.

Information_schema.TABLE_CONSTRAINTS: Returns information on all constraints. Users can get information on specific tables. The Constraints are identified by the CONSTRAINT_TYPE column. For example, to get all constraints on Users Table you can write SQL as:

```
SELECT * FROM INFORMATION_SCHEMA.TABLE_CONSTRAINTS Where Table_name = 'Users'
```

To get Primary key Constraint on the Users table you can write SQL as:

```
SELECT * FROM INFORMATION_SCHEMA.TABLE_CONSTRAINTS Where Table_name = 'Users' AND CONSTRAINT_TYPE =
'PRIMARY KEY'
```

Information_Schema.CONSTRAINT_COLUMN_USAGE: Returns column information and the constraint associated with it.

For example, in the above example we got PRIMARY KEY CONSTRAINT Information on Users table but we would like to have the column name. The SQL will look like:

```
SELECT COLUMN_NAME FROM INFORMATION_SCHEMA.CONSTRAINT_COLUMN_USAGE WHERE CONSTRAINT_NAME = 'PK_USERS'
```

Combining Information_schema.Table_constraints and Information_schema. CONSTRAINT_COLUMN_USAGE, SQL will look like

```
SELECT COLUMN_NAME FROM INFORMATION_SCHEMA.CONSTRAINT_COLUMN_USAGE JOIN
INFORMATION_SCHEMA.TABLE_CONSTRAINTS ON INFORMATION_SCHEMA.CONSTRAINT_COLUMN_USAGE.CONSTRAINT_NAME =
INFORMATION_SCHEMA.TABLE_CONSTRAINTS.CONSTRAINT_NAME WHERE
INFORMATION_SCHEMA.TABLE_CONSTRAINTS.TABLE_NAME = 'Users' AND CONSTRAINT_TYPE = 'PRIMARY KEY'
```

Information_schema.REFERENTIAL_CONSTRAINTS: Returns information about foreign key constraints.

For example, consider you have two tables in your database. One is users table and one is UserRoles table. Users table has UserID which is referenced in UserRoles table. To get the foreign key column information your SQL will look like

```
SELECT fkey.Table_name, fkey.Column_name FROM INFORMATION_SCHEMA.CONSTRAINT_COLUMN_USAGE rkey JOIN
Information_schema.REFERENTIAL_CONSTRAINTS Ref on rkey.CONSTRAINT_NAME = Ref.Unique_Constraint_Name
JOIN INFORMATION_SCHEMA.CONSTRAINT_COLUMN_USAGE fkey ON Ref.CONSTRAINT_NAME = fkey.CONSTRAINT_NAME
WHERE rkey.Table_Name = 'Users'
```
The above SQL will get you the table name and column names which reference the UserID table in the Users table.

Information_Schema.ROUTINES: Returns information on Stored Procedure and functions. To get information on all Stored Procedures in your database your SQL will be:

```
SELECT * FROM Information_Schema.ROUTINES Where Routine_type = 'PROCEDURE'
```
Information_Schema.PARAMETERS: Returns information on Parameters for stored procedure. To get information on Parameters for AddUser stored procedure your SQL will be:

```
SELECT PARAMETER_NAME, DATA_TYPE, CHARACTER_MAXIMUM_LENGTH FROM Information_Schema.PARAMETERS Where
Specific_name = 'AddUser'
```
This section explained how you can use some of the information schema views to extract data about your database.

Putting it to work

This section will give you two examples. The first one explains how you can create Delete Stored Procedure for your table and the second example explains how you can build VB declaration function using Stored Procedures created. You can create Insert, Update, Get and GetSingle stored procedures OR you can check the references section for information on downloading free code.

Example 1: Stored Procedure Generation

This Stored Procedure was designed following these standards -

1. Tables start with tbl and lookup tables start with tlkp.
2. All Stored procedures will have the format of procedure type and tablename without tbl and tlkp. For example, tblUsers table will have Get procedure name as GetUsers. In the following example it is going to be DeleteUsers.

```
CREATE    Procedure prCreateDeleteProcedure
@table_Name nvarchar(128),
@print bit
AS
Declare @SQLStatement varchar(8000), --Actual Delete Stored Procedure string
 @parameters varchar(8000), -- Parameters to be passed to the Stored Procedure
 @deleteStatement varchar(8000), -- To Store the Delete SQL Statement
 @procedurename nvarchar(128), -- To store the procedure name
 @DropProcedure nvarchar(1000) --To Store Drop Procedure SQL Statement
-- Initialize Variables
SET @parameters = ''
SET @deleteStatement = ''
--Get Parameters and Delete Where Clause needed for the Delete Procedure.
SELECT @parameters = @parameters + Case When @parameters = '' Then ''
     Else ', ' + Char(13) + Char(10)
     End + '@' +  INFORMATION_SCHEMA.Columns.COLUMN_NAME + ' ' +
     DATA_TYPE +
     Case When CHARACTER_MAXIMUM_LENGTH is not null Then
     '(' + Cast(CHARACTER_MAXIMUM_LENGTH as varchar(4)) + ')'
      Else ''
     End,
  @deleteStatement = @deleteStatement + Case When @deleteStatement = '' Then ''
     Else ' AND ' + Char(13) + Char(10)
     End + INFORMATION_SCHEMA.Columns.COLUMN_NAME + ' = @' + + INFORMATION_SCHEMA.Columns.COLUMN_NAME
FROM INFORMATION_SCHEMA.Columns,
 INFORMATION_SCHEMA.TABLE_CONSTRAINTS,
 INFORMATION_SCHEMA.CONSTRAINT_COLUMN_USAGE
WHERE  INFORMATION_SCHEMA.TABLE_CONSTRAINTS.CONSTRAINT_NAME =
INFORMATION_SCHEMA.CONSTRAINT_COLUMN_USAGE.CONSTRAINT_NAME AND
 INFORMATION_SCHEMA.Columns.Column_name = INFORMATION_SCHEMA.CONSTRAINT_COLUMN_USAGE.Column_name AND
 INFORMATION_SCHEMA.Columns.table_name = INFORMATION_SCHEMA.TABLE_CONSTRAINTS.TABLE_NAME AND
 INFORMATION_SCHEMA.TABLE_CONSTRAINTS.table_name = @table_Name AND
 CONSTRAINT_TYPE = 'PRIMARY KEY'
-- the following logic can be changed as per your standards. In our case tbl is for tables and tlkp is
for lookup tables. Needed to remove tbl and tlkp...
SET @procedurename = 'Delete'
If Left(@table_Name, 3) = 'tbl'
Begin
 SET @procedurename = @procedurename + SubString(@table_Name, 4, Len(@table_Name))
End
```

```
Else
Begin
 If Left(@table_Name, 4) = 'tlkp'
 Begin
  SET @procedurename = @procedurename + SubString(@table_Name, 5, Len(@table_Name))
 End
 Else
 Begin
  -- In case none of the above standards are followed then just get the table name.
  SET @procedurename = @procedurename + @table_Name
 End
End
--Stores DROP Procedure Statement
SET @DropProcedure = 'if exists (select * from dbo.sysobjects where id = object_id(N''[dbo].[' +
@procedurename + ']'') and OBJECTPROPERTY(id, N''IsProcedure'') = 1)' + Char(13) + Char(10) +
    'Drop Procedure ' + @procedurename

-- In case you want to create the procedure pass in 0 for @print else pass in 1 and stored procedure
will be displayed in results pane.
If @print = 0
Begin
 -- Create the final procedure and store it..
 Exec (@DropProcedure)
 SET @SQLStatement = 'CREATE PROCEDURE ' + @procedurename +  Char(13) + Char(10) + @parameters + Char
(13) + Char(10) + ' AS ' +
     + Char(13) + Char(10) + ' Delete FROM ' + @table_Name + ' WHERE ' + @deleteStatement + Char(13) +
Char(10)
 -- Execute the SQL Statement to create the procedure

 Exec (@SQLStatement)
End
Else
Begin
 --Print the Procedure to Results pane
 Print ''
 Print ''
 Print ''
 Print '--- Delete Procedure for ' + @table_Name + '---'
 Print @DropProcedure
 Print 'GO'
 Print 'CREATE PROCEDURE ' + @procedurename
 Print @parameters
 Print 'As'
 Print 'DELETE FROM ' + @table_Name
 Print 'WHERE ' + @deleteStatement
 Print 'GO'
End
GO
```

Example 2: Building VB functions based on Stored Procedures created -

This example is specifically designed for DotNetNuke 2.0. The following Stored procedure will generate
function declaration for Data Access Layer for specific stored procedure. This function needs to be
overridden.

```
CREATE PROCEDURE prCreateDataProviderSubs
@TableName nvarchar(4000)
AS
Declare @routineName nvarchar(128), -- To Store Stored Procedure Name
 @functionname nvarchar(4000) -- Actual VB Function or Sub
-- As in our case, we are removing tbl and tlkp from Table Names when creating stored procedure.
SET @TableName = Replace(@TableName, '|tbl', '|')
SET @TableName = Replace(@TableName, '|tlkp', '|')
-- To loop through all Stored Procedures to create Subs and Functions.
Declare curRoutineName cursor For
SELECT  Routine_name
FROM  INFORMATION_SCHEMA.ROUTINES
WHERE  (CharIndex('|' + SubString(Routine_name, 4, Len(Routine_name)) + '|', @TableName) > 0 OR
 CharIndex('|' + SubString(Routine_name, 7, Len(Routine_name)) + '|', @TableName) > 0 OR
 CharIndex('|' + SubString(Routine_name, 10, Len(Routine_name)) + '|', @TableName) > 0)
Order by 1
Open curRoutineName
FETCH NEXT FROM curRoutineName INTO @routineName
WHILE @@FETCH_STATUS = 0
Begin
 If @routineName is not null AND @routineName <> ''
 Begin
  -- In case of Add, Get and GetSingle the routines might return something.
  If Left(@routineName, 3) = 'Add' OR Left(@routineName, 3) = 'Get'
   SET @functionname = 'Public MustOverride Function ' + @routineName + '('
```

```
   Else
     SET @functionname = 'Public MustOverride Sub ' + @routineName + '('
 End
 -- Get all the parameter information and build the parameter string for the function and sub.
 SELECT @functionname = @functionname + Case When Right(@functionname, 1) <> '(' Then ', '
       Else ''
       End +
       'ByVal ' + SubString(PARAMETER_NAME, 2, Len(PARAMETER_NAME)) + ' as ' +
       Case When DATA_TYPE = 'int' or DATA_TYPE = 'smallint' Then 'integer'
         When DATA_TYPE = 'nvarchar' or DATA_TYPE = 'Char' or DATA_TYPE = 'varchar' Then 'string'
         When DATA_TYPE = 'datetime' Then 'date'
         When DATA_TYPE = 'bit' Then 'boolean'
         Else 'object'
       End
 FROM INFORMATION_SCHEMA.PARAMETERS
 WHERE  Specific_name = @routineName
 -- In case of Add then the return is going to be integer. In case of Get or GetSingle the return
 value is going to be IDataReader
 If Left(@routineName, 3) = 'Add' OR Left(@routineName, 3) = 'Get'
 Begin
   If Left(@routineName, 3) = 'Add'
     SET @functionname = @functionname + ') as integer'
   Else
     SET @functionname = @functionname + ') as IDataReader'
 End
 Else
   -- In case of Update and Delete it is sub.
   SET @functionname = @functionname + ')'
 -- Print the function
 Print @functionname
 FETCH NEXT FROM curRoutineName INTO @routineName
 End
 Close curRoutineName
 Deallocate curRoutineName
```

References:

www.etekglobalinc.com - Free Downloads of Stored Procedure Generator and DNN Middle Tier Function Generator.

CodeSmith - Automatically build sprocs from templates using this free tool.

Stored Procedures vs. Triggers

By G Vijayakumar

Last time, I wrote an article that focused on Using SELECT, Views and Stored Procedures in SQL Server. I was quite glad to differentiate the three and the Pros & Cons. I did not even give much importance of Trigger, but not because of lack of TIME. To be honest, I was just a beginner in use of Triggers. In this article I decided to write about Triggers and its difference with Stored Procedure. We had a team meeting to incorporate the audit information in our organization.

After a few months, we had a debate to incorporate the audit information either in Stored Procedure or Trigger. In the meeting, the set of team member has suggested having audit statements in Triggers and another set of team member has recommended having audit statements in Stored Procedures. I was totally too confused to make a decision. Then, I told my team members to stop the debate. I requested my team members to involve in R&D for few days before coming to a conclusion and judge the Pros & Cons of the two. This is how the article has been born; to have audit information in our project. I devoted my influence to write an article on Stored ProcedureVsTrigger and to differentiate the two and the Pros & Cons.

So, how do I start! I decided to use some information from my previous article http://www.sql-server-performance.com/gv_sp_views_selects.asp. I have introduced the characters that would be involved in the article before the initiative. These characters would play important role in the article.

1. Syscacheobjects
2. DBCC FREEPROCCACHE
3. Stored Procedure

4. Trigger
5. Select
6. Create
7. Truncate
8. Insert
9. Exec and,
10. Drop

How do I incorporate my audit work for tables in my database? Should I use Stored Procedure or Trigger? This is "Sub-Title" for the article. I have divided this article into three parts to better explain this information. I created two virtual teams with a set of three members. Team A will work on Trigger and Team B will work on Stored Procedure. I have provided scripts and examples to both teams.

I will not explain the definition for Stored Procedure and Trigger. I would recommend you read the MS-SQL Server BOL definition for Stored Procedure and Trigger.

Introduction

To learn the differences between the Stored procedure and Trigger, I need to mention the syscacheobjects system table. It is used to store information about compiled objects and their execution plans. The reason for this is because compiled source are stored here, and I have used this table to experiment the article. I have used one more DBCC FREEPROCCACHE consultant in the article. This command clears the syscacheobjects table of any current cached objects.

I presume that you have rudiment knowledge in database and use of DDL and DML commands. If you do not have much knowledge on DDL and DML commands, this article will help you learn both the types of commands.

Now, let's create a table and input a few rows in the table before we commence at taking a look at the differences between the Stored Procedure and Trigger.

Create Sample Table

I assume you have a database you can use for this. If not, you will want to create one at this time. Now, we need to create a table for our experimentation.

```
Create Table DummyTable1
(
        EmpId Int,
        EmpName Varchar(8000)
)

Create Table DummyTable1_Audit
(
        EmpId Int,
        EmpName Varchar(8000),
        AuditFlag  Char (1)
)
```

Now, let's add a few records in this table using this script:

```
Insert Into DummyTable1 Values (1, Replicate ('a',20))
Insert Into DummyTable1_Audit Values (1, Replicate ('a',20), 'N')
GO
Insert Into DummyTable1 Values (2, Replicate ('b',20))
Insert Into DummyTable1_Audit Values (2, Replicate ('b',20), 'N')
GO
Insert Into DummyTable1 Values (3, Replicate ('c',20))
Insert Into DummyTable1_Audit Values (3, Replicate ('c',20), 'N')
GO
Insert Into DummyTable1 Values (4, Replicate ('d',20))
Insert Into DummyTable1_Audit Values (4, Replicate ('d',20), 'N')
GO
Insert Into DummyTable1 Values (5, Replicate ('e',20))
Insert Into DummyTable1_Audit Values (5, Replicate ('e',20), 'N')
GO
Insert Into DummyTable1 Values (6, Replicate ('f',20))
Insert Into DummyTable1_Audit Values (6, Replicate ('f',20), 'N')
GO
Insert Into DummyTable1 Values (7, Replicate ('g',20))
Insert Into DummyTable1_Audit Values (7, Replicate ('g',20), 'N')
GO
```

```
Insert Into DummyTable1 Values (8, Replicate ('h',20))
Insert Into DummyTable1_Audit Values (8, Replicate ('h',20), 'N')
GO
Insert Into DummyTable1 Values (9, Replicate ('i',20))
Insert Into DummyTable1_Audit Values (9, Replicate ('i',20), 'N')
GO
Insert Into DummyTable1 Values (10, Replicate ('j',20))
Insert Into DummyTable1_Audit Values (10, Replicate ('j',20), 'N')
GO
```

DummyTable1 and DummyTable1_Audit has contains sufficient rows.

SELECT Statement

Now, let's view the contents of the table by executing the following command in Query Analyzer for our new table.

```
SELECT EmpId, EmpName
 FROM DummyTable1
GO
```

EmpID	EmpName
1	aaaaaaaaaaaaaaaaaaaa
2	bbbbbbbbbbbbbbbbbbbb
3	Cccccccccccccccccccc
4	dddddddddddddddddddd
5	eeeeeeeeeeeeeeeeeeee
6	Ffffffffffffffffffff
7	gggggggggggggggggggg
8	hhhhhhhhhhhhhhhhhhhh
9	iiiiiiiiiiiiiiiiiiii
10	Jjjjjjjjjjjjjjjjjjjj

```
SELECT EmpId, EmpName, AuditFlag
FROM DummyTable1_Audit
GO
```

EmpID	EmpName	AuditFlag
1	aaaaaaaaaaaaaaaaaaaa	N
2	bbbbbbbbbbbbbbbbbbbb	N
3	cccccccccccccccccccc	N
4	dddddddddddddddddddd	N
5	eeeeeeeeeeeeeeeeeeee	N
6	Ffffffffffffffffffff	N
7	gggggggggggggggggggg	N
8	hhhhhhhhhhhhhhhhhhhh	N
9	iiiiiiiiiiiiiiiiiiii	N
10	Jjjjjjjjjjjjjjjjjjjj	N

As you would expect, the data we inserted earlier has been displayed.

Truncate Statement

Now, let's execute the following commands to clear the table. I have used "Truncate" statement instead of "Delete" because I do not want to rollback my data.

```
Truncate Table DummyTable1
```

```
Truncate Table DummyTable1_Audit
GO
```

Trigger using Insert Statement – Part I

Let us begin with the Trigger statement. I have created an Insert Trigger for audit work. I have divided the DML statement task in two objects, one using Trigger and another using direct INSERT statement using query analyser. Part I will focus on insert statement for DummyTable1 table using query analyzer and the audit work for DummyTable1_Audit table using trigger. Part I will not differentiate from stored procedure. Let's start to create the trigger.

```
CREATE TRIGGER TR_DummyTable1 ON DummyTable1 FOR INSERT AS

INSERT INTO DummyTable1_Audit
   SELECT *, 'N' FROM inserted
```

The Trigger has been created successfully. The trigger will execute automatically and insert a row in the DummyTable1_Audit table for every insert in the DummyTable1 table.

Now, let's execute the following commands to clear the cache.

```
DBCC FREEPROCCACHE
GO
```

Freeing the procedure cache prevents an ad-hoc SQL statement from being reused, assuming that it is currently in the cache. This means that the next time we run the same ad-hoc statement, that it must be newly recompiled.

I have selected three human beings from Team A. I have asked them to execute the insert statement for DummyTable1 using query analyzer. They have executed the insert statement in their own way.

Now, member I of team-A has executed the insert statement and following commands to display cache information for the trigger we created and that is now stored in SQL Server's syscacheobjects system table.

```
Insert Into DummyTable1
Values (1, Replicate ('a',20))
GO
SELECT cacheobjtype, refcounts, usecounts, sql
FROM master.dbo.syscacheobjects
GO
```

The result will display many columns but we are only interested in four of them, as shown below.

Cacheobjtype	Refcounts	Usecounts	Sql
Executable Plan	1	1	TR_DummyTable1
Compiled Plan	2	1	TR_DummyTable1

Here's what the information displayed means:

Cacheobjtype: The type of object stored in the cache, which can include:

- Compiled Plan
- Executable Plan
- Parse Tree
- Cursor Parse Tree
- Extended Stored Procedure

We will be concentrating mainly on the Compiled Plan and the Executable Plan cacheobjtype type objects.

Refcounts: Number of other cache objects referencing this cache object. A count of 1 is the base.

Usecounts: Number of times this cache object has been used since inception.

Sql: Text of the statement.

Now, let's execute the same INSERT statement with a different value and verify the result.

```
Insert Into DummyTable1 Values (2, Replicate ('b',20))
GO
SELECT cacheobjtype, refcounts, usecounts, sql
FROM master.dbo.syscacheobjects
GO
```

Cacheobjtype	Refcounts	Usecounts	Sql
Executable Plan	1	2	TR_DummyTable1
Compiled Plan	2	1	TR_DummyTable1

The value of **Usecounts** has been incremented. SQL Server has used the same compiled plan for the TR_DummyTable1 sql statement and incremented the **Usecounts** of the executable plan. N number user will use the same compiled plan when we execute the Trigger.

Member II of team-A has executed the insert statement with the username on the INSERT statement and following commands to display cache information.

```
Insert Into dbo.DummyTable1 Values (3, Replicate ('c',20))
GO
SELECT cacheobjtype, refcounts, usecounts, sql
FROM master.dbo.syscacheobjects
GO
```

Cacheobjtype	Refcounts	Usecounts	Sql
Executable Plan	1	3	TR_DummyTable1
Compiled Plan	2	1	TR_DummyTable1

No difference at all. SQL Server has used the same compiled plan for the stored procedure and incremented the **Usecounts** of the executable plan.

Member III of team-A has executed the insert statement with the database and username on the INSERT statement and following commands to display cache information.

```
Insert Into vijay.dbo.DummyTable1 Values (4, Replicate ('d',20))
GO
SELECT cacheobjtype, refcounts, usecounts, sql
FROM master.dbo.syscacheobjects
GO
```

Cacheobjtype	Refcounts	Usecounts	Sql
Executable Plan	1	4	TR_DummyTable1
Compiled Plan	2	1	TR_DummyTable1

No difference at all. SQL Server has used the same compiled plan for the trigger and incremented the **Usecounts** of the executable plan. Part I has explained one way to do audit work with two entities having one as "Trigger" and another as "Insert" statement using query analyzer. The INSERT statement could be written from different ways. It could be from a MS-SQL SERVER Job, MS-SQL SERVER DTS using VB Script, Application and using Query Analyzer. A different set of entities has incorporated the INSERT statement in different ways. How do we club these entities into one object? That's how Part II has cropped. Let us move on to Part II.

Trigger using Stored Procedure – Part II

I have experiment the last one using INSERT statement for DummyTable1 table in Query analyzer. I decided to incorporate the INSERT statement [DummyTable1 table] in stored procedure. A different set of entities will use INSERT statement in different ways. I clubbed those entities in a stored procedure to upgrade Network circulation.

I have created a stored procedure to encompass the INSERT statement for DummyTable1 table.

```
Create PROC spAddDummyTable1 (@EmpID Int, @EmpName Varchar(8000)) AS
Begin
```

```
Insert Into DummyTable1 Values (@EmpID, Replicate (@EmpName,20))

IF @@Error > 0
 Begin
        Return 1
 End
End

Return 0
```

Truncate Statement

Now, let's execute the following commands to clear the table. I have used "Truncate" statement instead of "Delete" because I do not want to rollback my data.

```
Truncate Table DummyTable1
Truncate Table DummyTable1_Audit
GO
```

Now, let's execute the following commands to clear the cache before the Trigger using stored procedure experiment.

```
DBCC FREEPROCCACHE
GO
```

I have selected three human beings from the same team. I have asked them to execute the spAddDummyTable1 using query analyzer. They have executed the spAddDummyTable1 stored procedure in their own way. Now, member I of team-A has execute the spAddDummyTable1 and following commands to display cache information for the table.

```
Exec spAddDummyTable1 1, 'a'
GO
SELECT cacheobjtype, refcounts, usecounts, sql
FROM master.dbo.syscacheobjects
GO
```

The result will display many columns, but we are only interested in four of them, as shown below.

Cacheobjtype	Refcounts	Usecounts	Sql
Executable Plan	1	1	TR_DummyTable1
Compiled Plan	2	1	TR_DummyTable1
Executable Plan	1	1	spAddDummyTable1
Compiled Plan	2	1	spAddDummyTable1

Now, Let's execute the same spAddDummyTable1 stored procedure with a different value and verify the result.

```
Exec spAddDummyTable1 2, 'b'
GO
SELECT cacheobjtype, refcounts, usecounts, sql
FROM master.dbo.syscacheobjects
GO
```

Cacheobjtype	Refcounts	Usecounts	Sql
Executable Plan	1	**2**	TR_DummyTable1
Compiled Plan	2	1	TR_DummyTable1
Executable Plan	1	**2**	spAddDummyTable1
Compiled Plan	2	1	spAddDummyTable1

The value of **Usecounts** has been incremented. SQL Server has used the same compiled plan for the TR_DummyTable1 and spAddDummyTable1 sql statement and incremented the **Usecounts** of the executable plan. N number user will use the same compiled plan when we execute the statement.

Member II of team-A has executed the spAddDummyTable1 stored procedure with the username on the stored procedure and following commands to display cache information.

```
Exec dbo.spAddDummyTable1 3, 'c'
GO
SELECT cacheobjtype, refcounts, usecounts, sql FROM master.dbo.syscacheobjects
GO
```

Cacheobjtype	Refcounts	Usecounts	Sql
Executable Plan	1	**3**	TR_DummyTable1
Compiled Plan	2	1	TR_DummyTable1
Executable Plan	1	**3**	spAddDummyTable1
Compiled Plan	2	1	spAddDummyTable1

No difference at all. SQL Server has used the same compiled plan for the stored procedure, trigger and incremented the **Usecounts** of the executable plan.

Member III of team-A has executed the spAddDummyTable1 stored procedure with the database and username on the stored procedure and following commands to display cache information.

```
Exec vijay.dbo.spAddDummyTable1 4, 'd'
GO
SELECT cacheobjtype, refcounts, usecounts, sql FROM master.dbo.syscacheobjects
GO
```

Cacheobjtype	Refcounts	Usecounts	Sql
Executable Plan	1	**4**	TR_DummyTable1
Compiled Plan	2	1	TR_DummyTable1
Executable Plan	1	**4**	spAddDummyTable1
Compiled Plan	2	1	spAddDummyTable1

No difference at all. SQL Server has used the same compiled plan for the trigger and incremented the **Usecounts** of the executable plan. We have finished the experiment for the last two parts. Let us move on to Stored Procedures – Part III.

Stored Procedures – Part III

Part I has executed different INSERT statement using Query analyzer and for every insert statement, trigger has been executed automatically for audit work. Part II has executed stored procedure using Query analyzer and for every execution, trigger has been executed automatically for audit work. I realized that why do we need two objects separately. I decided to club two objects into one. I have decided to drop the trigger and move the INSERT statement for both DummyTable1 & DummyTable1_Audit table in a stored procedure.

Now, let's execute the following commands before creating Stored procedure experiment. Drop the existing stored procedure using the following command.

```
Drop Proc spAddDummyTable1
GO
```

Drop the existing trigger using the following command.

```
Drop Trigger TR_DummyTable1
GO
```

Truncate Statement

Now, let's execute the following commands to clear the table. I have used "Truncate" statement instead of "Delete" because I do not want to rollback my data.

```
Truncate Table DummyTable1
Truncate Table DummyTable1_Audit
GO
```

Now, let's execute the following commands to clear the cache before the Trigger using stored procedure experiment.

```
DBCC FREEPROCCACHE
```

```
GO
```

We will create a stored procedure with two parameters, and see how it is differs from the Part I and Part II.

```
Create PROC spAddDummyTable1 (@EmpID Int, @EmpName Varchar(8000))
AS
Begin

Insert Into DummyTable1 Values (@EmpID, Replicate (@EmpName,20))

IF @@Error > 0
 Begin
        Return 1
 End

Insert Into DummyTable1_Audit (EmpID, EmpName, AuditFlag)
 Select EmpID, EmpName, 'N'
  From DummyTable1 Where EmpID = @EmpID

IF @@Error > 0
 Begin
        Return 1
 End

End

Return 0
```

I have selected three human beings from the Team B. I have asked them to execute the spAddDummyTable1 using query analyzer. They have executed the spAddDummyTable1-stored procedure in their own way.

Now, member I of team-B has execute the spAddDummyTable1 and following commands to display cache information for the spDummyTable1 we created.

```
EXEC spAddDummyTable1 1, 'a'
```
GO SELECT cacheobjtype, refcounts, usecounts, sql FROM master.dbo.Syscacheobjects GO

Cacheobjtype	Refcounts	Usecounts	Sql
Executable Plan	1	1	spAddDummyTable1
Compiled Plan	2	1	spAddDummyTable1

SQL Server displays the compiled and executable plan for the spAddDummyTable1 stored procedure. Let's execute the same stored procedure with a different parameter value and view the cache details.

```
EXEC spAddDummyTable1 2, 'b'
GO
SELECT cacheobjtype, refcounts, usecounts, sql
 FROM master.dbo.Syscacheobjects
GO
```

Cacheobjtype	Refcounts	Usecounts	Sql
Executable Plan	1	2	spAddDummyTable1
Compiled Plan	2	1	spAddDummyTable1

The value of **Usecounts** has been incremented. Although we have given different parameter value, SQL Server has used the same compiled plan for the stored procedure and incremented the **Usecounts** of the executable plan. N number user will use the same compiled plan when we execute the stored procedure.

Now, let us execute the stored procedure with the username and see the cache details. Member II of team-B has executed the spAddDummyTable1 stored procedure with the username with different value on the stored procedure and following commands to display cache information.

```
Exec dbo.spAddDummyTable1 3, 'c'
GO
SELECT cacheobjtype, refcounts, usecounts, sql FROM master.dbo.syscacheobjects
GO
```

Cacheobjtype	Refcounts	Usecounts	Sql
Executable Plan	1	3	spAddDummyTable1

Compiled Plan	2	1	spAddDummyTable1

No difference at all. SQL Server has used the same compiled plan for the stored procedure and incremented the **Usecounts** of the executable plan. Now, member III of Team B has executed the spAddDummyTable1 stored procedure with the database and username with different values on the stored procedure and following commands to display cache information.

```
Exec vijay.dbo.spAddDummyTable1 4, 'd'

GO
SELECT cacheobjtype, refcounts, usecounts, sql
 FROM master.dbo.syscacheobjects
GO
```

Cacheobjtype	Refcounts	Usecounts	Sql
Executable Plan	1	**4**	spAddDummyTable1
Compiled Plan	2	1	spAddDummyTable1

No difference at all. SQL Server has used the same compiled plan for the stored procedure and incremented the **Usecounts** of the executable plan.

Summary

All three parts have shown no difference in the article. Part I has executed different INSERT statement using Query Analyzer and for every insert statement, trigger has been executed automatically for audit work. Part II has executed stored procedure using Query analyzer and for every execution, trigger has been executed automatically for audit work. I realized that why we need two objects separately, I decided to club two objects into one. I have decided to drop the trigger and move the INSERT statement for both DummyTable1 & DummyTable1_Audit table in a stored procedure. Part III has executed stored procedure using Query analyzer that will INSERT a row in DummyTable1 & DummyTable1_Audit table.

Part I is not good for programmer practice to have an INSERT statement in different places. We will avoid using Part I method. The Part II and Part III method have differences. I would straight away recommend and conclude Part III is better than Part II method. You would start asking how and why? Let me derive in short note.

Part II and Part III both are applicable for Maintainability, Flexibility and Manual Intervention. I have created a DummyTable1 table. I should have audit work for every DML action for DummyTable1 table. I have created three trigger and stored procedure for Part II method. Insert, Update and Delete trigger and spAddDummyTable1, spUpdateDummyTable1 and spDeleteDummyTable1 stored procedure. Insert trigger will execute automatically and will insert a post row in DummyTable1_Audit table for every INSERT action DummyTable1 table via spAddDummyTable1stored procedure. Update trigger will execute automatically and will insert a pre and post row in DummyTable1_Audit table for every UPDATE action DummyTable1 table via spUpdateDummyTable1 stored procedure. Delete trigger will execute automatically and will insert a pre row in DummyTable1_Audit table for every DELETE action DummyTable1 table via spDeleteDummyTable1 stored procedure. We have created three trigger and stored procedure to do a set of DML action. It is expensive. Yes, I agree with your point. We have created, in total, six objects in our database. As you assume, I have a database that has hold 150 tables. I would be creating three sets of trigger and stored procedure object [150 * (3+3) = 900 objects] for tables in my database and we need manual intervention to execute the stored procedure to execute the trigger automatically.

Part III could have three stored procedures and contains DML statements. spAddDummyTable1, spUpdateDummyTable1 and spDeleteDummyTable1 stored procedure. spAddDummyTable1 contain the INSERT statement for DummyTable1 and post INSERT statement for DummyTable1_Audit table. spUpdateDummyTable1 contain the pre and post INSERT statement for DummyTable1_Audit table and UPDATE statement for DummyTable1 table. spDeleteDummyTable1 contain the pre INSERT statement for DummyTable1_Audit table and DELETE statement for DummyTable1 table. Part III has got only three objects. I have a database that holds 150 tables. I would be creating three sets of stored procedure object [150 * 3 = 450 objects] for tables in my database. Part III would have only manual intervention to execute the stored procedures. No automatic execution.

As you assume, we would be incorporating the same stored procedure [i.e. spUpdateDummyTable1] in more than one stored object [stored procedure]. As you assume, we have changed the signature of the stored procedure [i.e. spUpdateDummyTable1]. Maintenance work has to happen for the stored procedure in reference place and no difference in Part II and Part II. It has an impact on Maintenance work and Part II and Part III both are applicable for maintenance work. But, Flexibility is better in Part III comparatively to Part II because of less stored objects available in database. Part II and Part III both need Manual Intervention to executed the stored procedure.

Note: You should try the UPDATE and DELETE trigger and stored procedure yourself.

Performance

In almost every interview that a DBA is in, someone asks how they performance tune a system. While there are some stock answers, the tuning in SQL Server is mostly based on good design, enough hardware, and a few basic guidelines.

We've culled the articles that give us a few ideas on how you can evaluate and improve the performance of your system. Indexes and fragmentation are the key topics in this volume.

Analyzing Data Storage - Ten SHOWCONTIG Queries

By Joe Sack

DBCC SHOWCONTIG allows you to report on fragmentation information for the data and indexes of a specified table. If neither an index nor table is specified, DBCC SHOWCONTIG will report on all tables within the database. You can capture this output by adding "WITH TABLERESULTS" to the DBCC SHOWCONTIG call. SHOWCONTIG allows you to grab all sorts of useful information, so that you can report or act upon it with your Transact-SQL code. In this article, we will be reviewing how you can use Transact-SQL queries to probe your database's potential trouble areas...

Prerequisites: The basics of SHOWCONTIG are not reviewed here, and if you're in need of this background, check out SQL Server Books Online's topic "DBCC SHOWCONTIG".

Query #1 - List all the tables that don't have clustered indexes (excluding system tables).

Prior to running this first query, we first need to create the #SHOWCONTIG temporary table. This table will be used to hold the results of the DBCC SHOWCONTIG result set.

```
CREATE TABLE #SHOWCONTIG (
    ObjectName CHAR (255),
    ObjectId INT,
    IndexName CHAR (255),
    IndexId INT,
    Lvl INT,
    CountPages INT,
    CountRows INT,
    MinRecSize INT,
    MaxRecSize INT,
    AvgRecSize INT,
    ForRecCount INT,
    Extents INT,
    ExtentSwitches INT,
    AvgFreeBytes INT,
    AvgPageDensity INT,
    ScanDensity DECIMAL,
    BestCount INT,
    ActualCount INT,
    LogicalFrag DECIMAL,
    ExtentFrag DECIMAL)
```

Next, populate the #SHOWCONTIG table with all heaps and clustered indexes within the database you wish to analyze. (If you wish to report on all indexes within the database, add the ALL_INDEXES keyword to your DBCC SHOWCONTIG execution).

```
INSERT #ShowContig
EXEC ('DBCC SHOWCONTIG WITH TABLERESULTS')
```

Now we are ready to list all the tables that don't have clustered indexes (excluding system tables). Within the #ShowContig table, if a specific row has an index name, this means the row is for a clustered index. If the index name is blank, the row represents a heap (no clustered index).

```
SELECT  ObjectName,
        ObjectID
FROM    #ShowContig
WHERE   LEN(IndexName)=0 AND
        ObjectName NOT LIKE 'dt%' AND
        ObjectName NOT LIKE 'sys%'
ORDER BY ObjectName
```

For tables that appear in this result set, consider adding a clustered index. Some DBAs argue that it isn't necessary for all tables; however, I think that clustered indexes should be added by default - and only removed if you have a very good reason to do so.

Query #2 - Show the top ten tables with the most data pages (does not include non-clustered index pages).

```
SELECT   TOP 10
         ObjectName,
         IndexName,
         countpages
FROM     #ShowContig
WHERE    ObjectName NOT LIKE 'dt%' AND
         ObjectName NOT LIKE 'sys%'
ORDER BY  countpages DESC
```

This query is mostly for informational purposes. You may be surprised by the results.

Query #3 - Show the top ten tables with the highest row counts.

```
SELECT   TOP 10
         ObjectName,
         IndexName,
         CountRows
FROM     #ShowContig
WHERE    ObjectName NOT LIKE 'dt%' AND
         ObjectName NOT LIKE 'sys%'
ORDER BY  CountRows DESC
```

Once again, this query is mostly for informational purposes. If the row counts surprise you - investigate.

Query #4 - List the top ten tables with the largest average record size.

```
SELECT   TOP 10
         ObjectName,
         IndexName,
         AvgRecSize
FROM #ShowContig
WHERE    ObjectName NOT LIKE 'dt%' AND
         ObjectName NOT LIKE 'sys%'
ORDER BY  AvgRecSize DESC
```

The smaller the average record size, the more rows you can fit on a single page. The more you can fit on a page (assuming a high index fill factor), the fewer pages you have to read in order to fulfill the query requirements. In other words, smaller average record sizes mean less I/O.

If the average is high, see if all the table columns are being used, and that the column data types are appropriate.

Query #5 - List the top ten tables with the largest record sizes.

```
SELECT   TOP 10
         ObjectName,
         IndexName,
         MaxRecSize
FROM #ShowContig
WHERE    ObjectName NOT LIKE 'dt%' AND
         ObjectName NOT LIKE 'sys%'
ORDER BY  MaxRecSize DESC
```

Like the average record size, this query can help you determine which tables have at least one large row. Keep in mind that all it takes is ONE large row within a table to get on the top 10 of this list - so consider this in the context of the average row width. If you see tables falling into both lists (average row width and largest record size), see if all the table columns are being used, and that the column data types are appropriate.

Query #6 - Show the top ten tables with the highest average bytes free per page.

```
SELECT   TOP 10
         ObjectName,
         IndexName,
         AvgFreeBytes
FROM #ShowContig
WHERE    ObjectName NOT LIKE 'dt%' AND
         ObjectName NOT LIKE 'sys%'
ORDER BY  AvgFreeBytes DESC
```

Generally, the average bytes free value should be low, so investigate high values (for larger tables). "Low" and "high" are relative terms to your database , but be sure to check your index fill-factor. Is your index fill-factor too low? If you're not performing that many insert/update operations, consider increasing the fill-factor and rebuilding your indexes - thus decreasing I/O.

Query #7 - Show the top ten tables with the LOWEST average page density.

```
SELECT  TOP 10
        ObjectName,
        IndexName,
        AvgPageDensity
FROM #ShowContig
WHERE   ObjectName NOT LIKE 'dt%' AND
        ObjectName NOT LIKE 'sys%'
ORDER BY  AvgPageDensity ASC
```

Generally, average page density should be high. Investigate low densities (for larger tables) closely. If you determine that fragmentation is an issue, recreating/rebuilding the clustered index will reorganize the data, resulting in full data pages (depending on the index fill-factor). If rebuilding the indexes or using DBCC DBREINDEX is not possible (the index is offline during the drop/re-create cycle), consider the less effective DBCC INDEXDEFRAG.

Query #8 - List the top ten tables with the highest amount of logical fragmentation.

```
SELECT  TOP 10
        ObjectName,
        IndexName,
        logicalfrag
FROM #ShowContig
WHERE   ObjectName NOT LIKE 'dt%' AND
        ObjectName NOT LIKE 'sys%'
ORDER BY  logicalfrag DESC
```

Investigate larger tables that appear on this list. Like the previous query, if you determine that fragmentation is an issue, adjust the fill-factor if necessary, recreate/rebuild the clustered index or execute the less effective DBCC INDEXDEFRAG.

Query #9 - List the top ten tables with the highest extent fragmentation.

```
SELECT  TOP 10
        ObjectName,
        IndexName,
        ExtentFrag
FROM #ShowContig
WHERE   ObjectName NOT LIKE 'dt%' AND
        ObjectName NOT LIKE 'sys%'
ORDER BY   ExtentFrag DESC
```

Extent fragmentation should be as low as possible. Investigate larger tables that appear on this list. Like the previous query, if you determine that fragmentation is an issue, recreate/rebuild the clustered index or execute the less effective DBCC INDEXDEFRAG.

Query #10 - List the top ten tables with the lowest scan density.

```
SELECT  TOP 10
        ObjectName,
        IndexName,
        ScanDensity
FROM #ShowContig
WHERE   ObjectName NOT LIKE 'dt%' AND
        ObjectName NOT LIKE 'sys%'
ORDER BY    ScanDensity ASC
```

Scan density should be as high as possible. If low, consider recreating/rebuilding the clustered index or executing the less effective DBCC INDEXDEFRAG.

Conclusion

After examining the output from #ShowContig, don't forget to issue a "DROP TABLE #ShowContig" as a final step.

```
DROP TABLE #SHOWCONTIG
```

Use these ten queries to get to know your database better. You may be surprised by what you find. For example: gigantic tables that you were not aware of, tables without clustered indexes, tables with wide row lengths, and tables with significant fragmentation.

Run these queries periodically to help manage both the size of your database and the performance of your queries.

Checking Your Database Fragmentation Level

By Nicholas Cain

There are a lot of posts on the site regarding index fragmentation and possible ways to deal with this. You could certainly use the Database Maintenance Plans built into SQL Server to handle your re-indexing needs; however, frequently you want something a little more directed than the catch-all solution provided by the maintenance plan.

In this article I will take you through the steps of building a dts package to run either on an ad-hoc or scheduled basis that goes out to your databases to grab the index fragmentation levels and email you a script to run to defrag those indexes that are fragmented beyond the level that you select. As a part of the dts it will archive the index information to archive tables so that you can go back over time and trend the fragmentation, which will allow you to investigate possible changes to the fill factor that you are using.

Creating the Database Objects

First things first, we are going to need a database to hold the information if you already have a database for this purpose. Otherwise, we'll create one and call in AdminDB.

CREATE DATABASE ADMINDB
In this database we are going to create four tables:

1. Index_Info_Northwind to hold the information from each database that we want to check. The table columns match the output columns from a DBCC SHOWCONTIG with two additional columns (with default values) to hold the database name and the current date. For the sake of this article we are going to use the Northwind database. Change the suffix of the table to match the database from which you want to capture the results.
2. DefragText to hold the text of the DBCC DBREINDEX statements when they are created.
3. Index_Info_Daily to hold the list of indexes that we will be creating the re-index script for (population of this table will be based upon criteria specified later).
4. Index_Info_Archive to hold historical index data. This will allow trending of indexes to see their fragmentation over time, helping you to decide on fill factors that might need to be changed or to allow you to alter the job schedule to fit better with the amount of fragmentation that occurs within your databases.

```
USE ADMINDB
GO
CREATE TABLE [INDEX_INFO_NORTHWIND] (
        [dbname] [varchar] (50) NOT NULL CONSTRAINT [DF_DB] DEFAULT ('NORTHWIND'),
        [ObjectName] [varchar] (50) NULL ,          [ObjectId] [int] NULL ,
        [IndexName] [varchar] (100) NULL ,          [IndexId] [int] NULL ,
        [Lvl] [int] NULL ,          [CountPages] [int] NULL ,
        [CountRows] [int] NULL ,          [MinRecSize] [int] NULL ,
        [MaxRecSize] [int] NULL ,          [AvgRecSize] [int] NULL ,
        [ForRecCount] [int] NULL ,          [Extents] [int] NULL ,
```

```
            [ExtentSwitches] [int] NULL ,          [AvgFreeBytes] [int] NULL ,
            [AvgPageDensity] [int] NULL ,          [ScanDensity] [decimal](9, 0)  NULL ,
            [BestCount] [int] NULL ,         [ActualCount] [int] NULL ,
            [LogicalFrag] [decimal](9, 0) NULL ,  [ExtentFrag] [decimal](9, 0) NULL ,
            [CAPTURE_DATE] [datetime] NULL CONSTRAINT [DF_DATE] DEFAULT (getdate())
        )
  ON [PRIMARY]
GO
CREATE TABLE [dbo].[DEFRAGTEXT] (
        [THETEXT] [varchar] (2000) COLLATE SQL_Latin1_General_CP1_CI_AS NULL
)
  ON [PRIMARY]
GO
CREATE TABLE [dbo].[INDEX_INFO_DAILY] (
        [dbname] [varchar] (50) COLLATE SQL_Latin1_General_CP1_CI_AS NULL ,
        [ObjectName] [varchar] (50) COLLATE SQL_Latin1_General_CP1_CI_AS NULL ,
        [ObjectId] [int] NULL ,
        [IndexName] [varchar] (100) COLLATE SQL_Latin1_General_CP1_CI_AS NULL ,
        [IndexId] [int] NULL ,       [Lvl] [int] NULL ,
        [CountPages] [int] NULL ,        [CountRows] [int] NULL ,
        [MinRecSize] [int] NULL ,        [MaxRecSize] [int] NULL ,
        [AvgRecSize] [int] NULL ,        [ForRecCount] [int] NULL ,
        [Extents] [int] NULL ,        [ExtentSwitches] [int] NULL ,
        [AvgFreeBytes] [int] NULL ,    [AvgPageDensity] [int] NULL ,
        [ScanDensity] [decimal](9, 0) NULL ,
        [BestCount] [int] NULL ,        [ActualCount] [int] NULL ,
        [LogicalFrag] [decimal](9, 0) NULL ,        [ExtentFrag] [decimal](9, 0) NULL ,
        [CAPTURE_DATE] [datetime] NOT NULL ,      [THEID] [int] IDENTITY (1, 1) NOT NULL
)
  ON [PRIMARY]
GO
CREATE TABLE [dbo].[INDEX_INFO_ARCHIVE] (
        [DBNAME] [varchar] (50) COLLATE SQL_Latin1_General_CP1_CI_AS NULL ,
        [OBJECTNAME] [varchar] (50) COLLATE SQL_Latin1_General_CP1_CI_AS NULL ,
        [INDEXNAME] [varchar] (100) COLLATE SQL_Latin1_General_CP1_CI_AS NULL ,
        [SCANDENSITY] [decimal](9, 0) NULL ,
        [CAPTURE_DATE] [datetime] NULL
)
  ON [PRIMARY]
GO
CREATE CLUSTERED INDEX [INDEX_INFO_ARCHIVE_OBJECTNAME] ON [dbo].[INDEX_INFO_ARCHIVE]([OBJECTNAME])
  ON [PRIMARY]
GO
```

Next we'll need a stored procedure to do the work of pulling the showcontig results into the table.

```
SET QUOTED_IDENTIFIER ON
GO
SET ANSI_NULLS ON
GO
CREATE PROCEDURE USP_DBshowcontig_single_db @name varchar(50)
AS
SET NOCOUNT ON

DECLARE @tablename VARCHAR (128)
DECLARE @dbname VARCHAR(20)
DECLARE @sql VARCHAR(1000)
DECLARE @inserttable VARCHAR(3200)

-- Create the table
CREATE TABLE #DBFRAGMENT (
    ObjectName VARCHAR (50), ObjectId INT,
    IndexName VARCHAR (100), IndexId INT,
    Lvl INT,                 CountPages INT,
    CountRows INT,           MinRecSize INT,
    MaxRecSize INT,          AvgRecSize INT,
    ForRecCount INT,         Extents INT,
    ExtentSwitches INT,      AvgFreeBytes INT,
    AvgPageDensity INT,      ScanDensity DECIMAL,
    BestCount INT,           ActualCount INT,
    LogicalFrag DECIMAL,     ExtentFrag DECIMAL)

create table #tablename (table_name varchar(400))

--DECLARE DB Cursor
DECLARE databases CURSOR FOR
  SELECT NAME
   FROM MASTER.DBO.SYSDATABASES
   WHERE NAME = @NAME
```

```
--Open the cursor
OPEN databases
FETCH NEXT FROM databases INTO @dbname

WHILE @@FETCH_STATUS = 0
 BEGIN
   set @sql = 'SELECT TABLE_NAME = NAME FROM ' + @dbname + '..SYSOBJECTS WHERE XTYPE =' + '''' + 'U' +
''''
   print @sql
   insert into #tablename exec(@sql)
   -- Declare cursor
   DECLARE tables CURSOR FOR
        SELECT TABLE_NAME
           FROM #tablename
   -- Open the cursor
   OPEN tables
   -- Loop through all the tables in the database
   FETCH NEXT FROM tables INTO @tablename
   WHILE @@FETCH_STATUS = 0
    BEGIN
       PRINT @TABLENAME
       -- Do the showcontig of all indexes of the table
       INSERT INTO #DBFRAGMENT
       EXEC ('USE ' + @dbname + ' DBCC SHOWCONTIG (''' + @tablename + ''') WITH TABLERESULTS,
ALL_INDEXES, NO_INFOMSGS')
       FETCH NEXT FROM tables INTO @tablename
    END
  set @inserttable ='INSERT INTO ADMINDB.DBO.INDEX_INFO_'+@NAME+'(ObjectName,
     ObjectId, IndexName, IndexId, Lvl, CountPages, CountRows,
     MinRecSize, MaxRecSize, AvgRecSize, ForRecCount, Extents, ExtentSwitches,
     AvgFreeBytes, AvgPageDensity, ScanDensity, BestCount, ActualCount,
     LogicalFrag, ExtentFrag)

  select ObjectName, ObjectId, IndexName, IndexId, Lvl, CountPages, CountRows,
     MinRecSize, MaxRecSize, AvgRecSize, ForRecCount, Extents, ExtentSwitches,
     AvgFreeBytes, AvgPageDensity, ScanDensity, BestCount, ActualCount, LogicalFrag,
     ExtentFrag
  FROM #DBFRAGMENT where ltrim(rtrim(#DBFRAGMENT.indexname))<> ''''

   --PRINT @INSERTTABLE
   EXEC (@inserttable)

   -- Close and deallocate the cursor
   CLOSE tables
   DEALLOCATE tables
   delete from #tablename
   delete from #DBFRAGMENT

   FETCH NEXT FROM databases INTO @dbname
 END

CLOSE databases
DEALLOCATE databases
drop table #tablename
--Delete the temporary table
DROP TABLE #DBFRAGMENT
GO
SET QUOTED_IDENTIFIER OFF
GO
SET ANSI_NULLS ON
GO
```

We will create one more procedure; this one will do the work of pulling the data from the Index_Information table and making it into a reindex statement that can be run or exported to a text file for execution later. The script as stands will re-index the tables as you go along, to prevent this comment out the line "exec (@sql)".

```
SET QUOTED_IDENTIFIER ON
GO
SET ANSI_NULLS ON
GO
CREATE PROCEDURE USP_Create_Reindex_Script
AS

SET ARITHABORT ON
DECLARE @DBNAME VARCHAR(50),
        @OBJECTNAME VARCHAR(100),
        @INDEXNAME VARCHAR(100),
```

```
      @SQL VARCHAR(2000),
      @THEID INT

SELECT @THEID = MIN(THEID) FROM INDEX_INFO_DAILY WHERE THEID > 0

WHILE @THEID IS NOT NULL
 BEGIN
   SELECT @DBNAME = DBNAME FROM INDEX_INFO_DAILY WHERE THEID = @THEID
   SELECT @OBJECTNAME = OBJECTNAME FROM INDEX_INFO_DAILY WHERE THEID = @THEID
   SELECT @INDEXNAME = INDEXNAME FROM INDEX_INFO_DAILY WHERE THEID = @THEID

   SET @SQL = 'USE '+@DBNAME+'; DBCC DBREINDEX ('+@OBJECTNAME+','+@INDEXNAME+',80);'
   INSERT INTO DEFRAGTEXT(THETEXT) VALUES (@SQL)
   exec(@sql) --Comment out if you don't want to automate the reindex

   SELECT @THEID = MIN(THEID) FROM INDEX_INFO_DAILY WHERE THEID > 0 AND THEID > @THEID
 END
GO
```

Creating the DTS Package

Now we have all of the objects it's time to create the package. It will be laid out as shown below.

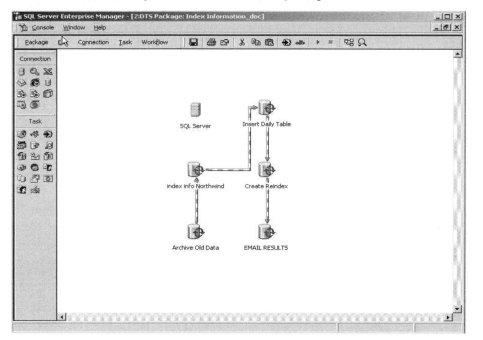

Firstly, you will need to make the connection to your SQL Server, make the default database whatever you are using. In our example here it's AdminDB, then we go through the steps:

1. "Archive Old Data" – This takes the previous days data from the Index_Info_Daily table and inserts it into the Index_Info_Archive table.

```
INSERT INTO INDEX_INFO_ARCHIVE
  SELECT
    DBNAME, OBJECTNAME, INDEXNAME, SCANDENSITY, CAPTURE_DATE
  FROM INDEX_INFO_DAILY
```

2. "Index Info Northwind" – Executes the procedure USP_DBshowcontig_single_db and passes the database name as a parameter (in this case Northwind).

```
EXEC USP_DBshowcontig_single_db 'Northwind'
```

3. "Insert Daily Table" – This truncates the daily table (removing yesterdays entries) and inserts the data for today based upon set criteria. In this case we are just inserting those objects with a scan density of less than 75% and that have more than 5000 rows.

```
TRUNCATE TABLE INDEX_INFO_DAILY
GO
INSERT INTO INDEX_INFO_DAILY
  SELECT * FROM INDEX_INFO_NORTHWIND
    WHERE CAPTURE_DATE > DATEADD (HOUR, -12, GETDATE())
    AND SCANDENSITY < 75
    AND COUNTROWS > 5000
GO
```

4. "Create Reindex" – This truncates the DefragText table, then executes the USP_Create_Reindex_Script which populates the DefragText table with the new reindex script and (if you have not uncommented that section of the procedure) will also reindex those objects inserted into Index_Info_Daily in the previous step.

```
TRUNCATE TABLE DEFRAGTEXT
GO
EXEC USP_CREATE_REINDEX_SCRIPT
GO
```

5. "Email Results" – This just uses xp_sendmail to send out the reindex script in an email allowing you to run it manually should you not wish to use the automated reindex functionality (which you should not do initially until you are confident of the impact that the reindex will have upon your server and the potential impact to users).

```
Exec master..xp_sendmail @recipients = 'recipient@email.com',
  @subject = 'Database Reindex Script',
  @query = 'SELECT * FROM ADMINDB.DBO.DEFRAGTEXT'
```

Further Enhancements

This is the basic package; it can be spruced up a lot and more functionality added. For example, you can add as many databases as you like, just add another table for each one and repeat step 2 of the DTS package for each one, remembering to include those tables in the insert in step 3. The script created will change databases as it needs to, so the single reindex script is as simple as copying the text from the email into query analyzer and hitting F5.

Currently, on my servers I am running this against 30 databases on a nightly basis and having the script automatically reindex. As I have few, if any, users overnight this is not a problem for me; however, you should make sure that you are not impacting users when you do this.

I am also running a data pump to put the object information into an excel spreadsheet, which then gets emailed to my manager and a couple of the development staff. While it's not a complete trending report, it does serve to identify some problem indexes.

You might want to add some kind of advanced reporting functionality into this at a later point to show the trend of the indexes. I've used this in the past for a couple of indexes that were showing up on an almost nightly basis, where I changed the fill factor on those indexes and now weeks go by before I see them appear in the report again.

If there are any enhancements you would like me to add, or functionality that you would like to see improved let me know, or if you come up with an improvement please 'share the wealth'.

Nicholas Cain - April 2004

Index Creation Guidelines

By Leo Peysakhovich

Often times index placement is a confusing task for many SQL Server developers. We all have been told that indexes do boost performance. The problem is how to select the ideal type of index, the number of columns to index, which columns should be indexed, and how to answer all these questions without using query analysis tools.

Not many people recognize the fact that indexes can cause a certain degree of performance degradation. Yes, indexes indeed can contribute to decreased database responsiveness if inappropriately selected. There are a lot of articles that tell developers how to analyze queries, how to use query execution plans, the SQL Server profiler, etc., at the time when the query is being defined. But what do you need to do as developer if it is not clear what kind of queries the application(s) will be using or is already using? What if there are a number of various applications accessing the database?

Is there any reasonable rule of thumb, some general index creation guidelines, that will allow to come up with indexes disposition simply by looking at the database layout? And what about those numerous cases when a developer is not designing a database but adding a few new tables and/or a few new columns to existing tables? Let's try to look at some examples and establish basic rules where indexes are useful and where they are useless. I will try to summarize some ideas from various sources and add my own experience from the development, architecture, and DBA prospective. And let's remember that these rules are approximate and may not work properly in all cases, but, based on my experience and my students' experience, they point to the right direction and work in 80-90% of all cases. (Besides working as an Architect and DBA, I am teaching courses in 'Database design and development' and 'Application design and development'). Remember, as well, that these guidelines are geared toward developers when they have limited knowledge about potential queries and applications.

There are 2 types of indexes: clustered and non-clustered. Without going in-depth discussion about differences between indexes, let's just note that a clustered index is the actual data. Rows are stored in index order. This means you can have only one clustered index per table, because rows can have only one physical order. Non-clustered indexes are pointer to data: the physical order of rows bears no relationship to a non-clustered index.

The Main Rule: every table should have a clustered index! It will make table maintenance easier and keep data stored in index order. Plus, a clustered index is the faster than a non-clustered. The primary key for a table should not always be a clustered index. If you create the primary key and don't specify otherwise, then SQL Server automatically makes the primary key a clustered index.

In most cases a unique column or a set of columns are good candidates for the clustered index. Do not try to place a clustered index on a column that can be updated or in the table were the INSERT is a frequently issued command and clustered index column is randomly defined. It will force the engine to physically rearrange pages allocated for the table, which will slow the system down. In a lot of cases, identity column can be subject for clustered index given the lack of a better candidate.

For example:

```
create table test (callerid char(5), name varchar(50)
   , address varchar(50), recordnum int identity(1,1)
      )
```

Column recordnum is a good choice for the clustered index. If the business rule for the callerid values is the sequence of characters following a pattern: 'AAAA[A-Z]', then callerid can be a candidate for the clustered index. If callerid can be any combination of characters and the table can grow rapidly (for telemarketing company, for example, 10,000 to 50,000 callers a day is a normal growth rate) then the field should not be clustered index.

Where indexes should be used ?

- Primary keys. As mentioned above, if you create the primary key and don't specify otherwise, then SQL Server automatically makes the primary key a clustered index. It is true in most cases. What are situations when it may not be true?

For example, the database has the following tables:

```
Create table notes ( noteid int not null PRIMARY KEY
      , userid varchar(50), notedt datetime, siteno char(5)
      )

Create table note_text (noteid int not null
      , seqno int not null, notetext varchar(8000)
      )
```

Primary key is the combination of noteid and seqno. What is the most likely way for the note's text to be retrieved or the table note_text to be joined with the table notes? By noteid column, right?

```
select notetext FROM note_text
 WHERE noteid = 10
 ORDER BY noteid, seqno
```

So, indexing of both columns is not necessary and (even it will be created as a part of the primary key constraint) a developer can redefine the index only to use noteid column in table note_text.

- Foreign keys defined by a foreign key constraint or logical foreign keys that may not be defined by constraint but will be used in table join.

For example:

```
Create table address (address_id int Primary Key, address_1 varchar(50), state char(2), zip char(5))

Create table orders (ordered int primary key, main_address_id int, location int)
```

main_address_id may be setup with foreign key constraint to address table and location is not. But location, according to business rules, logically refers to an address. Then location will be used in the table join to get an address and is the subject for an index creation.

- Index columns often used for a search query, grouping or sort purposes.

How one does identifies such columns if there are no queries or applications yet? Let's examine some examples of such prediction. Check out the previous example for note tables. It is easy to predict that people may often want to look up notes by a specific site number and not so often by userid. _By knowing the business of your company_, most search fields can be predicted easily. If a table keeps some personal information, the prediction process can tell us that social security number or phone number will be a searchable field in a lot of situations (phone number field(s) design can vary and it will impact your index decision). In a lot of cases it is very easy make a reasonable prediction about 85-90% of searchable criteria.

Now let's determine cases where indexes most likely should not be created. And this is the most interesting part.

Where indexes should not be used

- If a column in a table is not at least 80 - 85% unique values, then most likely the SQL Server Query Optimizer will not use a non-clustered index based on that column.

For example: index on column gender with values 'M', 'F', and NULL is not a subject for the index creation. The same rule can be applied to the flag and status columns with 5-6 different values.

- Do not create index on free form text columns.

Columns such as comment, name, address, legal name, and so on are considered free form columns. In general, almost any column with data type varchar to text can be considered as a free form text column. I have seen developers making flag columns with varchar(1) data type or social security number as varchar (50) but we are not talking about poor database design.

- Small tables (30 – 300 rows or about 10K of data)

In most cases such tables require 1 index for the primary key (most likely clustered) and most lookup tables like state, status_code_description are falling into this category.

- Do not create more indexes than is required.

Some developers think that the more indexes that are created, the better the performance. It doesn't work that way. An index can speed up data access, but it can also degrade performance for INSERT, UPDATE, or DELETE because SQL Server must maintain indexes every time. And if you determine that five or more indexes are required, then it may be time to stop and revisit your indexes design. Ideally, especially initially, you want to define as few indexes as possible. It is often a balancing act to select the ideal number of indexes for a table in order to find optimal performance. And don't automatically add indexes to a table because it seems like the right thing to do. Try to make an educated guess but remember that it is quite easy to make a guess, create indexes, and then later find out that guesses were wrong.

- Composite index is only useful for a query when the WHERE clause of the query matches the column(s) that are leftmost in the index. If the index has been created for the columns (address_id, address_type) but the query is using only address_type the index will not be used by Query Optimizer. Basically saying, it is very difficult to guess properly for the composite index without seeing the actual queries.

- Do not create duplicate indexes.

For example: index created for the columns noteid , seqno (see table note_text above). And then another index on the column noteid is created. Second index is the duplicate for the first one because Query Optimizer will use noteid from the first index when only one is created. So, the only one more appropriate index should be created. And, as it was discussed above, it may be the index on single column noteid.

- In most cases an index for datetime column is not required (and may be a bad idea as well). So do not create it until you know and test your query. If the search will use a datetime function in 'where' clause or some conversion mechanism, most likely the index will not be used by the Query Optimizer but performance will suffer.

Basically saying, the part '**Where indexes should not be used** ' may help you not only with index design, but with existing index analysis to get rid of some unnecessary indexes. I was doing the index analysis for one of my clients' database that had about 15G of space occupied by 247 indexes. After preliminary analysis, without even looking at the queries used by applications in database, I was able to drop more than 70 indexes, increase performance, and release 6G of wasted hard drive space.

Conclusion

Indexing can be quite a challenging task if you are not familiar with your databases, the relationships between tables, etc.. You must know the type of queries that will be run against your data, and then these need to be analyzed to determine the most appropriate indexes. In some cases a DBA should determine if fillfactor for an index should be setup differently from the default value, and some other factors could be examined when necessary. Only after all those steps the indexes must be created and tested to see if they any help.

This article, while not pretending to be 100% accurate for the final index definition in all situations, provides basics for the index definition while designing the database tables without resorting to some deep query analysis tools.

Indexing Strategies

By Ramesh Gummadi

Introduction

When we run a query, the choice of whether to use an index or not is decided by the query optimizer. Using appropriate indexes on tables so that the query optimizer chooses the most efficient strategy can yield significant performance gains. We will try to examine a few scenarios to familiarize ourselves with the way indexes are used to retrieve data and also try to figure out which index, clustered or non clustered, is good on each occasion.

Let us create a sample table so that we can use it for our purpose.

```
CREATE TABLE MEMBERS
( member_number    INT NOT NULL,
  account_number   INT NOT NULL,
  member_SSN       INT  NOT NULL,
  account_balance  MONEY NOT NULL,
  member_name      VARCHAR(30) NOT NULL,
  member_address   VARCHAR(60) NOT NULL )
```

We will use a number of scenarios here.

Retrieving a single row from the members table

Select account_balance from members where member_number = 9000

Let us say there is a **clustered index on the member_number column**.

SQL Server will first obtain the page number of the root page of the index from the sysindexes table. Then it will traverse through the index pages looking for a key value that is not greater than the current key value. In a clustered index the index consists of index key and a pointer which is the Page ID. So just one level above the leaf level it gets the page pointer to the data page holding the particular row and it scans the data page for the row containing the key.

Let us say there is a **non clustered index on the member_number column**.

In case of a non clustered index, too, the traversal works in a similar manner; the pointer to the key value we want to retrieve is found in the leaf level which is the Row ID of the data row. Using the Row ID sql server pulls the data row. The difference here is the non clustered index has one more logical read. The performance difference is very less between the two indexes here.

Retrieving a range of rows

Select account_balance from members where member_number between 9000 and 10000

In case of a **clustered index on member_number column** sql server will look again for the highest key value not greater than the lowest key we wish to retrieve. It will traverse through the index and will find the data page that contains the lowest key value, which is 9000 in our case. It scans the data page for 9000 and when it finds it, it then retrieves the rows sequentially until it reaches 10000, as we know in a clustered index the data rows are in arranged in the same order as the clustered index key.

In case of a **non clustered index on member_number column** the traversal of the index happens in a similar way. But once the leaf level is reached and the key value is found, the index entry contains the Row ID of the data row to be found which in this case will be the Row ID for member_number 9000. Using this Row ID, sql server will pull the data page holding that row. In a similar way it has to pull all the other rows for member_numbers between 9001 and 10000. We have to note a difference here. The key values are in sequence in a non clustered index, but the data pages are not. Let us say we have 50 rows satisfying the query and approximately 10 rows are present in each data page. So sql server has to retrieve the 50 rows in 50/10 = 5 logical reads to the data pages using a clustered index and sql server will need 50 logical reads to the data pages using non clustered index. This is a significant performance difference.

So it is always better to create a clustered index when we are accessing a range of rows.

Covered queries

Select account_balance from members where member_number between 9000 and 10000

Same query as before, but this time let us say that the members table has a **composite non clustered index on member_number and account_balance columns**. The query is called a covered query since the items in the where clause and select clause belong to the index. The query optimizer will realize that this is a covered query. In this case the sql server does not have to go to data level to work on the query. It can find the results in the leaf level of the non clustered index. It traverses the index based on the member_number and when it reaches the leaf level , it finds the account_balance information next to it in the key itself without having to access the data page through the pointer.

Let us say there are 500 rows that satisfy this query and there are 100 index entries per data page. So to get the results, sql server has to do 5 logical reads of data pages. This is more efficient than having a clustered index on the member_number column since we do not have to access data pages at all.

So, sometimes a covered non clustered index is more efficient than an equivalent clustered index.

Retrieving rows with clustered index and non clustered index on the table

Select account_balance from members where member_number between 9000 and 10000

Here we will examine a different scenario where there is a **non clustered index on the member_number**

column and **clustered index on the account_number column**. The main thing to note here is that the members table will now have leaf level index entries containing the clustered index key as a pointer instead of Row ID when there is no clustered index on the table. So in order to access the data rows, sql server has to traverse through the clustered index. In our example in order access row with member_number 9000, sql server will traverse through the non clustered index and in the leaf level it will find the index entry for 9000 having a clustered index key which will be the account_number. Based on this account_number it traverses through the clustered index and finds the data row. Suppose we have 100 rows to fetch; we have to access the clustered index 100 times to fetch the data pages containing the rows.

This is very inefficient and probably the query optimizer will choose a table scan instead of an index scan. In the same scenario let us change the query and execute the following query.

Select account_number from members where member_number between 9000 and 10000

So sql server will traverse through the non clustered index as before until the leaf level where it finds the clustered index key which is the account_number in this case. So sql server need not go fetch the data pages traversing through the clustered index again, since it found the member_number and account_number side by side in its index entries. So the query optimizer will choose the index scan since it is very efficient in this case.

Retrieving rows with multiple non clustered indexes on the table

Select * from members where account_balance between 500 and 5000 and member_number between 9000 and 9500

Let us say there is a **non clustered index on account_balance column and another non clustered index on the member_number column** without any clustered index on the table. In this case the query optimizer can use both the indexes. Since there is no clustered index, the leaf level of the indexes has Row IDs as pointers to the rows. So the query optimizer examines both indexes and gets the sets of Row IDs that match the given selection.Then it gets the intersection of both the sets of Row IDs. So instead of pulling the individual data pages, the query optimizer first gets a result set of all the RowIDs that match both the criteria. Based on how many rows satisfy the condition it estimates whether to make use of the indexes or to do a table scan to retrieve the rows. Let us say there are 100 rows that satisfy this query and there are 10,000 rows spread over 500 data pages (20 rows per page) in the table. It may be efficient to use the index scan and do 100 logical reads to get the data pages than scanning all the 500 data pages.

Conclusion

The decision of the query optimizer depends on the cost it would incur, or in other words, how many logical or physical reads it has to do to retrieve the result of a query. Hopefully these different scenarios will help a little bit in better understanding the usage of indexes by query optimizer.

Any comments are welcome.

References

Microsoft SQL Server 2000 Performance Optimization and Tuning Hand Book by Ken England.

Security

Security, it seems, is in the news constantly these days. Viruses, spyware, phishing, and the every increasing and more creative exploits ensure that anyone in the IT business must be constantly on their toes.

But how do you build a secure SQL Server? In SQL Server 2000, the security model would not be called robust. Functional and easy to understand, but hardly a bulletproof vault of data.

We bring you a collection of articles on various parts of the SQL Server security subsystem. Passwords, ports, encryption and using an anti-virus program on your server are the most interesting articles from this period in SQLServerCentral.com's history.

How to Make Sure You Have Good Passwords

By Robin Back

As many articles have covered, SQL passwords are very easy to figure out. SQL passwords are stored in the sysxlogins table in master database. To access this table you have to be a member of the fixed role sysadmin or sysadministrator. Still, there are programs out there that use the lack of SQL accounts lockout to hack a password. What can we do to prevent this or at least make it harder for them?

Log logins

When performing an installation of SQL server, you will be asked to use SQL Server and/or Windows authentication; default it is set only to Windows authentication. Even though you choose not to allow SQL logins, this is not that hard to change in the registry and then allow SQL accounts to login as well. There is always at least one SQL account to hack - **sa**.

If you change to do some type of log of logins, you will have a fair chance to trace someone trying to hack your SQL server through a SQL password. To change so that SQL server log logins in the errorlog you right-click on the server in SQL Server Enterprise Manager and select **Properties**. Change to the **Security-**tab and review your options:

Audit level
- None
- Success
- Failure
- All

Choose carefully, since **All** and **Success** might cause your errorlog to fill up the disk rather quickly depending on the applications/users using your SQL server.

Any changes made at the **Security-**tab needs a restart of SQL server to take affect. After changing you are able to use different ways to check the SQL server errorlog for any login attempts, but that "how to" will not be covered in this article.

Safe passwords

Dictionary word are one of the first ways any hacker will try to crack a password. That is why a combination of letters, digits, and special characters are required in order to have a really safe password. Making any password to hard to remember will end up in users writing their passwords in a document or even on a "post it".

My idea of a safe password that is not to hard to remember:

Password requirements
- Minimum 6 characters long
- Minimum 1 uppercase letter
- Minimum 2 alphanumeric characters
- Maximum 2 equal letters after each other
- Not the same as the login

There are only two sp's that perform any type of password check **sp_addlogin** and **sp_password**. It is not recommended to make any changes in any stored procedures shipped by MS but this is the only way you can check for password requirements.

Update stored procedures

After updating the two stored procedures and inserting a password check for new or existing users can add a insecure password. Then trying to, an error message will appear prompting for a safer password:

Microsoft SQL-DMO (ODBC SQLState: 42000)

Error 50000: Password requirements: Minimum 6 characters long, minimum 2 alphanumeric characters, minimum 1 uppercase character, max 2 equal characters after each other and can not be same as login.

OK

First, make a backup of your master-database, then run the two scripts:

- alter_sp_addlogin.sql
- alter_sp_password.sql

Remember that both scripts may be updated in hotfixes and servicepacks. So, remember to check the password requirements after applying a SQL update.

Note: None of the existing password will be checked. This will only affect existing users that change their current password and new users that will be added to SQL server.

Existing passwords

This is only a fairly easy check of the existing passwords in your SQL server. The only things that will be checked is if the password is:

- *NULL*
- Same as login name *
- Same as login name but reversed *
- Only one char long

Run this script in Query Analyzer:

- check_weak_passwords.sql

The script will generate a list of the SQL users passwords that are fairly easy figure out. Talk to the users and make them understand about the password sequrity, and what they should do about it.

* Same does not check for upper- and lower cases. SQL login "abc" and password "Abc" will report as same.

Summary

Even if you do all of above, your SQL server will not be safe from hackers. Your environment is always a potential target of any hackers out there. But at least you have made it harder for them.

Port Blocking, SQL Server, and the Internet

By Denny Figuerres

While random blocking of ports by ISP's could lead to a severely crippled Internet I do not believe that it is in the best interests of most users (private or business) to leave all ports open to all users. As an example of this let's take a look at the "MSBlast" worm and the damage it caused the IT community. The while no one can deny that Microsoft had a bug in the code that needed to be patched we can also see that 1) a fix was available and that 2) many servers were not patched and were left open to infection due to the ports used by SQL server being left open to the Internet.

Now let's consider what would have happened if say 70% of the Internet routers and firewalls as whole simply dropped traffic for that port. Sure, the worm would have still spread and done harm but how much less damage would it have done? How many millions of dollars would have been saved?

Look at the SPAM problem--many experts agree that a large amount of it is coming from "rogue" SMTP servers often running on home PC's that the owner is unaware of. If many ISP's blocked home user machines from making outbound connections as SMTP servers, it could block much of the SPAM we see every day.

Yes, there are issues; yes, legitimate traffic should be allowed across the networks.

But I think we as IT professionals have to assess:

1. Does this service need to be open to the public?
2. What is the possible impact to the business if this service is exposed?
3. Is this service secure?
4. Is there a better way to accomplish the same work or task?

In the case of a SQL Server I see almost no case where the ports should be left open. By default SQL server transmits plain text data. This means that it is trivial to hack.

Here are some options for connection:

Remote administration:

- VPN
- Remote Desktop
- VNC
- A secured web site with custom pages

Server to server data exchange:

- VPN between sites

Remote Clients such as applications:

- Web Services interface
- Web pages called "Inside" an application
- Custom binary protocol with encryption and authentication
- VPN tunnel to the server

So given that list of options, considering how many of them should take less than 20 minutes to implement (Like remote desktop or VNC), I have to ask why you would ever want to risk the valuable data and resources of that SQL server?

After all, your clients and/or your boss may not understand the problems but if you don't put up a good set of security methods and practices and the network or data is compromised, it may well be your job and your future credibility that are one the line. I, for one, would rather not be in the hot seat if I can avoid it. I would say it's time well spent.

Denny Figuerres ©June, 2004

RC4 Encryption in a Stored Procedure

By Joseph Gama

RC4 Encryption SP's/UDF's with TSQL calling activeX

These are stored procedures and functions to encrypt/decrypt data using the RC4 or Rijndael encryption algorithm. This is an interesting and useful example of calling COM objects with TSQL.

For learning purposes the examples are very simple and based on a few lines of code, something similar to:

```
declare @hr int
exec @hr =sp_oacreate 'OLEComponent.Object', @object out
```

```
exec @hr =sp_oamethod @object, 'RC4ED', ReturnValue out,@parameter,@parameter
EXEC @hr = sp_OADestroy @object
```

The variable @hr will store the return value from the system stored procedure call to ensure that the call was successful. If the value is other than zero it means that an error occurred. sp_oacreate will create an instance of the object previously created with VB6 and properly registered as an ActiveX control. VB6 will do that automatically when compiling the code. The next line of code uses sp_oamethod which will call a method of the ActiveX control. In this example, there are only two methods, encrypt and decrypt, but there could be properties, too. Finally, sp_OADestroy will destroy the instance we used before.

The system stored procedures used are the following:

sp_oacreate-Creates an instance of the OLE object.
sp_OAMethod-Calls a method of an OLE object.
sp_OADestroy-Destroys an instance of an OLE object.

Other useful ones:

sp_OAGetProperty-Gets a property value of an OLE object.
sp_OASetProperty-Sets a property of an OLE object.
sp_OAGetErrorInfo-Returns an error code from the latest OLE Automation operation.

RC4 Encryption

Stored Procedures

Sp_RC4- Encrypts any data type input to a varchar data type. Used to encrypt character data, such as text.

Sp_RC4Bin- Encrypts any data type input to a varbinary data type. Used to encrypt binary data, such as numbers or pictures.

```
declare @s varchar(255), @t varchar(255)
exec dbo.sp_RC4 'hello','abc',@s out
print @s
exec dbo.sp_RC4 '¥øµE7','abc',@s out
print @s
```

¥øµE7
hello

User Defined Functions

XRC4- Encrypts any data type input to a varchar data type. Used to encrypt character data, such as text.

XRC4Bin- Encrypts any data type input to a varbinary data type. Used to encrypt binary data, such as numbers or pictures.

```
print dbo.XRC4('hello','abc')
print dbo.XRC4('¥øµE7','abc')
```

¥øµE7
hello

Rijndael Encryption

Stored Procedures

Sp_EncRijndael- Encrypts any data type input to a varchar data type. Used to encrypt character data, such as text.

Sp_DecRijndael- Decrypts any data type input to a varchar data type.

Sp_EncRijndaelBin- Encrypts any data type input to a varbinary data type. Used to encrypt binary data, such as pictures.

Sp_DecRijndaelBin - Decrypts any data type input to a varbinary data type.

```
declare @s varchar(255), @t varchar(255)
exec dbo.sp_EncRijndael 'hello','abc',@s out
print @s
exec dbo.sp_DecRijndael @s,'abc',@t out
print @t
```

```
ž`'í□□□hÄи□ZyÊ"□.□Ù>ÿ»-□?.÷ATÔT^
hello
```

User Defined Functions

EncRijndael- Encrypts any data type input to a varchar data type. Used to encrypt character data, such as text.

DecRijndael- Decrypts any data type input to a varchar data type.

EncRijndaelBin- Encrypts any data type input to a varbinary data type. Used to encrypt binary data, such as pictures.

DecRijndaelBin - Decrypts any data type input to a varbinary data type.

```
print 'Character input:'
print dbo.EncRijndael('Hello!','password')
print dbo.DecRijndael('□~ÿ□Ù*ð¤i~á×õ§$Ih4ø□(,□Y)□&)z*¦□','password')
print 'Binary input:'
print dbo.EncRijndaelBin('Hello!','password')
print dbo.DecRijndaelBin(0x067EFF18D92AF5A46993E1D7F5A724496834F8187B2C17592981267D7AAAA604,
'password')
print convert(varchar(8000),0x48656C6C6F21)
```

```
Character input:
□~ÿ□Ù*ð¤i~á×õ§$Ih4ø□(,□Y)□&)z*¦□
Hello!
Binary input:
0x067EFF18D92AF5A46993E1D7F5A724496834F8187B2C17592981267D7AAAA604
0x48656C6C6F21
Hello!
```

It works by calling an activeX DLL which has to be created first.

Files

RC4 files
Rijndael files

To create and use the activeX DLL:

1-Open the project in VB6.
2-Compile the DLL.
3-Copy the DLL to c:\winnt\system32
4-Register the DLL using the START MENU: START/RUN regsvr32 c:\winnt\system32\crypt.Dll

The stored procedures will work fine now.

RC4 code based on Eric Hodges' RC4 Implementation
http://www.planet-source-code.com/vb/scripts/showcode.asp?lngWId=1&txtCodeId=29691

He deserves the credit for it.

I used the code from Queen City Software - Rijndael Encryption - to create the activeX dll http://www.planet-source-code.com/vb/scripts/ShowCode.asp?txtCodeId=24820&lngWId=1

They deserve the credit for it.

Joseph Gama

SQL Server Security: Dealing with Anti -Virus Programs

By Brian Kelley

With the recent slate of "virus" attacks plaguing us, a question that has come up fairly often is how to handle anti-virus programs running on the same system as SQL Server. If you tried to do an Internet search on SQL Server and anti-virus best practices you've probably been left with a bunch of links to descriptions of the SQL Slammer worm but not a whole lot else. I won't say this is unexpected because in an ideal world we'd want SQL Server to have the system all to itself without any other agents or programs running at the same time. Also, SQL Slammer's effects were felt far and wide and it dominates any searches that don't specifically exclude "slammer" in the search criteria.

But we don't live in an ideal world. Once upon a time running without anti-virus software may have been possible but it is no longer. Then again, virus definitions would come out monthly. Then the pace accelerated to weekly. Now it's not unusual, especially given rapid variants like with Beagle/Bagle and NetSky, to see multiple definition downloads in one day. With the change in the environment, anti-virus programs are now deployed on servers without a second thought. However, there are some considerations to take into account when deploying anti-virus agents and SQL Server in conjunction. I'll cover them in this article.

The Paging File

The Microsoft operating systems all make use of a paging file in order to "expand" memory virtually. Named pagefile.sys, the operating systems needs unfettered access to this file. This file is usually opened and locked by the operating system and there's no point to scanning it. As is pointed out in the Small Business Server FAQ, this is one of the files you want to exclude from scanning. I've included a link to that FAQ in the Additional Resources section.

While .sys files aren't executable, that's not to say some savvy virus writer won't decide to use the name "pagefile.sys" as part of his or her overall attack. When configuring what **not** to scan, only mark the actual paging files the operating system is going to use. For instance, a pagefile.sys entry under c:\winnt\ or c:\windows\ is not an actual paging file for the system. The paging files would only be found in the root directory of any drives they are configured to reside on. We would want our anti-virus solution detecting such "out-of-place" files.

Recommendation: This recommendation is true regardless of the application running on the server. Configure the anti-virus software to exclude pagefile.sys in its scanning but ensure you match this exclusion to what the operating system is actually using as the paging file.

Database Files (.mdf, .ndf, .ldf)

The standard extensions for SQL Server database files are .mdf, .ndf, and .ldf. Theoretically, these should never get infected as they aren't "run" like a .exe or .com file and they don't have the ability to execute macros like Microsoft Office documents (of which .doc for Word and .xls for Excel are the most prevalent for having macro viruses). Therefore, there's not a whole lot of reason to scan these files. In fact, there's a very good reason to exclude them from your anti-virus scans.

Microsoft KB article 309422 points out that if a virus sweep has a database file open when SQL Server tries to open the database, the database may be marked suspect. SQL Server is going to need exclusive access to the files and an anti-virus agent touching one at the same time SQL Server is trying to open it is going to cause a conflict. Of course, the same is true of any agent software, such as with backup software. The question that comes to mind is, "How often does SQL Server attempt to open the file?" The short answer is, "It depends." SQL Server will always attempt to open all the database files when it first starts up. In fact, you can often see entries in the log which begin with "Starting up database" and the database name:

```
2004-04-01 10:18:04.59 spid3 Starting up database 'master'.
2004-04-01 10:18:06.98 server Using 'SSNETLIB.DLL' version '8.0.818'.
2004-04-01 10:18:06.98 spid5 Starting up database 'model'.
2004-04-01 10:18:07.20 spid3 Server name is 'MySQLServer'.
2004-04-01 10:18:07.39 spid8 Starting up database 'msdb'.
2004-04-01 10:18:07.39 spid9 Starting up database 'pubs'.
2004-04-01 10:18:07.58 spid10 Starting up database 'Northwind'.
2004-04-01 10:18:07.58 spid11 Starting up database 'distribution'.
2004-04-01 10:18:08.98 server SQL server listening on 192.168.1.101: 1433.
2004-04-01 10:18:08.98 server SQL server listening on 127.0.0.1: 1433.
2004-04-01 10:18:11.35 server SQL server listening on TCP, Shared Memory, Named Pipes.
2004-04-01 10:18:11.35 server SQL Server is ready for client connections
2004-04-01 10:18:11.37 spid5 Clearing tempdb database.
2004-04-01 10:18:18.25 spid5 Starting up database 'tempdb'.
2004-04-01 10:18:20.15 spid3 Recovery complete.
```

The other time SQL Server may attempt to open a database is if a database is set to AutoClose. When someone attempts to access the database, SQL Server will have to open up the files and bring the database on-line. Since it is typically rare for production databases to be configured to AutoClose, generally the only time we'd see SQL Server attempt to open a database file is when SQL Server first starts up. However, while SQL Server has the file open the anti-virus software isn't going to be able to scan it. Therefore, there's really no point in attempting to scan files ending in these extensions.

Recommendation: Exclude files of .mdf, .ldf, and .ndf extensions from scanning.

Backup Files

In my environment we typically let SQL Server backup a database to a file on the local system and then copy that file to a central server. Nightly, backups run on both the SQL Server and the central backup repository, meaning we tend to have two copies of critical backup files on tape. Every once in a while we'd notice that the backup agents would be busy reading the file and writing to tape at the same time SQL Server would attempt to do its backup to the very same file. Now, the backup agent had opened the file first and therefore SQL Server was unable to lock the file. SQL Server would give up and the backup wouldn't run. The reason we had this problem is we were simply re-using the same backup file names. When we switched over to Perl scripts and an enterprise job engine, we started time stamping the backup files in the names themselves. That didn't eliminate the contention with the backup agent but what it did do was ensure SQL Server was always the winner. Given we're copying the file to a second server as well as a few other steps we took, we've minimized the overall risk of not having the right backup.

Needless to say, if SQL Server and a backup agent can contend over a backup file, so too can SQL Server and an anti-virus agent. Therefore some folks recommend excluding .bak and .trn files (or whatever extensions they prefer) from scanning as well. I have seen a case where we think the anti-virus agent was jumping in between the closing of the backup and a renaming process to do its scan. The rename failed as a result and the next step to copy didn't execute either. We have since gone to a strategy of excluding the backup files from scanning.

As for risk, these files aren't typically executable programs so the risk isn't very great if they aren't scanned. If you're reusing the same names, such as with a backup device or just a standard script that doesn't timestamp or do something to make the names different, you may want to exclude the backup extensions as well. It's better not to scan a file that you can't execute than have SQL Server fail out trying to write a backup you very well may need.

Recommendation: Exclude file extensions corresponding to backup files if you reuse file names.

Full Text Catalogs

KB article 309422 also states if an anti-virus agent is scanning a full-text catalog at the same time as the Microsoft Search service (MSSearch AKA Full Text Indexing), "you may experience problems with the full text catalog." Therefore, if you're using full-text indexing be sure to exclude the directories containing the full-text catalog files. By default this is the **FTDATA** directory underneath your SQL Server instance directory. A completely default install would have the full-text files under **C:\Program Files\Microsoft SQL Server\MSSQL\FTDATA**. However, you can specify the location of the files when creating the catalog. If you need to check the paths, take a look at **sp_help_fulltext_catalogs**.

Recommendation: Exclude any full-text catalog directories if you use full-text indexing.

System Directories

Once upon a time I saw literature recommending the exclusion of C:\Windows when doing anti-virus scans. At the time, though, definitions were showing up about once a month or so and the danger was the "rogue floppy" being brought into the office. Those days are long gone and I would say this recommendation should be as well. I've heard it repeated from time to time, but for me it doesn't make sense any longer. So why was it ever a suggestion?

The main rationale was the same one used for the paging file: the system should be using the file(s) in question and we don't want to take a chance on an anti-virus agent locking the file when the operating system needs it. While these points may have been of great concern in the past, I don't feel they outweigh the risk nowadays, especially with efforts to make the OS more reliable and fault tolerant. Let's face it: a lot of viruses and worms now drop their files in the system directories. For instance, the known Sasser variants drop their files in %WINDIR%, a known directory variable that corresponds to wherever Windows is installed (C:\WINNT or C:\WINDOWS usually). Welchia's variants tended to use %SYSTEM%, which typically corresponds to the System32 directory (C:\WINNT\SYSTEM32 or C:\WINDOWS\SYSTEM32). Therefore, choosing to exclude the system directories is no longer a viable option.

Recommendation: Scan system directories as you would any other directory.

Program Directories

I put program directories in the same category as system directories. "Old school" viruses would often attach themselves to already existing .exe and .com files. While the latest batch of viruses and worms haven't taken this approach, it never goes out of style. One need only look back as far as Nimda for a very widespread worm that went after executable files. Therefore, program directories should be scanned as well.

Recommendation: Scan program directories as you would any other directory.

Summary

Here is a summary of the recommendations.

Don'ts:

- Do not scan the paging file(s) on the system.
- Do not scan the SQL Server database file extensions: .mdf, .ndf, and .ldf.
- Do not scan extensions for backup files.
- Do not scan Full-Text directories.

Do's:

- Do scan system directories.
- Do scan program directories.

Concluding Remarks

This article presents my opinion and recommendations for how to handle SQL Server and anti-virus agents in conjunction. Yours may differ and I hope this article spurs some discussion on the topic. I've tried to explain why I've made a recommendation to offer up for consideration. Ultimately your organization is the final arbiter of how you go about implementing anti-virus agents in your environment. Carefully consider all the factors when determining how to implement anti-virus and SQL Server on your systems.

Additional Resources

SQL Server Related Resources:

- Frequently Asked Questions About Small Business Server - http://www.microsoft.com/sbserver/community/sbs_faq.asp
- INF: Consideration for a Virus Scanner on a Computer That Is Running SQL Server - http://support.microsoft.com/default.aspx?scid=kb;en-us;309422
- Running Virus-Scanning Software on the Same Server as SQL Server - http://www.microsoft.com/sql/techinfo/tips/administration/virusscanning.asp
- MVP N. Vyas Kondreddi's Overview of SQL Server security model and security best practices -

http://vyaskn.tripod.com/sql_server_security_best_practices.htm

Anti-Virus Providers

- AVG Anti-Virus Virus News, Warnings page - http://www.grisoft.com/us/us_vir_tt.php
- F-Secure Virus Info page - http://www.f-secure.com/virus-info/
- Kaspersky's VirusList - http://www.viruslist.com/
- McAfee Security Virus Info page - http://us.mcafee.com/virusInfo/default.asp
- Sophos Virus Info page - http://www.sophos.com/virusinfo/
- Symantec Security Response site - http://securityresponse.symantec.com/

This list is by no means exhaustive. However, these are the pages I most often use when looking for information about a new outbreak.

© 2004 by K. Brian Kelley. http://www.truthsolutions.com/
Author of *Start to Finish Guide to SQL Server Performance Monitoring* (http://www.netimpress.com).

XML

XML Integration with SQL Server 2000 was an afterthought and it shows. No native handling of the XML datatypes exist, something that seems like it will be rectified in SQL Server 2005. But for the time being, dealing XML remains a cumbersome process.

Nevertheless, it's an important technology in the world today, so we've brought you some examples on how you can work with and use XML in a few practical ways.

An Alternative XML Solution

By Wayne Fillis

Introduction

XML is a great tool for sharing and manipulating data. It is becoming (or is already!) a de facto standard in the Enterprise for the sharing of data in the form of XML documents, saved as .XML files (which can be opened and viewed in Internet Explorer) or imported directly into SQL Server. SQL Server 2000 introduced functionality for XML in the form of the FOR XML clause, which you can use in your SELECT statements. This is used to convert your queries into XML. However, the reality for SQL Server 2000 users is not quite so simple.

The Problem

The first problem with the FOR XML clause is that it does not create a well-formed XML document, in other words you can't just save the result of your query as a XML file and expect to be able to open it in Internet Explorer. You have to programmatically append ROOT tags at the beginning and end of your document. In addition to this, if used from BCP or Query Analyser, the XML result set is split over several rows. This may not seem too bad, until you realize that this splitting of rows MAY have chopped a tag in half - this will cause an error when you open the XML file in Internet Explorer. You will have to manually or programmatically string the lines in the resultset into one line. If you use another method to retrieve results (HTTP access, stream object in ADO), you shouldn't have this problem - but how do you plug an ADO solution into SQL Server unless you use ActiveX scripting in a DTS?

There are many possible solutions

An article called 'A Survey of Microsoft SQL Server 2000 XML Features' published by Microsoft in July 2001 (recently published on SQLServerCentral.com) documents various XML solutions. Some of these are simple, some are complex. Unfortunately, while these solutions are really powerful, most of them require ADO programming, and a lot of knowledge of XML - not so good for a newbie or someone who needs to put out a quick solution.

The easiest solution is, of course, to wait for SQL Server 2005 to be released. The new version of SQL Server has introduced impressive XML functionality in the Beta versions. If you don't want to wait, however, you could use an ActiveX script in a DTS package to prepare an XML document. This is very easy to code, and offers great flexibility, but you will need to code a separate lengthy script for each XML file you need to generate. Or you could use the same script and call the ADO Stream object to parse an XML Template - but again, you must do this in a DTS package. The system sproc sp_makewebtask can also create XML documents in the form of a HTML document. This is useful if you want to view your file on the Internet, but not for creating files.

Another way (we're getting closer now!) is to write a VB or C# program and use the Save method that is part of the RecordSet object in ADO. This method will save an ADO resultset as a XML document. Information on how to accomplish this can be found on the Internet in many places. Unfortunately, the ADO resultset is a denormalised resultset (i.e. no nesting - which is useful in XML documents), and you have no control over the layout of the XML document - unless you build in functionality for stylesheets. I wanted a more flexible, simple solution (i.e. I was too lazy to learn stylesheets!). I found it with XML Templates. The FOR XML clause offers great flexibility and variation to your XML documents, but what if you want to combine several queries into one document? XML Templates offers this solution. You prepare a template, which is an actual XML document, and place your SQL queries in the document. Once again though I was trapped by the need to write ADO code in an ActiveX script - i.e. DTS.

There is functionality embedded in SQLXML (included in SQL Server 2000 Web Release, and available for download at SqlXml 3.0 SP2 - make sure you download version 3 SP2), MSXML 4.0 SP2 (also downloadable from Microsoft), and ADO.NET enabling you to programmatically apply a XML Template to a database without any security risk. You can format the XML Template to meet any requirement, and embed as many queries and scripts as you need. The result is saved to a XML file, which contains your formatting and the data returned from the queries. If you don't want to use embedded SQL, put the SQL in a stored procedure (the sproc must return a resultset and must use FOR XML) and execute the sproc from your Template. You can even code your XML Templates with parameters, which can be passed to your queries.

To add more flexibility you can save the XML Template in a table in text format instead of having to deal with Dos files. Using the power of XML Templates, you can extend your functionality even further by specifying an XSD mapping schema and an XPath query instead of using SQL Queries in the Template.

To quote Microsoft:

"We feel that the use of templates with XSD mapping schemas and XPath queries is the most powerful mechanism for getting XML-based data directly from SQL Server 2000." - *http://msdn.microsoft.com/msdnmag/issues/02/01/SQLXML/default.aspx*

XML Templates is a productive alternative to the XML newbie. My next requirement was to be able to execute this XML Template from <u>anywhere</u> within SQL Server, and to re-use this solution with minimal effort. I also wanted to option of bypassing the template by executing a simple query string using FOR XML and have this converted into an XML file.

To achieve this, I coded all this functionality into an extended stored procedure. You can call the extended stored procedure from anywhere in SQL, passing the server and database to connect to, the name of the resultant XML File, and the ID key to the table containing the XML Template you want to process. You can also pass up to 10 parameters, which can be used in the template. Instead of passing the ID of the XML Template, passing a SQL query string will cause the resultset to be written to a XML file.

To code an extended stored procedure, you need to use Delphi or C++ (I used Visual C++.NET). Visual Studio .NET provides a template for creating extended stored procedures, and if you navigate to 'C:\Program Files\Microsoft SQL Server\80\Tools\DevTools\Samples\ods' you will find a self-extracting ZIP containing samples on how to create extended stored procedures. The readme document in the .NET project will give you some guidelines. You should be able to use native C++ to create an extended stored procedure as this functionality has been around for a while.

Once the code is completed, build the DLL and save it to 'c:\Program Files\Microsoft SQL Server\80\Tools\Binn'. Use sp_addextendedproc to add the extended proc to your database. You do NOT need to register the DLL in the usual way (i.e. using regsvr32).

Creating an Extended Stored Procedure using VC++.NET

The first step is to use Visual C++.NET to create the basic extended stored procedure, which accepts parameters when called from SQL Query Analyzer.

Install SQLXML, MSXML, .NET Framework and .NET Framework SDK and open a VC++.NET project using the Extended stored procedure template.

Add the following references:

- System.XML
- System.Data
- System
- mscorlib
- Microsoft.Data.SqlXml

and set the project properties to 'Use Managed Extensions'. Here is the code - it is not too long.

NOTE : I don't pretend to be a C++ expert, but I have had an expert QA this code, and have used it fairly extensively. Use at your own risk! If you are unfamiliar with C++, read the comments in the code - it should be clear enough, but please feel free to contact me if you require any clarification. Start reading from function 'xp_XMLTemplate_WriteFile' near the end of the code. This function calls class 'CXTWFile' which does most of the work.

Download alternativexml.cpp

Once the code has been compiled, copy the DLL to 'c:\Program Files\Microsoft SQL Server\80\Tools\Binn'

Create the extended stored procedure using:

```
master..sp_addextendedproc 'xp_XMLTemplate_WriteFile', 'XMLTemplate.dll'
```

Drop the extended stored procedure using:

```
master..sp_dropextendedproc 'xp_XMLTemplate_WriteFile'
```

The documentation says you are supposed to use 'DBCC xp_XMLTemplate_WriteFile(FREE)' to release the DLL so you can replace it, but I couldn't get this to work. I had to stop and start SQL to free the DLL

Next, create your table to hold the template and insert a template into the table:

```
CREATE TABLE [dbo].[XMLTemplate] (
        [XMLTemplateID] [int] IDENTITY (1, 1) NOT NULL ,
        [XMLTemplateDate] [datetime] NOT NULL ,
        [XMLTemplate] [varchar] (8000) NOT NULL
) ON [PRIMARY]
GO

ALTER TABLE [dbo].[XMLTemplate] WITH NOCHECK ADD
        CONSTRAINT [PK_XMLTemplate_XMLTemplateID] PRIMARY KEY  CLUSTERED
        (
                [XMLTemplateID]
        ) WITH  FILLFACTOR = 90  ON [PRIMARY]
GO

ALTER TABLE [dbo].[XMLTemplate] ADD
        CONSTRAINT [DF_XMLTemplate_XMLTemplateDate] DEFAULT (getdate()) FOR [XMLTemplateDate]
GO
```

Note that the stored procedure should return a resultset and must use the FOR XML clause.

```
INSERT INTO XMLTemplate (XMLTemplate)
VALUES (
'<XMLTemplateFile xmlns:sql="urn:schemas-microsoft-com:xml-sql">
<sql:header>
        <sql:param name="Param1"/>
        <sql:param name="Param2"/>
        <sql:param name="Param3"/>
        <sql:param name="Param4"/>
        <sql:param name="Param5"/>
        <sql:param name="Param6"/>
        <sql:param name="Param7"/>
        <sql:param name="Param8"/>
        <sql:param name="Param9"/>
        <sql:param name="Param10"/>
</sql:header>
<Param1 xmlns:sql="urn:schemas-microsoft-com:xml-sql">
        <sql:query>
                SELECT @Param1
        </sql:query>
</Param1>
<Param2 xmlns:sql="urn:schemas-microsoft-com:xml-sql">
        <sql:query>
                SELECT @Param2
        </sql:query>
</Param2>
<Part1 xmlns:sql="urn:schemas-microsoft-com:xml-sql">
        <sql:query>
                EXEC sproc @Param1 = @Param1, @Param2 = @Param2
        </sql:query>
</Part1>
<Part2 xmlns:sql="urn:schemas-microsoft-com:xml-sql">
        <sql:query>
                SELECT * FROM abc WHERE xyz = @Param3 FOR XML AUTO
        </sql:query>
</Part2>
</XMLTemplateFile>')
```

Create your XML file as follows:

```
EXEC master.dbo.xp_XMLTemplate_WriteFile
        @XMLFileName    = 'C:\testfile.XML',
        @XMLInput       = '1',
        @Server         = '(local)',
        @Database       = 'DatabaseName',
        @Param1         = @Param1,
        @Param2         = @Param2,
        @Param3         = @Param3,
```

```
@Param4      = ' ',
@Param5      = ' ',
@Param6      = ' ',
@Param7      = ' ',
@Param8      = ' ',
@Param9      = ' ',
@Param10     = ' '
```

If you don't want to use an XML Template, run the following:

```
EXEC master.dbo.xp_XMLTemplate_WriteFile
    @XMLFileName  = 'C:\testfile.XML',
    @XMLInput     = 'SELECT * FROM ABC WHERE xyz = 'ABC' FOR XML AUTO',
    @Server       = '(local)',
    @Database     = 'DatabaseName',
    @Param1       = ' ',
    @Param2       = ' ',
    @Param3       = ' ',
    @Param4       = ' ',
    @Param5       = ' ',
    @Param6       = ' ',
    @Param7       = ' ',
    @Param8       = ' ',
    @Param9       = ' ',
    @Param10      = ' '
```

Conclusions

This solution may be difficult to maintain, as it is written in C++, but it will offer great flexibility to your enterprise. By simple coding a new query, you can create a new XML file. Using the more advanced aspects of FOR XML, you can create impressive XML documents.

Knowing how to write your own Extended Stored Procedures is a great advantage to the SQL programmer, as it offers the ability to extend the functionality of SQL Server 2000.

Wayne Fillis @ SoftwareFutures

contact me at: wayne.fillis@cpt.softwarefutures.com

Changing Databases Using XML

By Dinesh Asanka

Introduction and Scope

As a database developer, you may be fed up with the never ending customer changes. Actually, this is not only relevant to database developers but for all of the other developers. But for database developers to meet the customer requirements, they may need to change the databases. But if these changes are done manually, you must list out all the changes to be done and do it perfectly. It is not sound methodically, is it? So, we have to find out an elegant way of doing it.

What are the changes?

What are the changes that you may need to do for the databases? They can be creating a new table, dropping an existing table, altering an existing table, deleting existing data of a table, or inserting some data. These changes may need to be done for more than one database. There can be more than one database depending on the customer's needs. For example, I have a done a project which contains configuration data in one database and day-to-day transactions are saved in some other database.

How can we do this?

We can simply write a VB application so that it can change the databases. These changes may not be done at once. There can be changes for two three times. If we use a simple VB application every time we need to change application so that it does the necessary changes to the relevant database, the problem will become worse, especially if you are having several customers and they are asking several changes. Then you will have to keep more than one EXE for this simple and straightforward task. We have made our life uneasy ourselves, haven't we?

If we can write an exe so that it reads some other source which users can change and do the changes it will be handy. We just need to change the source file rather than the VB application. Text file would do the job for us. But XML file be the most suitable one. This gives you another advantage over the VB application. That is XML file size will be just over 2-3 KB which you can send it through an e-mail.

XML File

Let's first create the XML file.

```
- <Change Ver="1.20">
  - <DBChanges>
    - <Database Name="Config">
        <Command>Drop Table Schdules</Command>
        <Command>CREATE TABLE Devices ([ID] int ,[Tire] int ,[Outputs] int ,[Inputs] int ,[TrendSamplesMax] int ,[Arrays] int)
        </Command>
      </Database>
    - <Database Name="Transacation">
        <Command>alter table TrendViewCache add ControllerTrend Bit</Command>
      </Database>
    </DBChanges>
  - <CopyData>
    - <Database Name="Config">
        <Table>Devices</Table>
      </Database>
    </CopyData>
  </Change>
```

Figure 1

Figure 1 is the listing of the XML file. we may call it SCRIPT.XML.

There are are several things in the XML file which I have not discussed earlier. First of them is the Version. This is for the reference. Version would be enough to identify the changes that were done to the database. As I discussed earlier, commands are separated for the databases. Here I have used two databases which are Config and Transaction. As you can see, there is a another XML tag called CopyData. Sometimes you need to store some information which may be entered by users. For an example, if you want to store country list in a table (of course you can get the country list from the windows registry) which you haven't sent it to customers earlier. Still, you can use INSERT command and do it. But better way is sending the template data in a MSAccess table and copy those data with the aid of a VB application.

VB Application

For this VB application I have used Microsoft XML ,v 3.0 and Microsoft Activex Data Objects (ADO) 2.7 library.

```
Private Sub cmdContinue_Click()
Dim xmldoc As New MSXML2.DOMDocument30
Dim XMLNode1 As IXMLDOMNode
Dim XMLNode2 As IXMLDOMNode
Dim XMLNode3 As IXMLDOMNode
Dim XMLNode4 As IXMLDOMNode
If xmldoc.Load(App.Path & "\Script.XML") Then
    lblVersion = "Version: " & xmldoc.childNodes(0).Attributes(0).nodeValue
    For Each XMLNode1 In xmldoc.childNodes
        For Each XMLNode2 In XMLNode1.childNodes
            For Each XMLNode3 In XMLNode2.childNodes
                For Each XMLNode4 In XMLNode3.childNodes
                    Select Case UCase(XMLNode2.baseName)
                      Case "DBCHANGE"
                         call_DbChange UCase(XMLNode3.Attributes.Item(0).nodeValue), XMLNode4.Text
                      Case "COPYDATA"
                         call_CopyData UCase(XMLNode3.Attributes.Item(0).nodeValue), XMLNode4.Text
                    End Select
                Next
            Next
        Next
    Next
End If

End Sub
```

Figure 2

Above function will load the XML and read its content. From the XMLNode2.baseName it will identify whether it has to change the database or it has to copy the data, depending on that it calls the two functions.

```
Private Sub call_DbChange(strDbName As String, strCommand As String)
Dim rstConn As New ADODB.Connection
Select Case strDbName
Case "CONFIG"
    rstConn.ConnectionString = TARGET_CONFIG_CONNCETION_STRING
Case "TRANSACTION"
    rstConn.ConnectionString = TARGET_TRANS_CONNCETION_STRING
End Select
    rstConn.Open
    rstConn.Execute strCommand
    rstConn.Close
End Sub
```

Figure 3

Figure 3 shows how it changes the database which is self introductionery. TARGET_CONFIG_CONNCETION_STRING, TARGET_TRANS_CONNCETION_STRING are connection strings which you can build depending on your database.

```
Private Sub call_CopyData(strDbName As String, strTable As String)

Dim rstSourceRst As New ADODB.Recordset
Dim rstTargetRst As New ADODB.Recordset
Dim i As Integer
Dim f As Field

Select Case strDbName
Case "CONFIG"
    rstSourceRst.Open strTable, SOURCE_TRANS_CONNCETION_STRING, adOpenForwardOnly, adLockReadOnly
    rstTargetRst.Open strTable, TARGET_TRANS_CONNCETION_STRING, adOpenDynamic, adLockOptimistic
Case "TRANSACTION"
    rstSourceRst.Open strTable, SOURCE_TRANS_CONNCETION_STRING, adOpenForwardOnly, adLockReadOnly
    rstTargetRst.Open strTable, TARGET_TRANS_CONNCETION_STRING, adOpenDynamic, adLockOptimistic
End Select

    Do While rstSourceRst.EOF = False
        rstTargetRst.AddNew
        For i = 0 To rstSourceRst.Fields.Count - 1
            rstTargetRst.Fields(i) = rstSourceRst.Fields(i)
        Next
        rstTargetRst.Update
        rstSourceRst.MoveNext
    Loop

    rstSourceRst.Close
    rstTargetRst.Close
End Sub
```

Figure 4

Figure 4 shows how to copy the template data to the customers table.

Improvements

This can be improved to keep the updated version in the customer's computer, say in windows registry, so that when you are running the next upgrade you can check the existing version. It is better if you can keep the date as well there.

Conclusion

My idea is to introduces a simple way to the database upgrades with using the power of XML. You may have greater ideas than this. Fell free to share your experience and creative ideas with us and let's make database upgrade an normal work from what it looks like--a mess!

Handling Simple XML Using T-SQL

By Eli Leiba

This article describes how to traverse a simple XML file that has only 2 attributes (name and value, like a dictionary). And get the results in a single column in SQL SERVER result set

When dealing with interfaces to other applications that are not SQL SERVER based or even not even RDBMS based, the best (and simplest) media for communicating is the XML file.

When the data required can be arranged in a dictionary manner (name and value), the remote application can make an XML file in the following form at :

```
<ROOT>
<LINE>
        <NAME>NAME1</NAME>
        <VALUE>VALUE1</VALUE>
</LINE>
<LINE>
        <NAME>NAME2</NAME>
        <VALUE>VALUE2</VALUE>
</LINE>
        .
        .
        .
        .
</ROOT>
```
I wrote a procedure that gets the XML file full path and name and traverses the XML file and the output is a single column result set where the odd rows are the "name" tags value and the even rows are the "value" tags value.

I used the BULK INSERT t-sql Statement combined with dynamic sql execution in order to "bulk copy" the XML file Inside SQL Server. This is the code implementation of the XML traversing process :

```
create  proc sp_translate_simple_xml
  (@XMLfile varchar(100))

as

begin

declare @idoc int
declare @doc varchar(8000)
declare @xml_line varchar(200)
declare @bulkinscmd varchar(500)

set @doc =''

-- insert XML file into temporary table

Create table #tempXML
  (line varchar(8000))

set @bulkinscmd = 'BULK INSERT #tempXML FROM ' +
        '''' + @XMLfile + ''''

exec (@bulkinscmd)

DECLARE xml_cursor CURSOR
    FOR SELECT * FROM #tempXML

-- create XML string in SQL SERVER memory
OPEN xml_cursor
FETCH NEXT FROM xml_cursor INTO @xml_line
WHILE @@FETCH_STATUS = 0
 BEGIN
    SET @doc = @doc + rtrim(ltrim(@xml_line))
    FETCH NEXT FROM xml_cursor INTO @xml_line
 END

close xml_cursor

deallocate xml_cursor

drop table #tempXML

--Create an internal representation of the XML document.
exec sp_xml_preparedocument @idoc OUTPUT, @doc

-- SELECT statement using OPENXML rowset provider
SELECT  text
 FROM  OPENXML (@idoc, '/ROOT/LINE')
 WHERE text is not null

EXEC sp_xml_removedocument @idoc
END
Go
```

Example of a call to the procedure. Suppose an XML called <u>dict.xml</u> is in C:\sql. That looks like this:

```
<ROOT>
```

```
<LINE>
      <NAME>SUBJECT</NAME>
      <VALUE>ELI SECTION</VALUE>
</LINE>
<LINE>

      <NAME>THE PLANT</NAME>
      <VALUE>IEC factory</VALUE>
</LINE>
<LINE>

      <NAME>CREATE DATE</NAME>
      <VALUE>01/07/2004</VALUE>
</LINE>
</ROOT>
```

after running the procedure :

```
use master
go

exec sp_translate_simple_xml 'c:\sql\dict.xml'
```

this will traverse the dict.xml file and produce a single column result set with name in odd row numbers and values in even row numbers. We will get the following results (using this file - dict.xml):

```
text
-------------------------
SUBJECT
ELI SECTION
THE PLANT
IEC factory
CREATE DATE
01/07/2004

(6 row(s) affected)
```

Conclusion

The procedure can be used as an ideal tool for communicating with applications that cannot link directly to SQL server, must use an intermediate media, and a little amount of data is required for communication.

Reduce Database Round Trips Using XML

By Jon Winer

Connecting to and executing commands against a database is a simple task. We do it without much thought because in today's applications, data access is commonplace and necessary. For those of us who work in a Microsoft 'Shop', ADO and ADO.NET is the norm when it comes to reading and writing from and to a database.

Oftentimes, I need to execute the same command with different arguments repeatedly. This is easy to do and there are many methods of doing so. Developers could use a looping construct, holding open a connection until the process has exited the loop. Developers could use a 'bulk insert' by executing a SQL script similar to: "insert into table1 (field1, field2, field3) select field1, field2, field3 from table2". Most often, I see developers passing in a delimited list of values to a single stored procedure. The argument is then parsed and a cursor loops through the values executing the appropriate commands.

I would like to look at the latter option, but with a SQL XML spin to it. For those who are not familiar with FOR XML and OPEN XML, here is a brief intro. SQL 2000 supports two main methods for working with XML. FOR XML converts a recordset to XML. This output XML can be customized to either be node or attribute centric. It also allows for highly customizable XML using the EXPLICIT key word. OPEN XML converts a Unicode XML string to a recordset. Using XPath type queries, the XML can be parsed and queried against much like a SQL table.

So what is the problem I am trying to solve? Typically, when submitting a delimited list of values to a single stored procedure, you must be mindful of the values you are passing in. You must make sure the values do not contain the same character as the delimiter you are using. Also, there is a max length of 8000 varchar (4000 nvarchar) to be mindful of. Not to mention, parsing out the delimited values can be a bit messy and SQL Server is not optimized for string parsing. To help describe my solution, let me give you an example.

I have a simple contact database with several tables:

```
ContactValue (lookup table)
  - ContactValueID (PK)
  - ContactValue

Contact
  - ContactID (PK)
  - FirstName
  - LastName
  - MiddleInitial
  - SSN
  - DateCreated (Default GetDate())

ContactLink
  - ContactID (PK)
  - ContactValueID (PK)
  - Value
  - DateCreated (Default GetDate())
```

The ContactValue table functions as a lookup table and contains a few of the different methods for contacting individuals (phone, fax, pager, email, etc). This table could grow to encompass many more contact methods. The Contact table contains basic information about a person that is not subject to frequent change. The ContactLink table establishes the one to many relationship between a contact and the possible contact methods and their corresponding values.

I have built a simple application to collect the contact information and submit it to the database. The details of the application are not important, but let me show you some pieces of the code that do the work.

```vb
Option Strict On
Option Explicit On

Imports System.Xml

Public Class ContactValue
        Implements IDisposable

        Private oXmlDoc  As XmlDocument
        Private oXmlRoot  As XmlElement

        Public ReadOnly  Property ContactValueXML()  As  String
        Get
                Return oXmlRoot.InnerXml
              End  Get
        End Property

        Public Sub  New(ByVal contactValueXML As  String)

              Try
                      oXmlDoc =  New XmlDocument
                      oXmlDoc.LoadXml("<ROOT>" & contactValueXML &"</ROOT>")
          oXmlRoot = oXmlDoc.DocumentElement()
                Catch ex  As Exception
                        Throw ex
                End  Try

End Sub

Public Sub SetXMLContactValue(ByVal contactValueID As Integer,
ByVal value As String)

  Dim oXmlNode  As XmlNode
  Dim oCData  As XmlCDataSection

  Try
    oXmlNode = oXmlRoot.SelectSingleNode("/ROOT/contactvalue[@id='" & contactValueID.ToString()& "']")
     If  Not oXmlNode Is  Nothing Then
          oCData = oXmlDoc.CreateCDataSection(value)
            oXmlNode.AppendChild(oCData)
     End  If

  Catch ex  As Exception
```

```
      Throw ex
  Finally
     oXmlNode = Nothing
  End  Try
End Sub

  Public Sub Dispose()   Implements System.IDisposable.Dispose
    oXmlDoc = Nothing
    oXmlRoot = Nothing
  End Sub

End Class
```

The code above does three things. Its constructor takes an XML string argument which functions as a 'template' for the values you wish to assign. It provides a method to pass in a name/value pair and have it written to the XML (SetXMLContactValue) and a property to retrieve the XML (ContactValueXML).

To generate the XML for the constructor, I make a stored procedure call passing in a comma delimited list of IDs from the ContactValue table. See the code snippet below:

```
oParam(0) = New SqlParameter("@ContactValueIDs", SqlDbType.NVarChar, 4000)
oParam(0).Value = "1,2,3,4"   'phone, fax, pager, email

sSql = "usp_GetContactValuesXML"

oXML = Database.RunSpReturnScalar(cn, sSql, oParam)
```

The stored procedure returns a single column of data containing the desired XML. The XML is generated using the FOR XML clause. The code then returns the XML as an object. If no results are returned, oXML = Nothing. Below is the stored procedure code:

```
CREATE PROCEDURE dbo.usp_GetContactValuesXML
(
  @ContactValueIDs nvarchar(4000)
)
AS

SET NOCOUNT ON

DECLARE @SQL nvarchar(4000)

--strip out any single quotes to help prevent SQL injection attack and return the XML
SET @SQL = N'SELECT contactvalueid ''id'', contactvalue ''name''
  FROM contactvalue WITH (NOLOCK)
  WHERE contactvalueid IN (' + Replace(@ContactValueIDs, CHAR(39), '') + ') FOR XML AUTO'

EXEC sp_ExecuteSQL @SQL

GO
```

The XML returned looks like this:

```
<contactvalue id="1" name="Phone"></contactvalue>
<contactvalue id="2" name="Fax"></contactvalue>
<contactvalue id="3" name="Pager"></contactvalue>
<contactvalue id="4" name="Email"></contactvalue>
```

If the stored procedure returns results, we then need to pass the resultant XML to ContactValue class constructor and assign the values collected from the application to the class.

```
If Not oXML Is Nothing Then
      oContactValue = New oContactValue(oXML.ToString())
      oContactValue.SetXMLContactValue (1, "5551212")              'phone
      oContactValue.SetXMLContactValue (2, "5553434")              'fax
      oContactValue.SetXMLContactValue (3, "5555656")              'pager
      oContactValue.SetXMLContactValue (4, "jwiner@jwiner.com")    'email
End If
```

If we then make a call to the oContactValue.ContactValueXML property, the XML returned should appear as below:

```
<contactvalue id="1" name="Phone"><![CDATA[5551212]]></contactvalue>
<contactvalue id="2" name="Fax"><![CDATA[5553434]]></contactvalue>
<contactvalue id="3" name="Pager"><![CDATA[5555656]]></contactvalue>
```

```
<contactvalue id="4"name="Email"><![CDATA[jwiner@jwiner.com]]></contactvalue>
```

At this stage, we are now ready to process the XML. To do so, we make a call to the stored procedure; passing in the ContactID and the XML returned from the oContactValue.ContactValueXML property. The code snippet is below:

```
sSql = "usp_SetContactValuesXML"

oParams(0) = New SqlParameter("@ContactID ", SqlDbType.Int, 4)
oParams(0).Value = ContactID
oParams(1) = New SqlParameter("@TemplateXML ", SqlDbType.NVarChar, 4000)
oParams(1).Value = oContactValue.ContactValueXML()

Database.RunSp(cn, sSql, oParams)
```

The stored procedure uses the OPEN XML clause to convert the XML into a logical table and then cursor through it, inserting the values into the ContactLink table. Another option would be to directly insert the results of the 'SELECT…FROM OPENXML(…)' query into the ContactLink table. There are pros and cons to each approach. The cursor approach is more resource intensive, but allows row by row manipulation of the data prior to any insert action. The set based approach performs much more efficiently, but does not yield the same flexibility.

The different options mentioned above are highlighted in version 1 and 2 of the stored procedures below:

Version 1:

```
CREATE PROCEDURE dbo.usp_SetContactValuesXML
(
    @ContactID int,
    @TemplateXML nvarchar(4000) = '<ROOT></ROOT>'
)

AS

SET NOCOUNT ON

DECLARE @iDoc int
DECLARE @Doc nvarchar(4000)
DECLARE @ContactValueID int
DECLARE @ContactName nvarchar(200)
DECLARE @ContactValue nvarchar(4000)

SET @Doc = '<ROOT>' + @TemplateXML + '</ROOT>'

EXEC sp_xml_preparedocument @iDoc OUTPUT, @Doc

DECLARE Contact_Cursor CURSOR FOR
--map to xml nodes and attributes and populate cursor
 SELECT
       id 'Id', name 'Name', contactvalue 'Value'
 FROM OPENXML (@iDoc, '/ROOT/contactvalue', 2)
 WITH (Id int '@id', Name nvarchar(200) '@name', ContactValue nvarchar(4000) '.')

OPEN Contact_Cursor

FETCH NEXT FROM Contact_Cursor INTO @ContactValueID, @ContactName, @ContactValue

WHILE @@FETCH_STATUS = 0
 BEGIN
   --if value is present
   IF Len(RTrim(LTrim(@ContactValue))) > 0
     BEGIN
       --insert into ContactLink table
       Insert into ContactLink(ContactID, ContactValueID, Value)
                   Values(@ContactID, @ContactValueID, @ContactValue)
     END
   FETCH NEXT FROM Contact_Cursor INTO @ContactValueID, @ContactName, @ContactValue
 END

CLOSE Contact_Cursor
DEALLOCATE Contact_Cursor

EXEC sp_xml_removedocument @iDoc

GO
```

Version 2:

```
CREATE PROCEDURE dbo.usp_SetContactValuesXML
(
  @ContactID int,
  @TemplateXML nvarchar(4000) = '<ROOT></ROOT>'

AS
SET NOCOUNT ON

DECLARE @iDoc int
DECLARE @Doc nvarchar(4000)

SET @Doc = '<ROOT>' + @TemplateXML + '</ROOT>'

EXEC sp_xml_preparedocument @iDoc OUTPUT, @Doc

Insert into ContactLink(ContactID, ContactValueID, Value)
 SELECT
    @ContactID, id 'Id', contactvalue 'Value'
 FROM
    OPENXML (@iDoc, '/ROOT/contactvalue ', 2)
 WITH (Id int '@id', Name nvarchar(200) '@name', ContactValue nvarchar(4000) '.')

EXEC sp_xml_removedocument @iDoc

GO
```

So there we have it. We've accomplished several things:

- To process multiple items, we've made only one call to the database (excluding the initial bootstrapping calls)
- Leveraged FOR XML and OPEN XML and created an object to encapsulate building of what used to be delimited values into a structured XML format
- Created a reusable object that can be used with other similar solutions
- Allowed for any and all values using the <![CDATA[]]> node within the XML

Limitations:

- Stored Procedure variable size is limited to nVarChar(4000)
- Must use SQL Server 2000, earlier additions do not offer XML support

Things to remember:

- Remember XML is case sensitive, so keep that in mind when writing your SELECT…FOR XML query

For more on XML support within SQL Server 2000:

- http://msdn.microsoft.com/library/default.asp?url=/library/en-us/tsqlref/ts_oa-oz_5c89.asp
- http://msdn.microsoft.com/library/default.asp?url=/library/en-us/xmlsql/ac_openxml_1hd8.asp

SQL Server 2005

As we write this book, we're in the post Beta 2 phase, with the 3rd Community Technical Preview of SQL Server 2005 having been recently released. And given the news lately, it doesn't seem to be much of a race to see if this book publishes before SQL Server 2005 released (it will).

But most of these articles have been written on Beta 2 or the first CTP release. Given that, have an open mind if you read them since it is likely that there will be changes in the final product.

Content on the new version of SQL Server has been fairly scarce, probably because most people know there will be changes and are waiting until at least Beta 3 to do any heavy duty writing. The changes from then to the RTM version, if this product follows a similar cycle to those in the past, will be mostly performance related.

So if you haven't seen the product, here's a small sample of what it's like.

Introduction to DTS in SQL Server 2005

By Vinod Kumar

Introduction

One of the key features introduced in SQL Server 2005 is the new DTS platform. With the new release of SQL Server Beta 2, you must be eager to get your hands dirty on this new amazing platform. This product does bring in a new perspective and new thinking the way we used to work with DTS. Most of the DTS architecture has undergone dramatic changes. In this article I will walk through an step-by-step easy uploading of a given datafile into SQL Server. This new version of DTS does go beyond the ETL (Extract, Transform, Load) tools definition. You can orchestrate your code and create an workflow with the same. DTS in Yukon is more manageable, usable and more mature from its previous version.

Understanding BI Project

To start creating the project, go to Start->All Programs->SQL Server 2005->Select Business Intelligent Development Studio. This will open up an environment that is very much familiar to all developers, VS Studio IDE. Press Crtl+Shift+N or Use File->New->New Project option. This will list all the business intelligent projects available. The BI "Workbench" doesn't require a direct connection to the SQL Server to design packages, nor does it require a connection to save work. Since this is an IDE that looks feels and does almost most of the VS Studio environment. It also allows us to integrate our DTS Projects with version control software like VSS.

For our exercise we will select Data Transformation Project as selected in the diagram above. After setting our project directory and the project name properly click on OK. This will create the necessary directory structure and all the project related files. The Solution explorer will open up with a default DTS Package. We will change our package name to your custom needs.

Most of the basic functionality and the explanation of various tasks can be found from my <u>first DTS article at my website</u>. Selecting the DTS Package we are presented in the main application frame and looking at the Design view, we find interesting tabs.

Control Flow: Gives a logical window to look at tasks. The concept is same to what it used to look in the DTS 2000 world too. This window contains some interesting new tasks, constraints and looping operators like the FOR Loop, FOR EACH Loop, SEQUENCE etc. This is the main task window. All the related control flow tasks are presented in the next task frame. Some of the interesting events are:

Looping Containers

ActiveX Script Task

Bulk Insert task

Data flow task

Execute DTS Package

File System Task

MSMQ Task

Send Mail task

Data Flow: The Data Flow designer manages all of the data movement and transformations between a source and target. In order to include data flow within your package, you must manually add a Data Flow task to the Control Flow designer or let DTS do it for you when you open the Data Flow designer window. All projects can have multiple Data Flow tasks and all tasks can have a source and destination activities. There can be various transformations possible like the Aggregation; Derived Columns are possible. This can also be considered as an aggregation of logical tasks.

Event Handlers: This is an interface through which the task raises events and exposes the opportunity for events to be handled. DTS events for every executable container task within the package's runtime environment are exposed in the user interface, with each event having the possibility of its own event handler design surface for implementing compound work flows. Some event handlers provided are: OnCustomEvent, OnError, OnExecStatusChanged, OnNMProgress, OnPostExecute, OnPostValidate, OnPreExecute, OnPreValidate, OnProgress. All the parameters available for the present package are displayed in this section.

Package Explorer: This gives us an interface through which we can execute the package and view the health of the running Package. It gives you statistics of the various pipelines available, how they were executed, and how they were synchronized. The total execution time is also monitored through this window.

Creating our project

In this demo our requirement is to upload windows an event viewer data into SQL Server tables. This might sound very simple. But let's see how we can make this requirement interesting. With a simple visual check at the datafile we can see there are multiple types available. A typical datafile looks like:

```
Type,Date,Time,Source,Category,Event,User,Computer
Information,05-Aug-04,8:14:39 AM,DataTransformationServices90,None,12289,N/A,VINODKNET01
Success Audit,05-Aug-04,8:14:39 AM,MSSQLSERVER,Logon ,18453,vinodk,VINODKNET01
Error,05-Aug-04,8:13:29 AM,DataTransformationServices90,None,12291,N/A,VINODKNET01
Success Audit,05-Aug-04,8:13:28 AM,MSSQLSERVER,Logon ,18453,vinodk,VINODKNET01
Information,05-Aug-04,8:13:28 AM,DataTransformationServices90,None,12288,N/A,VINODKNET01
Information,05-Aug-04,6:15:00 AM,MSDTC,TM,4097,N/A,VINODKNET01
Error,05-Aug-04,6:15:00 AM,Userinit,None,1000,N/A,VINODKNET01
Error,05-Aug-04,6:15:00 AM,Userenv,None,1054,SYSTEM,VINODKNET01
Success Audit,05-Aug-04,1:27:31 AM,MSSQLSERVER,Logon ,18453,vinodk,VINODKNET01
Error,05-Aug-04,1:24:04 AM,DataTransformationServices90,None,12291,N/A,VINODKNET01
Warning,14-Jul-04,7:24:46 PM,WinMgmt,None,62,N/A,VINODKNET01
```

As said before, we can find there are different types like Success, Information, Warnings, Error and so on. In this DTS Package we will try to upload each eventlog source type into respective tables of our choice. I've also added the sample datafile for your reference. Having laid our foundation in understanding our datafile structure, let's take a look at the tables these data would get into.

> Aggevnt - Get a distinct count of the source available in the datafile

> ErrorEvents - All error events are loaded into this table

> Evntlog - All information events are loaded into this table

> FailureEvents - All failure events are loaded into this table

> SuccessAuditEvents - All success events are loaded into this table

> WarningEvents - All warning events are loaded into this table

For the first step in our control flow window, we will truncate all the above tables before the data is inserted into the table. Drag and drop "Execute SQL Task" into the orchestration frame. You will find a "red cross". This represents an unavailability of database connection to execute the database task. Select the Connection information or create one. And last but not least, we need to provide the SQL Statement. After specifying the configuration our final SQL Task window would look like:

Next, drag and drop a Data flow task onto the Control flow window. Then connect the output of the Execute task onto the Data flow task. Now the final Control flow task would look like:

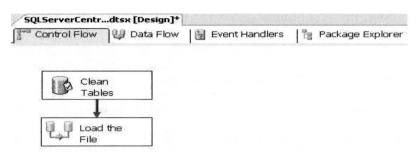

Double click on the data flow task. You will be presented with the Data flow frame window. As said earlier, this is the place where we would logically group tasks and perform units of work. And this is the window where we are going to perform the actual designing of our DTS Package. The first task is to get the input datafile into our DTS Package. So drag and drop the "Raw File Source" as the input. Double click on the package and give proper connection information to the flat file. The columns tab after the connection information would look like:

Flat File Source Editor

Configure the properties used to connect to and obtain data from a text file.

Connection
Columns
Error Output

Available External...

	Name
☑	Type
☑	Date
☑	Time
☑	Source
☑	Category
☑	Event
☑	User
☑	Computer

External Column	Output Column
Type	Type
Date	Date
Time	Time
Source	Source
Category	Category
Event	Event
User	User
Computer	Computer

OK   Cancel

Taking a closer look at the requirement, we can see that we have to get the distinct count of the Source and at the same time have to get the file data into our tables. For this task we need to use a Multicast task. The multicast transformation implements the functionality to distribute a single inbound dataset amongst several outputs. The benefits of the multicast are apparent when needing to push the identical dataset to two or more destinations. For our requirement we need to pipe it to a aggregate function and a character map function. The aggregate data flow transform allows for the aggregation of input data from a data stream to multiple aggregation outputs at varying aggregation grouping levels. A typical aggregate output can be as Sum, Count, Average, Maximum, Minimum etc. We can also group by input columns like:

And the character mapping allows us to change the characters input and in-line activity or can form as a new column to the input stream. For this basic task, we will change the input type information to upper case. This will be used for our bifurcation process. Hence the character mapping data will look like:

Finishing our first stage, let us look how our Data flow looks. It surely looks cool !!! But, I assure you, the final output would look even more beautiful.

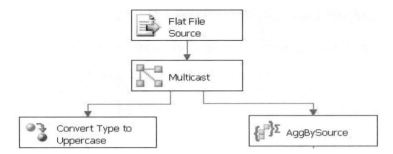

Our next step is to load all the data into SQL Server. For the same, just drag and drop an OLE DB Destination. The OLE DB destination is one of the destination types found in the DTS data flow architecture. This destination allows for the connectivity with destinations that are OLE DB compliant. Since SQL Server is also OLE DB Compliant, this task can be used effectively. Just connect the input flow and give the connection information. We are all set to play with the column mapping tab and finally the data gets into SQL Server. Typical OLE DB Destination connection information looks like:

Now we have accomplished one-half of our requirement. The other requirement is to insert data from the datafile into corresponding tables. For this we need to use an un-conditional split operation. The conditional split transformation handles the re-direction of data based upon conditions being met. These conditional expressions can be driven by columnar values or variables that are within scope for the data flow task and the transform. And for our requirement we can take a look at the conditional-split operation.

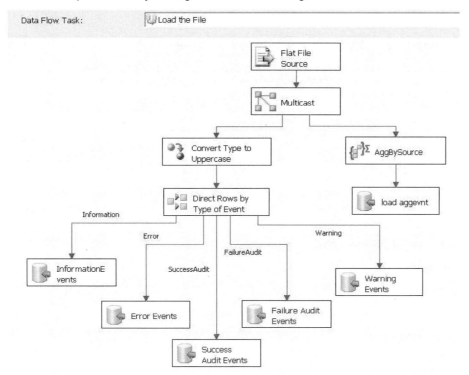

Hereafter, we are on course to insert data into our corresponding tables using OLE DB Destination. The final finished product surely looks graceful and more elegant !!!

If you wish to execute a package, you can click on the play icon on the toolbar, press F5, or choose Debug

-> Start from the menu. This puts the design environment into execution mode, opens several new windows, enables several new menu and toolbar items, and begins to execute the package. We can also optionally debug the package using the watch window. Just double click on the connecting arrows and set some watch variables and re-execute the package. Let's take a look at the number of rows loaded into the system.

```
Select
(Select Count(*) from [dbo].[aggevnt]) as [aggevnt],
(Select Count(*) from [dbo].[ErrorEvents]) as [ErrorEvents],
(Select Count(*) from [dbo].[evntlog]) as [evntlog],
(Select Count(*) from [dbo].[FailureEvents]) as [FailureEvents],
(Select Count(*) from [dbo].[SuccessAuditEvents]) as [SuccessAuditEvents],
(Select Count(*) from [dbo].[WarningEvents]) as [WarningEvents]
```

	aggevnt	ErrorEvents	evntlog	FailureEvents	SuccessAuditEv...	WarningEvents
1	32	222	1532	18	5052	160

With the minimum config and dry run on my personal laptop. I was able to run this package and load data into Yukon in less than 1.5 seconds. And I am amazed with the improvements DTS Pipelines have introduced.

Conclusions

I think in this article we have taken a sneak preview to what Yukon DTS is to offer us. I have been playing with this new DTS architecture for sometime now and I feel DTS has given a fresh look and feel to this ETL tool. I like DTS on its usability fronts and with a final word is: Yukon rocks !!!

SQL Server 2005 DBCC Command Quick Reference

By Jon Reade

New, undocumented and retired DBCC Commands in SQL Server 2005

Even new DBCC commands have been introduced by Microsoft's SQL Server development team. Unfortunately, little or no documentation is available on the new commands listed below, though some of them may be documented in the RTM release.
Those that are listed as being documented do not require a trace flag to be set before using them. However, to use the undocumented commands, you will need to turn on trace flag 2588.
This has changed since SQL Server 7.0/2000, where the trace flag was 2520.

Please note that the following is a result of investigations with the beta 2 release of SQL Server 2005. The final RTM release may differ slightly.

As always, **never** use an undocumented DBCC command on a production server unless advised by Microsoft, and never use a documented one unless you understand how it may affect the performance of your server.

DBCC commands new to SQL Server 2005

Documented new commands

freesessioncache () -- no parameters

requeststats ({clear} | {setfastdecayrate, rate} | {setslowdecayrate, rate})

Undocumented new commands

mapallocunit (I8AllocUnitId | {I4part, I2part})

metadata ({'print' [, printopt = {0 |1}] | 'drop' | 'clone' [, '' | ....]}, {'object' [, 'type',...}, {Id | Name}, [{Ownerid | Ownername}], [{Dbid | Dbname}]])

optimizer_whatif property, value

persiststackhash (hashfile, BUFLATCH_TIMEOUT | ATTENTION | OUTOFLOCKS | LATCH_ATTN | OUTOFLOG | OUTOFMEM | SOS [, SKIPLAST | INCLUDELAST])

semetadata (object id | name, index id | name [, partition id])

DBCC commands altered since SQL Server 2000

The following is presented as a list of pairs of commands. The first command is the old syntax, as used in SQL Server 2000. The second of each pair is the altered syntax new to SQL Server 2005. In most cases, the commands have been extended to take advantage of passing an object ID instead of a name, but if your scripts use any of these commands, it's probably worth checking them out before you migrate to SS2K5.

2000 : checkalloc [('database_name'[, NOINDEX | REPAIR])] [WITH NO_INFOMSGS[, ALL_ERRORMSGS] [, ESTIMATEONLY]]
2005 : checkalloc [('dbname'|dbid[, NOINDEX | REPAIR])] [WITH NO_INFOMSGS[,ALL_ERRORMSGS][, ESTIMATEONLY]]
Changes : SQL Server 2005 now accepts the dbid as well as the dbname

2000 : checkdb [('database_name'[, NOINDEX | REPAIR])] [WITH NO_INFOMSGS[, ALL_ERRORMSGS][, PHYSICAL_ONLY][, ESTIMATEONLY][, TABLOCK]
2005 : checkdb [('dbname | dbid'[, NOINDEX | REPAIR])] [WITH NO_INFOMSGS[,ALL_ERRORMSGS][, PHYSICAL_ONLY][, ESTIMATEONLY][, TABLOCK]]
Changes : SQL Server 2005 now accepts the dbid as well as the dbname

2000 : checkident ('table_name'[, { NORESEED | {RESEED [, new_reseed_value] } }])
2005 : checkident ('table_name'[, { NORESEED | {RESEED [, new_reseed_value] } }])
Changes :
Although the syntax is identical for SQL Server 2000 and 2005, there is a subtle change in the behaviour of this command.
In SQL Server 7.0 and 2000, running checkident would cause the identity column to be re-seeded, even if the table was empty.
In SQL Server 2005, if the table is empty when dbcc checkident is run, the reseed value will be ignored.

2000 : dbrepair ('dbname', DROPDB [, NOINIT])
2005 : dbrepair ('dbname', markdirty | {dropdevice, int} | {repairindex, int, int})
Changes : dropdevice syntax changed ; markdirty and repairindex options added
NB : It seems odd that this command has been extended with this release, as in the SQL Server 2005 setup help file, setupsql9.chm, it states that DROP DATABASE should be used instead of this command. It was included in SQL Server 2000 for backward compatibility only.

2000 : indexdefrag ({dbid | dbname | 0}, {tableid | tablename}, {indid | indname})
2005 : indexdefrag ({dbname | dbid | 0}, {tableid | tablename} [, {indid | indname} [, partition_number]])
Changes : An extra optional parameter has been added, partition_number

2000 : inputbuffer (spid)
2005 : inputbuffer (spid, [batchid])
Changes : An extra optional parameter has been added, batch_id

2000 : outputbuffer (spid)
2005 : outputbuffer (spid, [batchid])
Changes : An extra optional parameter has been added, batch_id

2000 : proccache
2005 : proccache ([compplan_ticks_threshold])
Changes : An optional parameter has been added, compplan_ticks_threshold

2000 : sqlperf (LOGSPACE)({IOSTATS | LRUSTATS | NETSTATS | RASTATS [, CLEAR]} | {THREADS} | {LOGSPACE})
2005 : sqlperf (LOGSPACE | IOSTATS | NETSTATS | RASTATS [, CLEAR]} | [THREADS])
Changes : As for 2000, but LRUSTATS has been removed as an option.

NB : Microsoft only document the LOGSPACE parameter of this command - use any others at your own discretion.

2000 : updateusage ({'database_name'| 0} [, 'table_name' [, index_id]]) [WITH [NO_INFOMSGS] [,] COUNT_ROWS]
2005 : updateusage ({'dbname' | dbid | 0} [, {'table_name' | table_id} [,{index_id | 'index_name'}]]) [WITH [NO_INFOMSGS] [,] COUNT_ROWS]
Changes : Can now specify db_id, table_id, or the index name as parameters, instead of just the db/table/index name.

Also note that there is a problem with the output generated by the dbcc showcontig command under certain conditions in the beta version of SQL Server 2005, where more than one block of information per index is generated for tables that contain text columns.

DBCC commands retired since SQL Server 2000

Many of us have used them at one time or another, and a few might even depend upon them. However, we can't say we have not been warned, and Microsoft has finally retired a whole raft of dbcc commands in SQL Server 2005.
Most of these were not particularly useful, but thoughtfully retained right up to SQL Server 2000 for backward compatibility with SQL Server 6.5 and earlier scripts.
The following dbcc commands are now dead and buried from SQL Server 2005 onwards:

```
adduserobject (name)
balancefactor (variance_percent)
bufcount [(number_of_buffers)]
cacheprofile [( {actionid} [, bucketid])
checkdbts (dbid, newTimestamp)]
des [( {'dbname' | dbid} [, {'objname' | objid} ])]
dropuserobject ('object_name')
getvalue (name)
iotrace ( { 'dbname' | dbid | 0 | -1 }, { fileid | 0 }, bufsize, [ { numIOs | -1 } [, { timeout (sec)
| -1 } [, printopt={ 0 | 1 }]]] )
lockobjectschema ('object_name')
matview ({'PERSIST' | 'ENDPERSIST' | 'FREE' | 'USE' | 'ENDUSE'})
memospy
memusage ([IDS | NAMES], [Number of rows to output])
monitorevents ('sink' [, 'filter-expression'])
newalloc (previously retired, use of checkalloc recommended instead)
perflog
pglinkage (dbid, startfile, startpg, number, printopt={0|1|2}, targetfile, targetpg, order={1|0})
procbuf [({'dbname' | dbid}[, {'objname' | objid}[, nbufs[, printopt = { 0 | 1 } ]]] )]
rebuild_log (dbname [, filename])
row_lock (dbid, tableid, set) - Not Needed
shrinkdb (previously retired, use of shrinkdatabase recommended instead)
tab ( dbid, objid )
tape_control {'query' | 'release'}[,('\\.\tape')]
textall [({'database_name'|database_id}[, 'FULL' | FAST] )]
textalloc ({'table_name'|table_id}[, 'FULL' | FAST])
upgradedb (db)
usagegovernor (command, value)
wakeup (spid)
```

DBCC commands included in SQL Server 2005, which will be retired at a later date

dbreindex
This will be replaced with the REBUILD option of the ALTER INDEX statement.

indexdefrag
This will be replaced with the REORGANIZE option of the ALTER INDEX statement.

showcontig
This command will be replace by the system function fn_indexinfo

Complete list of documented SQL Server 2005 DBCC commands

```
checkalloc [('dbname'|dbid[, NOINDEX | REPAIR])] [WITH NO_INFOMSGS[, ALL_ERRORMSGS][, ESTIMATEONLY]]
checkcatalog [('dbname'|dbid)] [WITH NO_INFOMSGS]
checkconstraints [( 'tab_name' | tab_id | 'constraint_name' | constraint_id )] [WITH ALL_CONSTRAINTS |
ALL_ERRORMSGS]
checkdb [('dbname | dbid'[, NOINDEX | REPAIR])] [WITH NO_INFOMSGS[, ALL_ERRORMSGS][, PHYSICAL_ONLY][,
ESTIMATEONLY][, TABLOCK]]
```

```
checkfilegroup [( [ {'filegroup_name' | filegroup_id} ] [, NOINDEX] )] [WITH NO_INFOMSGS[,
ALL_ERRORMSGS][, PHYSICAL_ONLY][, ESTIMATEONLY][, TABLOCK]]
checkident ('table_name'[, { NORESEED | {RESEED [, new_reseed_value] } } ] )
checktable ('table_name'[, {NOINDEX | index_id | REPAIR}]) [WITH NO_INFOMSGS[, ALL_ERRORMSGS][,
PHYSICAL_ONLY][, ESTIMATEONLY][, TABLOCK]]
cleantable ('dbname'|dbid, 'table_name'|table_id [, batch_size])
concurrencyviolation (reset | display | startlog | stoplog)
dbreindex ('table_name' [, index_name [, fillfactor]]) [WITH NO_INFOMSGS]
dbrepair ('dbname', markdirty | {dropdevice, int} | {repairindex, int, int})
dropcleanbuffers
free dll_name (FREE) e.g. DBCC xp_sample (FREE)
freeproccache
freesessioncache
help ('dbcc_command' | '?')
indexdefrag ({dbname | dbid | 0}, {tableid | tablename} [, {indid | indname} [, partition_number]])
inputbuffer (spid, [batchid])
opentran [({'dbname'| dbid})] [WITH TABLERESULTS[,NO_INFOMSGS]]
outputbuffer (spid, [batchid])
perfmon
pintable (database_id, table_id)
proccache ([compplan_ticks_threshold])
requeststats ({clear} | {setfastdecayrate, rate} | {setslowdecayrate, rate})
show_statistics ('table_name'[, 'target_name'])
showcontig ([table_id | table_name [, index_id | index_name]] [WITH FAST, ALL_INDEXES, TABLERESULTS
[,ALL_LEVELS]])
shrinkdatabase ({'dbname'|dbid}, [freespace_percentage [, {NOTRUNCATE | TRUNCATEONLY}]])
shrinkfile ({fileid | 'filename'} {[, EMPTYFILE] | [[, compress_size] [, {NOTRUNCATE |
TRUNCATEONLY}]]})
sqlperf (LOGSPACE)
traceoff [( tracenum [, tracenum ... ] )]
traceon [( tracenum [, tracenum ... ] )]
tracestatus (trace# [, ...trace#])
unpintable (dbid, table_id)
updateusage ({'dbname' | dbid | 0} [, {'table_name' | table_id} [, {index_id | 'index_name'}]]) [WITH
[NO_INFOMSGS] [,] COUNT_ROWS]
useroptions
```

Complete list of undocumented SQL Server 2005 DBCC commands

```
activecursors [(spid)]
addextendedproc (function_name, dll_name)
addinstance (objectname, instancename)
auditevent (eventclass, eventsubclass, success, loginname, rolename, dbusername, loginid, objname,
servername, providername)
autopilot (typeid [, dbid [, {maxQueryCost | tabid [, indid [, pages [, flag [, rowcounts]]]]} ]])
buffer ( {'dbname' | dbid} [, objid [, number [, printopt={0|1|2} ][, dirty | io | kept | rlock |
ioerr | hashed ]]])
bytes ( startaddress, length )
cacheprofile ( actionid [, bucketid])
cachestats
callfulltext - system sp use only
checkprimaryfile ( {'FileName'} [, opt={0|1|2|3} ])
clearspacecaches ('dbname'|dbid, 'table_name'|table_id, 'index_name'|index_id [, partition_number])
collectstats (on | off)
cursorstats ([spid [,'clear']])
dbrecover (dbname [, IgnoreErrors])
dbreindexall (dbname|dbid[, type_bitmap])
debugbreak
deleteinstance (objectname, instancename)
detachdb ( 'dbname' [, fKeep_Fulltext_Index_File (0 | 1)] )
dropextendedproc (function_name)
config
dbinfo [('dbname')]
dbtable [({'dbname' | dbid})]
lock ([{'DUMPTABLE' | 'DUMPSTATS' | 'RESETSTATS' | 'HASH'}]|[{'STALLREPORTTHESHOLD', stallthreshold}])
log (dbname | dbid [,{0|1|2|3|4}[,['lsn','[0x]x:y:z']|['numrecs',num]|['xdesid','x:y']|
['extent','x:y']|['pageid','x:y']|['objid',{x,'y'}]|['logrecs',{'lop'|op}...]|['output',x,
['filename','x']]...]]])
page ( {'dbname' | dbid}, filenum, pagenum [, printopt={0|1|2|3} ])
pss [(uid[, spid[, printopt = { 1 | 0 }]] )]
resource
dumptrigger ({'BREAK', {0 | 1}} | 'DISPLAY' | {'SET', exception_number} | {'CLEAR', exception_number})
errorlog
extentinfo [({'dbname'| dbid | 0} [, {'tablename' | tableid} [, {'indexname' | indexid | -1} [,
partition_number]]])]
fileheader [( {'dbname' | dbid} [, fileid])
fixallocation [({'ADD' | 'REMOVE'}, {'PAGE' | 'SINGLEPAGE' | 'EXTENT' | 'MIXEDEXTENT'}, filenum,
pagenum [, objectid, indexid, partitionid, allocUnitId])
flush ('data' | 'log', dbname | dbid)
flushprocindb (dbid)
```

```
freeze_io (dbname | dbid)
icecapquery ('dbname' [, stored_proc_name [, #_times_to_icecap (-1 infinite, 0 turns off)]])
Use 'dbcc icecapquery (printlist)' to see list of SP's to profile.
Use 'dbcc icecapquery (icecapall)' to profile all SP's.
incrementinstance (objectname, countername, instancename, value)
ind ( { 'dbname' | dbid }, { 'objname' | objid }, { indid | 0 | -1 | -2 } [, partition_number] )
invalidate_textptr (textptr)
invalidate_textptr_objid (objid)
latch ( address [, 'owners'] [, 'stackdumps'])
loginfo [({'dbname' | dbid})]
mapallocunit (I8AllocUnitId | (I4part, I2part})
memobjlist [(memory object)]
memorymap
memorystatus
metadata ({'print' [, printopt = {0 |1}] | 'drop' | 'clone' [, '' | ....]}, {'object' [, 'type',...},
{Id | Name}, [{Ownerid | Ownername}], [{Dbid | Dbname}]])
no_textptr (table_id , max_inline)
optimizer_whatif property, value
persiststackhash (hashfile, BUFLATCH_TIMEOUT | ATTENTION | OUTOFLOCKS | LATCH_ATTN | OUTOFLOG |
OUTOFMEM | SOS [, SKIPLAST | INCLUDELAST])
prtipage (dbname | dbid, objid | objname, indexid | indexname [, partition_number [, level]]). No
partition specified uses the first partition. No level specified prints root page.
readpage ({'dbname'|dbid}, fileid, pageid, formatstr [, printopt = { 0 | 1} ])
renamecolumn (object_name, old_name, new_name)
ruleoff ({ rulenum | rulestring } [, { rulenum | rulestring } ]+)
ruleon ( rulenum | rulestring } [, { rulenum | rulestring } ]+)
semetadata (object id | name, index id | name [, partition id])
setcpuweight (weight)
setinstance (objectname, countername, instancename, value)
setioweight (weight)
showdbaffinity
showfilestats [(file_num)]
showoffrules
showonrules
showtableaffinity (table_id | table_name [, partition_number])
showtext ('dbname' | dbid, {textpointer | {fileid, pageid, slotid [,option]}})
showweights
sqlmgrstats
stackdump [( {uid[, spid [, batchid [, ecid]]} | {threadId, 'THREADID'}] )]
tec [( uid[, spid[, batchid[, ecid]] )]
thaw_io (dbname | dbid)
useplan [(number_of_plan)]
writepage ({'dbname' | dbid}, fileid, pageid, offset, length, data)
Acknowledgements and references:
```

SQL Server 2005 Express Edition

Except where noted below, the above investigation was carried out on the Beta 2 release of SQL Server 2005 Express Edition.

At the time of writing (November 2004) this product was available as a free download at http://www.microsoft.com/sql/

SQL Server 2005 Setup Help (c) Microsoft Corporation 2004.

The information about future discontinued DBCC commands was sourced from Microsoft's SQL Server 2005 setup help file.

It is recommended reading for anyone who writes commercial database software that depends upon the lower-level functionality provided by SQL Server, as it includes details of discontinued commands and configuration options.

This document can be found at C:\Program Files\Microsoft SQL Server\90\Setup Bootstrap\Help\1033\setupsql9.chm, after installing SQL Server 2005 Express Edition to the default installation directory.

Search on "dbcc" to find this information.

Yukon Passwords

By Randy Dyess

Among the changes brought to you by the next version of SQL Server is the ability to tie SQL Server login passwords into the Windows 2003 local policy for passwords. This ability allows SQL Server login passwords to enjoy the same complexity and expiration policies long associated with Windows login passwords.

Not to take anything away from this nice step forward by Microsoft, there are a few limitations when dealing with the new password policies. One of the limitations is that the policy enforcement can only be initiated with SQL Server installations running on Windows 2003 servers. Windows 2000 installations will ignore some of the new changes, but a weak SQL Server only policy similar to the MBSA checks will be performed. Another limitation is the granularity of the policy choices. You must either turn all three choices on, only turn on the expiration policy, or only turn on the account lockout and password complexity policy. It would have been nice to be able to only enforce password complexity without having to accept the potential problems associated with account lockouts. Another limitation is the password policies must be the same as the local Windows password policy. This is a nice combination as it allows similar policies, but it would also be nice to be able to set up a separate policy structure for your SQL Server application.

Password Complexity

If you set the CHECK_POLICY property of the login to ON, which it is by default, then you will have the ability to control the complexity of your SQL Server login passwords during their creation and during any password reset.

The default behavior of Windows is to have the password complexity filter, **Passflt.dll**, inactive by default. You can activate this filter and all passwords will be required to have at least 8 characters and be created with characters from three of the four following lists:

- English Uppercase characters
- English Lowercase characters
- Numeric characters
- Special characters

You can alter this behavior with a custom password filter, but this filter will require advance C++ and Windows API skills.

YUKON installations running on Windows 2000 installations will not utilize the Windows Security API to enforce password complexity but will use policies similar to that of the Microsoft Baseline Security Analyzer and only check for the following conditions:

- Blank or Null passwords
- Passwords same as the user name
- Passwords same as the machine name
- Passwords of "Password", "Admin", or "Administrator"

Account lockout

If you set the CHECK_POLICY property of the login to ON, which it is by default, then you will have the ability to control whether your login will be locked-out when X login attempts fail. This policy is the same as when you forget your Windows account password and only have X number of times to guess before your account is locked-out for a set number of minutes or until it is reset by an administrator. This feature was included for SQL Server logins to prevent those brute-force password attacks that are common with SQL Server installations. While this is a great idea for some of your SQL Server logins, you may want to turn this feature off for your main application logins or you will find yourself the easy victim of DOS attacks that leave all your application users sitting there as the application continually fails because of the login lockout. This feature will need to be tested over time to see if it is worth utilizing or not. My feeling is that it would be great for human logins but not for application logins.

This policy is only available for YUKON installations running on Windows 2003 and above installations.

Password Expiration

If you set the CHECK_EXPIRATION property of the login to ON, which it is by default, then you will have the ability to control whether your SQL Server login passwords expire or not. Setting this property to OFF will have the same effect as using the "Password Never Expires" option available for Windows login. Like Windows logins, when the password is about to expire the users are given a warning to change them. This policy is another useful policy to use for your human logins but not for your non-human logins

This policy is only available for YUKON installations running on Windows 2003 and above installations.

Password Enforcement

Authentication:
Checks performed during authentication include both the check for account lockout and for password age restrictions.

Password Set/Change:
Checks performed during password creation or changes include both checks for password complexity and for password history rules. These checks allow for the same rules for the complexity of the password and to make sure the same set of passwords are not used over and over.

Client Side Support:
Another nice change is the ability to force users and allow users to change their SQL Server login passwords during logging in. This ability will give administrators some relief as they no longer have to let users change their passwords with the **sp_password** system stored procedure, nor do they have to change the password themselves if the users do not have the ability to execute the **sp_password** system stored procedure.

Transact-SQL Statements

CREATE LOGIN
Creates a new Microsoft Windows or SQL Server login account. Permissions default to members of the **sysadmin** and **securityadmin** fixed server roles and to logins with ALTER ANY LOGIN permission.

Syntax
CREATE LOGIN *login_name*
{ WITH *option_list1* | FROM WINDOWS [WITH *option_list2* [,...]] }

option_list1 ::=
PASSWORD *password* [HASHED] [MUST CHANGE] [, *option_list3* [,...]]

option_list2 ::=
DEFAULT_DATABASE = *database* | DEFAULT_LANGUAGE = *language*

option_list3 ::=
| SID = *sid*
| DEFAULT_DATABASE = *database*
| DEFAULT_LANGUAGE = *language*
| CHECK_EXPIRATION = { ON | OFF }
| CHECK_POLICY = { ON | OFF }

Arguments
login_name Specifies the name of the SQL Server or Windows login that is being created.

PASSWORD *password* Specifies the password for the login that is being created.

HASHED Applies to SQL Server logins only. Specifies that the password is already hashed.

MUST_CHANGE Applies to SQL Server logins only. If this option is included, SQL Server will prompt for an updated password the first time the new login is used.

SID = *sid* Applies to SQL Server logins only. Specifies the GUID of the new SQL login. If this option is not included, SQL Server will automatically assign a GUID.

DEFAULT_DATABASE = *database* Specifies the default database to be assigned to the login. If this option is not included, the default database will be set to MASTER.

DEFAULT_LANGUAGE = *language* Specifies the default language to be assigned to the login. If this option is not included, the default language will be set to the current default language of the server. If the default language of the server is changed in the future, the default language of the login will remain unchanged.

CHECK_EXPIRATION Applies to SQL Server logins only. Specifies that password expiration policy should be enforced on this login. The default value is ON.

CHECK_POLICY Applies to SQL Server logins only. Specifies that the Windows password policies of the computer on which SQL Server is running should be enforced on this login. The default value is ON.

Remarks
Pre-hashing of passwords is supported only when creating SQL Server logins

ALTER LOGIN
Changes the properties of a Microsoft Windows or SQL Server login account.

Syntax
ALTER LOGIN *login_name* WITH *set_option* [,...]
set_option::=
PASSWORD = *password* [OLD PASSWORD = *oldpassword*
| *secadmin_pwd_option* [*secadmin_pwd_option*]]
| SID =*sid*
| DEFAULT_DATABASE = *database*
| DEFAULT_LANGUAGE = *language*
| NAME = *login_name*
| CHECK_POLICY = {ON|OFF}
| CHECK_EXPIRATION = {ON|OFF}

secadmin_pwd_opt := MUST CHANGE | UNLOCK

Arguments
login_name Specifies the name of the SQL Server or Windows login that is being created.

PASSWORD *password* Specifies the password for the login that is being created.

HASHED Applies to SQL Server logins only. Specifies that the password is already hashed.

MUST_CHANGE Applies to SQL Server logins only. If this option is included, SQL Server will prompt for an updated password the first time the new login is used.

SID = *sid* Applies to SQL Server logins only. Specifies the GUID of the new SQL login. If this option is not included, SQL Server will automatically assign a GUID.

DEFAULT_DATABASE = *database* Specifies the default database to be assigned to the login. If this option is not included, the default database will be set to MASTER.

DEFAULT_LANGUAGE = *language* Specifies the default language to be assigned to the login. If this option is not included, the default language will be set to the current default language of the server. If the default language of the server is changed in the future, the default language of the login will remain unchanged.

CHECK_EXPIRATION Applies to SQL Server logins only. Specifies that password expiration policy should be enforced on this login. The default value is ON.

CHECK_POLICY Applies to SQL Server logins only. Specifies that the Windows password policies of the computer on which SQL Server is running should be enforced on this login. The default value is ON.

UNLOCK Specifies that a locked login should be unlocked.

LOGINPROPERTY

Syntax
LoginProperty ('*login-name*','*property*')

Arguments

login-name The name of the SQL Server login.
'property The property to be queried: .

> IsLocked If the login is currently locked out. .
> IsExpired If the login is has expired. .
> IsMustChange Checks to see if the login needs to change it's password on the next login.

sys.sql_logins

This catalog view contains a row for each security principal that is a SQL login (of type S).

name SYSNAME NOT NULL Name of principal, unique within the database.
principal_id INTEGER NOT NULL ID of principal, unique within a database.
sid VARBINARY(85) NULL SID (Security Identifier) if the principal is defined external to the database (type S, U, and G), else NULL
type CHAR(1) NOT NULL Principal Type, one of:

> S = SQL User
> U = Windows User
> G = Windows Group
> A = Application Role
> R = Database Role

create_date DATETIME NOT NULL Login create date
modify_date DATETIME NOT NULL Login modify date
default_database_name SYSNAME NULL Name of the login's default database.
default_lanugage_name SYSNAME NULL Name of the login's default language.
is_secure_access_required BIT NULL If 1, then session encryption is required.
is_basic_auth_disabled BIT NULL If 1, then basic authentication is disabled.
is_ntlm_auth_disabled BIT NULL If 1, then NTLM authentication is disabled.
is_kerberos_auth_disabled BIT NULL If 1, Kerberos authentication is disabled.
is_policy_checked BIT NULL Password policy is checked.
is_expiration_checked BIT NULL Password expiration is checked.

Conclusion

The new password policy enforcement rules are active by default in YUKON but can be turned off by the administrator if you do not want every password to be checked. It would be a better option to keep the policy checks active and configure each login as it is created to be checked or not.

As you can see, the new changes are not sweeping in scope but they do offer a great step forward in thinking for Microsoft. In the past I have often wrote that it felt like Microsoft was giving up on using SQL Server logins altogether but with these new changes I am no longer sure of this. It is nice for them to recognize that not every application will be ported to Windows Authentication and that they need to continue with the strengthening of SQL Server logins.

I would like to let you know that the YUKON Beta 1 release was used during the research for this article and the information contained within this article may change during the subsequent Beta and Market releases. I doubt this will happen, but please test any policies or scripts you may create with the information contained within this article against the final release before making it actual policy.

Everything Else

The stuff that doesn't really fit into any category, mostly things that might be related to the softer side of being a DBA, your career, getting better at the non-technical parts of your job.

Hopefully these are the articles that give you some ideas, make you think, and help you to differentiate yourself from others.

Becoming More Productive

By Haidong Ji

Readers who follow my writing may notice a theme in most of my articles: automation. After all, we are in the computer business and computer technology is supposed to make our life easier. Whenever we can, we want computers to do things for us, not the other way around. To that end, I am constantly looking for ways to automate tasks and increase my productivity. Giving the ever increasing workload on us all today, this is getting more and more important. After all, if we spend most of our time doing repetitive tasks, how can we find time to learn and do real creative stuff?!

In this article, I want to share with you some practical productivity tips that I learned over the years. Hopefully they will be helpful to you also. There are a lot of books on this subject. The famous ones are "Seven Habits of Highly Effective People"; and "Get things done: the art of stress-free productivity". I have not read the second one but have heard good reviews.

Touch type. Learn it if you are not doing it already

Touch typing is typing without looking at the keyboard. Not only you are typing faster, more importantly, when your eyes are off the keyboard and on the text you are typing, it feels like your thoughts are flowing through your fingers. Therefore, you are more likely to be "in the zone" and your thought process is not interrupted. This may sound trivial, but actually touches the core of high productivity. That is, to be highly productive, you need to concentrate for a period of time without interruptions.

Maybe a lot of readers out there do this already. For a non-native English speaker like me (my native language is Chinese), this does not come naturally. There are many different tutorial software packages that teach touch typing on the web. I've downloaded TypingMaster and followed that program. I cannot fully touch type yet, but feel that it has made a difference in my productivity, especially in composing emails.

Let's face it, most of us will spend a significant portion of our lifetime sitting in front of a computer. If you can type fast, imagine the time you could save over your lifetime. Download a touch typing program and practice for about 30 minutes or so after lunch every day for a few days. It is a very good investment of your time.

Master a good editor

As I mentioned above, we will spend a lot of time entering and editing text. Therefore, it is important that you use a text editor that you feel comfortable with and knows most of the functions and shortcuts (Avoid the mouse if you can, the time you have to move away from the keyboard and move the mouse is time wasted). The popular ones out there are EditPlus, UltraEdit, and TextPad. Steve Jones wrote his review on EditPlus; you can check it out here.

Don't use Microsoft Word to enter and edit your files. This is true almost in all cases. Word's many so-called features really are just distractions. If you have to, enter and edit text in your favorite editor first and format it in Word later after you are done. You probably end up saving time 9 out of 10 times. As for myself, for my own documentation purposes, I use plain text. If I need to make it look fancy, I just use HTML.

My personal favorite editor is VI. More specifically, it is VIM, because VIM is available in almost all platforms. I've heard many times before how great VI is. It really took a couple of years for me to get that and be productive in VI. (That is probably not strange. I read a very good essay somewhere that says it takes years to master a programming language. I've been learning C on and off for a few years now but still am not comfortable with it. I guess I need to use it to write something useful, instead of just following books and tutorials. If readers have or know of a project somewhere or on SourceForge that uses some beginning C skills, let me know, I'd like to participate). Once I learned a few VI commands, I was absolutely hooked. I now use VI for all my text editing tasks.

Handling emails

Email is such an important part of our life that we can hardly live without it, yet it can be a huge productivity killer if not handled properly. I will not waste my time here explaining why that is the case. I will just guide you to an excellent essay by Ole Eichhorn instead.

Things I do so that email enhances productivity, not diminishes it:

1. If you can, only check your email 3 or 4 times during the day. Leave your email software program closed the rest of the day. When I come to work every morning, I check my emails, tasks, and calendars within Outlook. I take note of tasks, appointments, and other things I need to do on a piece of paper and then promptly turn off Outlook. I then check again once after lunch, and once one hour before I go home. I may check more or less depending the tasks I have for that day;
2. If you have to leave your email open, turn off the new email notification feature if you have it on. It is such a distraction and a productivity killer;
3. Create folders within Outlook's inbox and create rules within Outlook to sort inbound emails automatically based on the sender, subject, etc. This way, your inbox is not going to be cluttered;
4. I classify my emails into 2 categories: Informational and Action-Oriented. For Informational emails, I will read them and decide if I want to keep them afterwards right away. This helps me to keep my mail box size under control.
   For Action-Oriented emails, if you use Outlook, you can create a macro that can automatically create an Outlook task for you. You can also set reminder in this task so that user request will never be buried in the email. Follow this link to get that macro.
5. If you use Outlook, get a plugin called Lookout from Microsoft. Lookout indexes all contents within Outlook. Afterwards, you can search your emails much, much faster. You usually get results within a second, much better than Outlook's built-in search function.
6. While on the topic of Lookout, I highly recommend you download Google's desktop search tool.

Conclusion and Resources

Let me know what you think by posting your comments on this article's forum. What are your favorite productivity enhancing tips?

Resources

1. TypingMaster, program that teaches touch typing;
2. Steve's review of EditPlus
3. VIM, one of the best editors;
4. an excellent essay by Ole Eichhorn on email;
5. Macro that creates a task when an email is selected;
6. Lookout, an excellent Outlook plugin for email, calendar, task, and contact search;
7. Google's desktop search tool.

Hidden Dangers!

By James Travis

Don't jump the gun before you read.

First let's discuss security at the personal level.

Many folks forget that the biggest threat is not outside their company, but inside. They walk away from their desk, forgetting to 3 finger salute and lock the desktop. While they are away and depending on where they are located, more people than they want could pass by and casually access the things they are responsible for or glean a bit of information.

Others receive emails with attachments that do bad things behind the scene but they run them anyway. Or they allow web pages to execute code without paying much attention. In this discussion it would be extremely hard to get required code executed unless the user lowers there IE security settings which in itself is not unheard of. Users have to be (especially those who are admins) more aware of holes in security and properly plan against them.

What the heck am I talking about?

It is simple--DMO opens you to potential attacks you may never have considered if you have any registered servers in Enterprise Manager. There are multiple security issues that may not have ever occurred to you as a user and thus you never gave them any thought.

Yes, I am being vague but let's jump in.

Saving your password when you use a SQL Account to attach to a remote server.

Bet more folks do this than anyone would ever imagine, but hackers surely have thought about it. But what does this have to do with danger; the password is encrypted in the registry, so unless they know the encryption schema they will be busy for a bit. So what is the danger?

Try this and you might be surprised. Create a VBS file name getit.vbs and enter the following code.

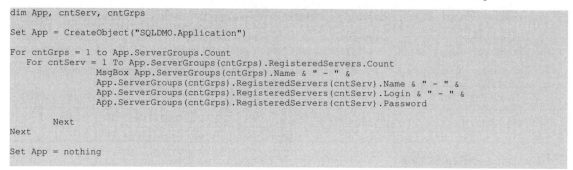

```
dim App, cntServ, cntGrps

Set App = CreateObject("SQLDMO.Application")

For cntGrps = 1 to App.ServerGroups.Count
    For cntServ = 1 To App.ServerGroups(cntGrps).RegisteredServers.Count
            MsgBox App.ServerGroups(cntGrps).Name & " - " &
            App.ServerGroups(cntGrps).RegisteredServers(cntServ).Name & " - " &
            App.ServerGroups(cntGrps).RegisteredServers(cntServ).Login & " - " &
            App.ServerGroups(cntGrps).RegisteredServers(cntServ).Password

        Next
Next

Set App = nothing
```

Recognize anything that popped up?

Maybe now you see the potential for mischief considering not only can they get your saved password quickly; many folks tend to use the same password for many things, especially when the user account is the same.

Using NT Authentication to attach to a remote server.

Ok, so you can get to the stored password via DMO. So what if a Trusted Login is used. Just add the following to the above code after "App.ServerGroups(cntGrps).RegisteredServers(cntServ).Password".

```
& " - " & App.ServerGroups(cntGrps).RegisteredServers(cntServ).UseTrustedConnection
```

So it would be easy for an attacker to determine you are using a trusted authentication to take advantage of an alternate choice of attack. Even then, though, if the code found no saved password the next best thing would be to try a trusted login. This is less of an issue other than it opens the one door.

So, what concern should you have?

Not that you need to run out and yell 'the sky is falling!', or anything, but consider these things. If a hacker gets a user's password what are the odds that password also works on most everything else--pretty high from my experience. If nothing more hackers have another potential method of attack on external machines that VPN into their companies or clients and cause a lot of havoc.

Final Thoughts

First off I hope I didn't scare anyone, but I have just made you aware of a potential security risk. A user who saves any password is as scary as the ones who write them on sticky note nearby. The last line of defense is always the user and they need to be schooled properly when using certain tools to avoid creating potential security hotspots for themselves.

You may ask what to do to keep safety up. Personally, I would avoid installing EM on any machine that does not absolutely need it and even then use a SQL Password with prompt for password set so it is not saved. If users of any level dial in from external and they use EM (including managers), do not allow trusted connections, and again have prompt for password set so as not to have saved.

The fewer clues you make available the better. So remember to always remove the key from the lock when you leave.

Is All Code Really Code? One Question From an Interview

By Andy Warren

When we hire new employees (at my day job) we start with a phone interview. I've got a list of a couple dozen questions we run through that give us an idea of whether we should consider bringing the person in for a more in depth interview. While a discussion of those questions is probably worth an article in itself, we'll stick closer to SQL today and talk about just one of the questions I ask of candidates for senior developer positions.

Here it is:

"A junior developer comes to you with the following problem. They have a SQL stored procedure comprised of about 200 lines of business logic. The procedure executes without error but does not return the expected results. Without looking at the code, what guidance would you offer that would help them solve the problem?"

Think on it for a minute; I imagine you'll think of a couple different options and maybe a couple questions. What do you think is the common answer?

Answer: Add print statements to the code.

Other answers I've been given:

- You shouldn't have that much code in a single stored procedure
- I'd have to look at the code
- Have them check the data

In 10% of the interviews they'll suggest using a debugger, either the one in Query Analyzer or the one in Visual Studio.Net.

So let's talk about what I think about the answers briefly. Adding print statements isn't the worst idea, similar to adding debug.print or debug.writeline statements or whatever your language of choice supports. What I look for is do they go the extra mile, suggest putting one inside every branch, or putting one halfway to cut in half the lines of code to inspect. Too much code in one proc? Hard to tell based just on lines of code, but I don't see 200 as excessive - still, I'm open to a discussion on that point. Looking at the code? Sure you want to look, but I'm looking for someone who doesn't HAVE to look, they can explain how they solve the problem to someone else in repeatable fashion. Checking the data? Definitely part of the process, bad data happens far too often, always a factor to be considered.

Possibly you can tell I'm a fan of the debugger approach. Why? Suppose we reframed the question to look something like this:

"A junior developer comes to you with the following problem. They have a VB6/VB.Net method comprised of about 200 lines of business logic. The method executes without error but does not return the expected results. Without looking at the code, what guidance would you offer that would help them solve the problem?"

I'd be willing to bet that almost every developer will say that you should step through the code. Why does the answer change? Developers think of VB6/VB.Net/C#/whatever as code, but stored procedures as *magical things on the server*. If you're using VB6 or whatever you have a very rich development environment - step through, watch variables, etc, but for some reason developers don't think of stored procedure code as code. Even when they make that leap, few stop to realize that they are debugging stored procedures with techniques worthy of the early nineties.

As far as the interview itself, this question lets me see if they can see outside their world a little, see how they react to a small challenge, how would they do as a mentor? Standard stuff I think. While you you might not agree with the question, I hope you'll think about the range of answers and why so few developers use a debugger on stored procedures.

The Danger of Hiring Stars

By David Poole

Introduction

In my father's day employment was simple. You joined a firm after leaving school at the age of 14 and at the end of 50 years you got a gold watch and the brush off. The company accepted that it had certain responsibilities and you understood that they expected loyalty and hard graft.

Moving jobs was frowned upon and seen as a sign of someone prepared to betray those loyalties. Almost as socially stigmatizing as someone changing the football team that they support!

In Britain this changed in the 1980's in the era of Margaret Thatcher and Ronald Reagan. The employment market was shaken up forever and in today's climate we are expected to be more flexible and to be prepared to change at the drop of a hat. The upshot of this is that you are likely to have several changes of employer during your career.

Let us suppose that you are a successful DBA. Being good at your job you may find that you are head-hunted by another company. If this is the case you should be careful because there are some things you need to think about.

The only three questions that you are ever asked in an interview

No matter how many questions you will ever be asked in an interview the recruiter is only really trying to answer three questions.

- Can they do the job?
- Will they do the job?
- Will they fit into the organization?

No matter how many questions you ask in your interview (and you should ask several) you should seek to answer these questions for your own personal benefit.

- Can I do this job?
- Do I really want to do this job?
- Will I fit into the organization?

Let us assume that as a DBA the "Can I do this job?" questions is a generally yes.

What makes you successful?

You are a being head-hunted because you have a reputation as a successful DBA, but do you ever stop to consider where that reputation came from?

It is not such a daft question as it sounds. I read an article in the Harvard Business Review entitled "The Risky Business of Hiring Stars" which asked why it was that a high flier recruited from one company performed disappointingly in their subsequent company.

How much of your success is due to the people you work with?

Your skills may be your own, but the way in which your colleagues support you can make a big difference. When I joined my current company I knew a fair bit about SQL Server but not an awful lot about web applications. The people I worked with were keen to learn from me and were equally keen to teach me. The result is that I thrived.

The Harvard Review article quoted one executive as saying that when a company gains a new employee it is a bit like a body receiving an organ transplant. A perfectly good DBA joins a perfectly good development team but they reject each other. The DBA does not fit into the organization.

The example given in the article was of resentments caused by the head-hunted employee's high salary and preferential treatment in terms of resources. It leads to the employee being ostracised by their colleagues and therefore unable to function within the organization.

How much of your success is due to the resources you have available to you?

I recently had a contract to work in a company where there were dual monitors on the developers' desks. It took some getting used to as I usually work on a laptop, but the benefits of having Books on-line on one screen and Query Analyzer on another were obvious. Moving back to my laptop I feel as if I've lost a limb.

How would you cope if your favorite 3rd party tool was not available to you? This rather sounds like a "Can you do the job" question but there is another element to this.

Assuming that your prospective employer does not have an equivalent tool, will they allow you to purchase your favorite tool?

I have worked in large organizations that wouldn't provide their employees with anything other than out-of-the-box tools and some that couldn't afford to. On balance I would prefer the latter because in the first there is nothing you can do to change the organization's policy whereas at least in the second you can earn the tool by improving productivity.

The questions being asked here are "Do I want the job?" & "Will I fit in?"

How much of your success is due to the processes and methodologies in a company?

I worked for a company with a very flat structure that one consultant called an "ad-hocracy". Productive work was done as a result of meetings in corridors and at coffee machines. Decisions were fast and working was flexible.

That is fine for a small organization or a department developing small projects, but if the organization grows beyond a certain point the lack of formal structure will be more of a hindrance than a benefit.

It is a two-edged sword. If you are moving between a rigid, formal environment and a very flexible one, then the culture shock is going to be severe. If you thrive in a rigid environment then will you cope when that structure isn't there?

Again, a point raised in the Harvard Business Review was that head-hunted staff tended to be less flexible in their thinking, principally because the way they worked before was successful and therefore they tended to hang on to their old way of working as a tried and tested method. They were slow to recognise that their old ways of working were a poor fit for their new environment.

In a purely technical IT role this might not be a major problem; after all, SQL is SQL. If you are being head-hunted as a DBA, then the chances are that you are moving beyond the purely technical towards a more managerial role, in which case you need to consider how flexible you are, or how flexible you are prepared to be.

This is a "Will I fit in?" question.

Are you a round peg in a round hole?

Think very carefully about this question, particularly in the context of the previous three.

If you say to yourself I am successful because

- I work well with my peers and colleagues and enjoy doing so.
- I have the tools I feel I need to do my job.
- I am comfortable with the way in which I have to work.

Then, frankly, you need to ask yourself why do you want to move?

Why do you want to move?

Assuming it is not a choice forced on you by circumstance you should consider this question very carefully. If you get it wrong then the chances are you will be moving again within six months of the initial move.

I have worked for two organizations that I have been very glad to leave. With hindsight being 20:20 moving to these companies was a mistake.

Even looking back at the preceding companies with nostalgia and the knowledge that I should not have accepted jobs in the companies that I moved to, the decision to move was the right one. I simply moved to the wrong place because I didn't ask the right questions.

The mix of factors that influence the decision to move jobs are complex.

Money

It is flattering to be offered a high salary. The prospective employer is saying that they value you and there is the subliminal implication that your current employer does not value you as highly as they should.

Don't be blinded by the salary. If someone is offering a telephone number salary there has to be a down side. It is easy to say that you can put up with a lot for the right money, but you would be surprised at how small "a lot" can be.

It is also easy to say that the salary will buy you a better lifestyle but the hours you will probably have to work to earn your salary will give you little chance to enjoy it. I know someone with a surround sound cinema system that would impress George Lucas, but the dust on it is inches thick!

At the risk of sounding old I can tell you that in my twenties I spent my money acquiring the usual toys a young man collects. In my thirties I realized that the things I spent so much on and considered important are not worth a damn.

Career progression

This is probably one of the best reason for changing jobs. It is a chance for you to extend yourself, to take on new challenges and responsibilities.

The downsides are that with extended roles and responsibilities comes additional pressure and demands on your time. You may move from a job you love to one you love less.

I once worked for an ambitious American boss who once said to me that he used to think that being number one would be the most satisfying position to be in. He subsequently found out that being number two for a good number one was by far the more satisfying position.

Chance to learn something new

In the IT field this is a very important consideration. That is providing the "something new" is an industry standard or up and coming technology. Alternatively it could be a chance to learn a new career skill such as project management.

If you are seeking to learn a new technical skill will it play to your existing strengths? For example, you may learn about some new data access technologies that are an enhancement to your SQL skills.

If you are moving to learn a new career skill other than a technical skill, how do you feel about potentially gaining the career skill at the expense of losing some of your technical skills?

Change of scene

There are some people who enjoy change for change sake. In the IT world we call them contractors.

Why do you want a change of scene? If it is to escape a general malaise then you should try and identify the source of that malaise; otherwise, you will have dealt with the symptom not the cause. I've made this mistake myself and have regretted it.

Does the change of scene mean a change in environment? Such a change can be enormously beneficial but you need to ask yourself if the change would suit you. For example, if you are a country person then would a move to a city area suit you?

To benefit your family

Robert Heinlen defined love as a condition experienced when the well-being and happiness of another is essential to your own. What he didn't say was that your happiness should also be intrinsic to theirs. In other words love is a two-way street.

Changing jobs in the mistaken belief that martyring yourself will make your family happy is a sorry mistake to make. I don't know many people who are totally able to disconnect their work life from their private life. If you are in a stressful situation at work you will inevitably bring this home.

Conclusion

Reviewing this article, it sounds as if I am suggesting that as a successful DBA you should stay put. This isn't the case at all. If you don't push yourself you will never find out where your limits lie. What I am saying is that the decision to change jobs needs to be taken with your eyes open and that you need to be brutally honest with yourself.

Think Like a DBA

By Andy Warren

I've been managing a small development team for a few months now and one of the more interesting comments has been that I think like a DBA, not a developer. This usually comes about whenever I offer a solution that is more sql based than 'code' based. This article will take about one particular instance. Will be interesting to see what comments are posted!

Recently I was doing one of my semi daily walk arounds, seeing if anyone needed anything, were on track, etc. Usually I stop in for a couple minutes, move on, then back to my office to do my own work. I noticed one of the developers writing code that I think you will all recognize, so I'll just present a vanilla representation - translate to your language of choice:

```
if rs.fields("lastname") is null
    somevar = ''
else
    somevar=rs.fields("lastname")
end if
```

Basically you've retrieved a value from a table into a recordset, datareader, whatever, and you're assigning the results to a variable or assigning an empy string to the variable if the value is null. In essense, you want a string value, you don't want a null.

This isn't uncommon by any means. DBAs love nulls (well, those of us who believe in allowing them); developers don't find them as useful in program code. Typically char/varchar/text values that are null become empty strings, null integers become 0, null dates become 1/1/1900 or something like that. Now keep in mind I'm not saying that developers don't understand nulls or ever find a use for them, but I think most common app code tends to convert them to something 'friendlier'.

Looking at the code lead to a whole different discussion, but essentially circled back to me asking if you're going to get rid of the nulls, why not do it 'upstream', in the stored procedure?

Basically if I were trying to accomplish the same task, I would change the stored procedure to look something like this:

```
select isnull(lastname, '') as LastName from sometable where ....
```

This eliminates the possibility that I can get a null back at all. Conversely, if I were writing the value back to the db, I'd typically do something like this:

```
update sometable set lastname = nullif(lastname, '') where ....
```

The last thing I want in the db is empty strings unless they truly mean something. In both cases I'm doing the work on the server, as close to the data as possible. To me, this means that from that point on I don't have to worry about the values, I can just work with what I get.

Is the SQL technique 'better'? Performance on either approach is close enough to being the same to worry about and too small to bother with testing it anyway! Quality? I'd say once tested both work equally well. I think the SQL version results in less code written fewer times.

As we continued the discussion, we finally got down to bare metal - should you put any code besides insert/update/delete/select code in a stored procedure, violating the rules of n-tier design? I don't know that I'm qualified to speak on what the rules are or should be, but I think when it comes to a database you have two choices. One is treat it like a dumb data store; keep your procs as simple as possible or even use dynamic sql exclusively, leaving yourself the ability to connect to whatever type of data store your customer may elect to use. The other is to leverage the strength of the platform, even if that means breaking some of those 'rules' about what code should reside where. I like code with as many layers as possible, stored procedures are a powerful layer that I like to fully exploit. Still, if you're sticking with the rules, that does null out the isnull/nullif scenario? Or does it?

Ultimately it's about knowing that there are different ways to solve a problem and understanding when best to apply each. A lot of it is style, but the style has to be based on merit, not just 'I like SQL' or 'I like code'! Talk to your developers about this: how do they handle nulls? Do they know isnull and nullif? Throw them a curve, get them to look at the coalesce function. Get them to think about the power of the db platform and how it might change how they solve problems.

About The Authors

Ameet Phadnis

Speed Up Development on Backend and Middle Tier with SQL Scripts – pg. 148

Amit Jethra

I started my career as Developer on VB/PB/ASP/APT - SQL/Sybase/Oracle. Moved to SQL Admin first in Nov 2000 on SQL 7.0 and later on to SQL 2000, but with more of a developer workload. Since last 2 years or so, I have been focusing more on SQL Admin stuff. and I have enjoyed working on SQL Server. My main areas of intrest in SQL are Database Design, Scripting, troubleshooting and Perfomance Tuning. Now, I am looking forward to SQL Server 2005 (Yukon) to arrive. Currently I am with Microsoft GTSC in SQL PSS Team.

Capturing the Error Description in a Stored Procedure – pg. 63

Andre Vigneau

I hold a college certificate in programming and analysis as well as another in finance accounting. I am MCSE certified since 1996 and also MCDBA since 2000. I have accumulated over 12 years experience in information technologies. I worked over 10 years in the database arena specializing on Microsoft SQL Server platform. Today, I can say that I am specialized in database architecture, management, performance optimization and applications analysis and development. I have defined administration automation procedures as well as a statistic collection system to ease databases maintenance and reveal usage trends. Always prepared to face new challenges, I have worked in various micro-computer environments. I am actually working as senior database administrator and database systems team leader, managing overall operations of development and test servers in a heterogeneous environment where database can range from MySQL, MSDE, SQL Server, and Oracle.

Versioning – Pg. 78

Andy Warren

Is All Code Really Code? One Question From an Interview – Pg. 211
Think Like a DBA – Pg. 215

Anthony Bressi

Anthony Bressi is owner of Agilist Technologies Inc. which specializes in software for SQL Server Database Administrators and SQL Server developers. Mr. Bressi has over 8 years of hands-on experience in the Microsoft SQL Server development environment.

Scheduled MS Cluster Failovers Using Automation Server Objects – pg. 33

Ashish Kaushal

I have 11 years of experience in varied computing trades, of which SQL Server has been an integral part of it for seven years. I presently work as freelance consultant and trainer. I hold B.S.E in Electronic & Communication; I have MCSE (Microsoft Certified System Engineer), MCDBA (Microsoft Certified Database Administrator), and MCT (Microsoft Certified Trainer) certifications.

How To Find SQL Server Objects – pg. 23

Brian Kelley

Brian is currently an Enterprise Systems Architect with *Ag*First Farm Credit Bank (http://www.agfirst.com) in Columbia, SC. Prior to that he served as a senior DBA and web developer with *Ag*First. His primary responsibilities include overhauling the current Windows NT infrastructure to provide for a highly available, network-optimized framework that is Active Directory ready. Brian assumed his Architect role in December 2001. He has been at *Ag*First since January of 2000 when he originally came on-board as an Intranet web developer and database programmer. In addition to his role at *Ag*First Farm Credit Bank, Brian heads Warp Drive Design Ministries (http://www.warpdrivedesign.org), a Christian ministry devoted to using technology for encouraging Christians in their faith as well as presenting the Gospel in a non-confrontational manner. He has been a columnist at SQL Server Central since July 2001.

SQL Server Security: Dealing with Anti-Virus Programs – pg. 172

Brian Knight

Brian Knight, MCSE, MCDBA, is on the Board of Directors for the Professional Association for SQL Server (PASS) and runs the local SQL Server users group in Jacksonville. Brian is a contributing columnist for SQL Magazine and also maintains a weekly column for the database website SQLServerCentral.com. He is the author of Admin911: SQL Server (Osborne/McGraw-Hill Publishing) and co-author of Professional SQL Server DTS (Wrox Press). Brian is a Senior SQL Server Database Consultant at Alltel in Jacksonville and spends most of his time deep in DTS and SQL Server.

Bruce Szabo

Bruce received his Master's degree in Nuclear Chemistry in 1992 from the University of Rochester in Rochester NY. In 1996 he entered the computer field working on an Informix database that ran on a DOS 386 computer. He has been working at an Internet firm (OEConnection, LLC) managing databases and publishing information using SQL 2000, BizTalk 2002 and Visual Basic .Net.

Chris Cathers

For over 9 years I've been playing with databases, I cut my databases teeth on SQL 6.5. Since then I've gotten my MCSE in windows 2000, and my MCDBA in SQL 7.0 & 2000. The MCDBA's have gotten me 4 jobs, the MCSE, 0. I enjoy coding in T-SQL, perhaps its because my colleagues think SQL is a black art, perhaps I just love computers. Whatever the case, Databases have taken me everywhere I wanted to go. And the future still looks good – (The black art thing :) For my next career though, I think I'd like to program video games, or write Sci-Fi books…

Chris Kempster

Chris has been working in the computer industry for around 8 years as an Application Development DBA. He began his career as an Oracle AP then moved into a DBA role using Oracle. From there he has specialised in DBA technical consulting with a focus to both Oracle and SQL Server. Chris has been actively involved with SQL Server since 1999 for a variety of clients and is currently working with a range of large scale internet based development projects. Visit www.chriskempster.com for further information and his ebook titled "SQL Server 2k for the Oracle DBA".

Christoffer Hedgate

Chris Hedgate is a consultant for Dotway AB in Sweden, where he works with SQL Server and .NET development. He has authored several articles, presentations and a SQL Server 2000 Performance Optimizing class, and is a frequent speaker and teacher. You can reach Chris through his blog at http://www.hedgate.net/blog.

Dale Elizabeth Corey

Dale Elizabeth Corey has 18 years of professional experience including IT/IS Management, DBA, Programmer, System/Network Administrator, and Software Instructor for such organizations such as the City of Titusville, FL, Brevard Community College, and McDonnell Douglas Space Systems at Kennedy Space Center. Her education credentials include a M.S. in Management Information Systems from Nova Southeastern University (4.0 GPA); and a B.B.A. in Computer Information Systems. Her membership and certification credentials include Upsilon Pi Epsilon (international honor society in the computing sciences); Microsoft Certified Systems Engineer; Microsoft Certified Professional + Internet; Association of Computing Machinery; and IEEE.

David Poole

Dave worked first for a French manufacturing company as an analyst/programmer working with mini-computers. He then spent five years as systems manager for an American 'direct mail' printing company, followed by five years with an global advertising agency as a database administrator and business analyst. He specialised in database analysis, particularly in the area of direct mail and response analysis, using a variety of tools, including SPSS, VB, SQL Server, Access, and Excel. He currently works as a DBA specialising in web content management systems for a technical documentation company near Manchester (UK).

Denny Figuerres

I started with computers about 24 years back. First PC was a Commodore VIC 20 and my "Mass Storage" was a cassette tape deck from my stereo gear with a home made A/D converter built from a 555 timer IC. I have worked at a large ISP for several years www.inreach.com based in Stockton California. I ran the support desk for a while and then the IT support including the adoption of RadiusNT form IEA software that logged dialup use form the modem banks to the tune of about 6 million SQL database records per month using SQL 6.5. For the last 4 years I have been working with a Billing and Ops' system company www.internetsupportsystems.com in florida

Port Blocking, SQL Server, and the Internet - pg. 168

Dinesh Asanka

I am living on a beautiful island called Sri Lanka, just beside India. I started my carrier as a simple data entry operator and was in the almost all the sections of Software. I have mote than ten years of experience in the IT field. Currently I am functioning for a company called Advance Data Technologies (Pvt) Ltd as a Senior Database Designer. I am working in SQL Server for just over five years. I have being involved in databases such as Dbase 3+, Clipper, MS Access, SQL Server, Oracle, DB2, mySQL at different scale. I am passionate in Cricket. I am enjoying the sharing my knowledge in SQLServerCentral.com as well.

Changing Database Using XML - pg. 180

Dinesh Priyankara

Dinesh is a Software Developer who started his career as "DataEntryOperator". He is currently working for Logical Systems, Colombo and he is MCSD, MCDBA, and MCSE. SQL Server 2000 and .NET are the current platforms he is working on. You can reach him at http://spaces.msn.com/members/dineshpriyankara/.

Null Functions (Aren't Those Meetings?) - pg. 73

Don Peterson

I am currently a Sr. Data Architect working in Lenexa, Kansas for Ingenix, a subsidiary of United Health Group. I started working with SQL Server in 1996 while on active duty in the U.S. Marine Corps. I was "volunteered" to learn SQL Server (6.0) in order to support the helpdesk system, and much to my surprise, I grew to like the job. After leaving active duty in 1998, I worked at a depressing series of failing dot-coms in southern California, more than half of which no longer exist. During that period I gained valuable experience in multiple business environments as a consultant and with a number of software packages and DBMS's. In my current position, database design and proper Enterprise Data Management are my primary focus and passion (while at work at any rate.)

Lookup Table Madness - pg. 130

Eli Leiba

Eli Leiba works at Israel Electric Company as a Senior Application DBA in Oracle and MS SQL Server. He also has certifications from Microsoft and BrainBench in Oracle and SQL Server database administration and implementation. Mr. Leiba holds a B.S. in Computer Science since 1991 and has 13 years' experience working in the databases field. Additionally Mr. Leiba teaches SQL Server DBA and Development courses at Microsoft CTEC and also serves as a senior database consultant for several Israeli start-up companies. (e-mail: iecdba@hotmail.com)

Handling Simple XML Using T-SQL - pg. 183

Frank Kalis

Started professional working with a small software company with responsibilities for implementing algorithms for derivatives pricing, risk management, portfolio management and other interesting stuff. In 1999 I change sides and started working as an asset manager for Germany's most successful bank insurer. It's been quite good since then.

An Introduction to Database Models - pg. 134

G Vijayakumar

G. Vijayakumar has worked in client server and web application. He is currently working for Transworld, which is located in Bangalore, India, working on an e-banking product.

Stored Procedures vs Triggers - pg. 142

Goce Smilevski

An Efficient Set-based Solution for Islands and Gaps - pg. 52

Haidong Ji

I was a developer, working with VB, SQL Server, Access and lots of other Microsoft stuff. I am currently a SQL Server DBA in my company in the Chicago area. In addition to SQL Server, I also do Oracle work on Linux and Solaris. I am MCSD and MCDBA certified. In my spare time, I like to do Linux, C and other open source project. I can be reached at Haidong.Ji AT gmail dot com.

Becoming More Productive - pg. 208

James Luetkehoelter

James Luetkehoelter is an MCSD, MCSE, MCDBA and MCT. He has been working in the database arena for the last nine years. He is currently the president of Spyglass LLC, a consultancy focusing on data-centric services, including data architecture, data quality analysis, database and application design, business intelligence and database administration. In his spare time, James documents the various attempts at pronouncing "Luetkehoelter". He is currently up to 1,456 distinct variations

From the Soapbox: Does Anyone Know What Disaster Recovery Is? - pg. 81
Reporting Services Part 1: Overview, Architecture, and Installation - pg. 114

James Travis

I currently work for a major US Bank in their internal support service area.
I develop tools and applications used by the call center, division, and corporate employees for various tasks.

Hidden Dangers! - pg. 209

Jeff Moden

Jeff Moden is a mostly self-taught SQL Developer and is a Senior Data Analyst for a billion-plus dollar world-wide multi-level marketing company that specializes in telephone services and DSL products. He has 10 years of SQL Server experience, 34 years of programming experience, and has both written and taught many computer based and electronics courses for the Navy and private industry. His passion for tight code and clear, easy to read embedded documentation is self evident in this, his first submittal to SQLServerCentral.com as a new author. We look forward to more articles by Jeff.

Calculating Work Days - pg. 60

Jeffrey Yao

Jeffrey Yao is a DBA with an MBA degree, who always try to manage database systems in a way that can squeeze out the most pleasure and benefits to both my company and myself. As a DBA, I do not like any news from the system I am managing, what I like is "no news is good news".

How To Be a Good DBA – Strategy and Tactics - pg. 132

Joe Sack

Joseph Sack, MCDBA, is a SQL Server consultant based in the Twin Cities. He is the author of SQL Server 2000 Fast Answers for DBAs and Developers (Apress) and the co-author of Beginning SQL Server 2000 DBA: Novice to Professional (Apress). He can be contacted via his website, http://www.SackConsulting.com.

Analyzing Data Storage – Ten SHOWCONTIG Queries - pg. 153

Jon Reade

Jon Reade is an independent consultant working as a SQL Server DBA for eight years, prior to which he specialised in database developement. His main specialities are performance tuning problematic SQL Server systems, and auditing database security for customers in the financial services sector. He also works on forensic database investigations for corporations.

SQL Server 2005 DBCC Command Quick Reference - pg. 198

Jon Winer

Jonathan Winer, a co-founder of SQLServerCentral.com has worked as an applications developer for the past 8 years. Jonathan has worked for many companies in his career. Jonathan spent some time at NASA where he was involved in building an energy management and reporting system. Jonathan is currently working for Channel Intelligence, a central Flordia company, whose emphasis is in online commerce services.

Reduce Database Round Trips Using XML - pg. 185

Joseph Gama

RC3 Encryption in a Stored Procedure- pg. 169

Keith Henry

An Introduction to MDX - pg. 109

Kevin O'Donovan

Software developer for the last 18 years, writing such things as compilers/debuggers, scientific libraries, radar image processing tools, etc, though mostly database apps for the last 9 or 10 years. Currently senior developer for a software development division for Mersey Docks & Harbour Company. Also run my own company writing bespoke software and selling a couple of almost shrink wrapped applications I've developed over the years.

Distributed Backup Checking - pg. 13

Krishna Sonti

An Introduction to Linked Servers - pg. 9

Leo Peyasakhovich

Leo Peysakhovich is consultant and president of ACCT INC. As a developer, DBA, and an architect he has been working with SQL Server since 1993. He has published multiple technical articles throughout his career. He provided training for more than hundred of people in SQL Server and Business Application Development. He immigrated to the United States from Minsk, Belarus in 1989. He holds a degree in Electrical and Automated System Engineering (equivalent to an M.S. in System Control Engineering). Leo lives in a suburb of Philadelphia with his wife Liana and 2 sons Felix and Nathan. He can be reached at leop@acctinc.com

Index Creation Guidelines - pg. 160

Mark Nash

Monitoring Drive and Database Free Space - pg. 27

Nicholas Cain

Nicholas Cain started out as the overnight guy at the now defunct MicroWarehouse a few years ago. There he got his first introduction to SQL Server where he found an interest and a little aptitude thanks to the help of some great workmates. He now works as a DBA at T-Mobile USA.

Checking Your Database Fragmentation Level - pg. 156

Patryk Nowakowski

Currently I'm working as an external consultant for UBS AG in Zurich, Switzerland. I specialize in Hyperion Essbase (OLAP) and Java development. Before that I've been developing mostly RDB systems and RDB related applications for BZWBK (one of the major polish banks). My experience to date includes mostly SQL Server, Essbase, Java and .NET. I have Master's degree in economics. I'm 26.

ADO.NET – A Data Access Layer - pg. 47

Paul Ibison

Currently work in London for central government as the SQL DBA in a team of Oracle DBAs. Specialize in replication, maintain www.replicationanswers.com and was awarded SQL Server MVP status for 2004-5.

Log Shipping vs. Replication - pg. 89

Randy Dyess

Randy has a large variety of experiences dealing with SQL Server over the past 8 years and has worked with environments with Terabytes of data and environments that had over a 1000 databases with only a few megabytes of data in each database. Randy is the author of *TransactSQL Language Reference Guide* and numerous magazine and newsletter articles pertaining to SQL Server security and optimization issues. Randy is also the founder of www.Database-Security.Info and www.TransactSQL.Com. Randy volunteers on the PASS DBA SIG national newsletter committee and is the Director of Programs for the North Texas SQL Server Users Group.

Ramesh Gummadi

Working as a DBA at Aegis Mortgage Corporation, Baton Rouge.LA

Ramunas Balukonis

Ramunas Balukonis works as Data Base Administrator for "VPMarket, UAB" (Lithuania), on of the biggest retail operator in the Eastern Europe. Current activity is to implement sql server data warehouse and ms OLAP solutions for enterprise.

Robert Marda

I have worked for bigdough.com since 18 May 2000 as an SQL Programmer. My duties include backup management for all our SQL Servers, mentoring junior SQL Programmers, and serving as DBA while our DBA is on vacation. I develop, test, and deploy stored procedures and DTS packages as well as manage most major SQL projects. Our offices are located in Bethesda, Maryland. Before working for bigdough, I worked for Telos Corporation in Ashburn, Virginia. I started learning T-SQL and using SQL Server 7.0 on 22 March 1999. In April 1999 I was given the position of Senior Database Analyst/Administrator at Telos Corporation. I have been married to Leoncia Guzman since 23 Jul 1994. We met in the Dominican Republic where I lived for about 2 years as a missionary. We have 4 children, Willem (age 9), Adonis (age 6), Liem (age 5), and Sharleen (age 4). My hobbies include spending time with our 4 children (we play chess, dominos, mancala, and video or computer games together), keeping tropical freshwater fish, breeding and training parakeets, coin collecting (US and foreign), playing on line chess (I am ZorroRojo at redhotpawn.com) and geneology.

Robert Pearl

Robert Pearl, President of Pearl Knowledge Solutions, Inc., has grown through the ranks as a solutions-oriented Senior Database Administrator with a proven track record in application development, system architecture & design, and database administration, as well as a skilled project leader, as demonstrated through 10+ years of experience in the management of critical database operations. His focus has allowed him to become a subject matter expert in MS SQL technology. In searching for a simple clear-cut solution to manage multiple SQL Servers, he has developed SQLCentric - a web-based database monitoring and alert system - with the DBA in mind. Now an industry recognized product, and winner of the SQL Server Magazine's Reader's Choice 2004 for best monitoring software, Robert Pearl has also contributed several articles on MS SQL Server.

Robin Back

Sanket Naik

Santveer Singh

Total 13 years of IT experience in manufacturing, consulting and financial industry. Career started with COBOL then moved to xBase, then to Oracle and finally switch to SQL Server. Having 8 years of Experience with SQL server. Presently working for Algomod Technologies, New York as DBA (SQL Server).

Sharad NandWani

Unique Identifier: Usage and Limitations - pg. 77

Shiv Kumar

Tracing Deadlocks - pg. 43

Sotiris Filippidis

I am a software developer located in Athens, Greece and I've been working with Microsoft-oriented technologies since 1996. I started as a Web author and moved on to more serious development some years later. I am currently enjoying my VS.NET 2003 experience with VB.NET as well as a range of languages & technologies such as XSLT,XML, JScript, VBScript, SQL, ASP 3.0, ASP.NET, VB6. Companies I've worked for so far: Axon Info Systems Ltd, the Greek National Documentation Centre, Istos Net S.A., Financial Technologies S.A., Key Systems S.A. I have also worked for Anubis Publications S.A. as a freelance computer book author-translator from 1994 to 2000 and for Ikon Porter Novelli as a freelance PR translator from 2000.

Conditional Statements in WHERE Clauses - pg. 64

Stefan Popovski

Be Prepared! - pg. 57

Stephen Lasham

Extract a String From Between Two Delimiting Characters - pg. 67

Steve Jones

With over a decade of working with SQL Server as well as many other aspects of the IT industry, Steve Jones brings a variety of viewpoints to many problems that DBAs face. As a founder of SQLServerCentral.com, Steve has worked to build a community that is practical, professional, and invaluable to SQL Server DBAs

Incident Reponse – The Framework - pg. 82
Incident Reponse – Responding to an Incident - pg. 85

Sureshkumar Ramakrishnan

I am a software Consultant with Capgemini India and have more than 4 years experience working on Microsoft technologies.

Deleting Duplicate Records - pg. 66

Vinod Kumar

Vinod Kumar has done his Bachelors in Mechanical Engineering from Anna University, Chennai. He has been very passionate about Microsoft SQL Server. In pursuit of this interest, he has been an awardee of Microsoft SQL Server MVP program since 2003. He is also an MCSE, MCSD, MCDBA, MCAD, MCSA. Vinod is a highly rated speaker at Microsoft forums like TechEd and MSDN. He is an active volunteer for INETA and PASS. Vinod manages SQL Server Usergroup (SQLBang - http://groups.msn.com/SQLBang) at Bangalore. You can read more of his resources and articles on SQL Server at the website www.extremeexperts.com he co-hosts.

Introduction to DTS in SQL Server 2005 - pg. 191

Wayne Fillis

An Alternative XML Solution - pg. 177

Wes Brown

I am currently working as a Senior Database Administrator for The SCOOTER Store in New Braunfels, Tx, the largest provider of powered mobility in the U.S.

Four of a Kind – Backup Software Shootout - pg. 17
Four of a Kind – Backup Software Shootout Part 2 - pg. 21